Praise *Sleep Like Starfish*

Sleep like Starfish is a fascinating excavation of the intricacies of love and trauma and how they intersect. This book is gripping, heartbreaking, and uplifting. Shel Atkins is a tireless researcher and an astute observer of life. If you've ever felt broken or lost—"like a body with no skin"—you'll find yourself in the pages of this very honest memoir.

—Judy Goldman, author of *Child: A Memoir*

How do you cope with a life of trauma, both from the inside out and the outside in? If you're Shel Atkins, you do it with grit and faith and humor. *Sleep like Starfish* will feel sharp and true to anyone who has spent any time in life's wringer—which is to say everyone.

—Tommy Tomlinson, author of *Elephant in the Room* and host of the *Southbound* podcast

Shel Atkins has a story to tell, and she does so with wisdom, grace, and heart in *Sleep like Starfish*. Through the lens of her experience, Atkins illuminates the journey to healing, peace, and joy. What an emotionally generous, profound, and beautiful human story!

—Allison Hong Merrill, author of *Ninety-Nine Fire Hoops*

Sleep like Starfish

Rachelle Atkins

Sleep like Starfish

Copyright ©2025 by Rachelle Atkins
Crabapple Press, Charlotte, NC

All rights reserved.

The author has tried to recreate events, locales, and conversations from her memories of them. In order to maintain anonymity in some instances, the names of individuals and places may have been changed, as well as identifying characteristics and details, such as physical properties, occupations, and places of residence.

No part of this book may be reproduced or used in any manner without written permission of the copyright owner except for the use of quotations in a book review.

Printed in the United States of America

ISBN: 978-1-5011-7321-9

Book design by Robert Kern, TIPS Publishing Services
Cover art by Gigi Dover
Cover design by Lib Ramos
Author photo by Piper Warlick

rachelleatkins@yahoo.com

29 28 27 26 25   5 4 3 2 1

*Dedicated to the family I came from
and the one I created.*

You're all I need in this world.

Contents

Prologue   vii
Author's Note   xvi

Once We Were a Family 1
The Lost Year 13
An Urban Cowboy 19
Barreling through like a Storm 33
We Were the Trees 39
Stone-Cold Sober, but Also Kind of Drunk 47
Teenage Musicians Are Jerks 51
Turns Out, Surfers Are Jerks Too 57
A Lullaby for the Reckless 67
Mama, He's a Bad, Bad Man 81
Leaving Shorty's 87
Fear of Sharks 91
Dorm Rooms and Teddy Bears 101
A Walking Achy Boo-Boo 111
An Inside Job 119
Sandy the Hippie 123
Your Corporate Barbie 131
A Gravitational Pull 141
I'm with the Band 147

Houses of the Holy............................155
Sleep like Starfish 159
The Biggest Damn Handgun 167
Feels like Home................................173
Hustling...179
A Ritual Prayer.................................199
Neurosis Diagnosis 207
Revelations 215
The Most Fragile of Us All 221
The Diner Prophet 229
We Are All Stories..............................235
Needling 247
My Alter Ego....................................255
Crying at Work..................................261
Strangers on a Plane...........................267
Love Thigh Self.................................271
The Woman Who Ironed the Sheets 279
What Does the Owl Say? 283
Trip, Fall, and Die...............................289
The Movie in My Head 297
The Dinner Party Guest 303
You're Exhausted 311
Going to California.............................319
A Streak of Tigers...............................337

Acknowledgments   345

Prologue

A blazing fire crackled in the fireplace and felt so good on my achy bones that I scooted off the sofa and perched right there on the stone hearth. I let the warmth get so close I wondered if we'd soon smell burning hair and the fibers of my black cashmere sweater. There were ten of us, all creatives of one type or another—writers, painters, poets, musicians—all gathered in a warm circle in the living room of our host's gorgeous home. We called ourselves The Bluestockings, a name borrowed from the groups of women who dared to gather for the sake of literary conversations in mid-eighteenth-century England. We took turns sharing our current work in progress and spent a few minutes explaining our state of mind and condition of heart at the time of inspiration, each of us offering thoughtful feedback to each artist.

During this time in my life, the promise of organic, vegan, gluten-free donuts at the nearby market could lure me out of the house on Saturday mornings when little else could. Any remaining energy I could muster would be saved for my day job as a construction project manager, food shopping, taking care of home and kids, a walk around the block to ease the pain in my joints, and of course, the ever-present doctor appointments.

I'd recently learned about the spoon theory. The theory goes like this: people with chronic illness start every day with a certain number of spoons that we use up with each activity in which we participate, whether it be attending a party, making dinner, or just taking a shower, until eventually we run out of spoons. Every day it seemed I had fewer and fewer spoons, but I was so keen to be with these kind, creative souls that I saved them up for this evening.

When it was my turn to share my work, I slid my computer in front of me, and without preamble, I read about my earliest memory. It's one that is so worn in my mind that I almost didn't expect the response it elicited from my peers. I'd written it, but had I ever allowed myself to truly consider how it had informed my view of myself and my place in the world? We are sometimes so close to our stories that familiarity blunts the hard edges that others see so clearly. I was surprised when my story moved them in a way that was tangible. Their collective affirmation of my work felt like the truest form of acceptance and belonging. In this moment, they understood and accepted the deepest, most damaged parts of me.

Tears filled my eyes, but I willed them not to drop. To those around me, the tears would have made sense considering what I had just read, and in this group, we often cried together, but it was also physical pain that wracked my body and brought tears to my eyes. Through my reading, I had been vulnerable, exposing my hidden self in the presence of these women I didn't know very well outside these meetings. Sharing your stories like this can feel like you've stripped naked in a room full of strangers, no matter how warm and welcoming they may be. My writing in particular reads like a roadmap of all my defects. By the time the evening was over, I was in so much physical pain I could hardly walk the short distance to my car.

On the drive home, I flicked on the seat heater, relaxing into it like a heating pad, and began to feel there may be a connection between the tension in my body and the essay about my childhood I had just shared. Was the accumulation of unaddressed traumas the cause of the debilitating fatigue and the very real pain of mysterious origin I now battled daily? Has this pain shown up to get my attention? Was there a connection between the emotional pain of my past and this physical pain of my present?

Over the past few years, I'd amassed an impressive collection of controversial diagnoses, such as chronic inflammatory response syndrome, known in functional medicine circles as CIRS; chronic late-stage Lyme disease which led to fibromyalgia; and a biotoxin illness due to mold exposure. Others were a little more mainstream like shingles (which I'd had twice on my body and once, most hideously, in my eye) and reactivated Epstein-Barr virus. I'd also discovered I was a carrier of streptococcal pneumonia. I was only in my fourth decade, but my body felt twice as old.

Some of these made sense. I could trace the CIRS back three decades to when I was sixteen years old. One night, out of the blue, my top lip started to tingle and go numb. I was on the phone with a boy I liked and checked myself out in the mirror. My lip was so swollen it had begun to block my nostrils, making it hard to breathe. The next morning, my mom threw back the covers, looked at my distorted face—think Will Smith's character in the movie *Hitch* after an allergic reaction to seafood—and declared I needed to get ready for school. Her blonde waves shook as she delighted in her own joke. While I enjoyed her momentary playfulness, I was mortified at the thought of showing up to my new school in this giant-lipped state. The thought of all the jokes that would have haunted me the rest of my high school years made me cringe. That afternoon, a doctor determined it was likely a reaction to the pesticides on the apple and grapes I had been eating just before the swelling began. The CIRS diagnosis, if accurate, would certainly make sense of this incident.

The mold illness made sense too because we'd spent twenty years living in a water-damaged home, and despite many costly remediations to the crawlspace, the air retained just enough mold spores to further deplete my already compromised immune system.

It is with curiosity, not blame or accusation, that I decided to call up the past in hopes of healing from it. A chaotic childhood gave way to an adulthood full of accumulated stress and sickness, devoid of any real respite and stillness. My marriage has been strained by the tough times that come when two traumatized, uneducated people marry and become parents at a young age. I can't help but wonder: If healing the wounds of the past can heal my body, does this mean illness has been my fault and within my control this whole time? How much of our wellness is truly within our control?

That night at Kelly's house made me consider how unprocessed grief and the resulting untreated anxiety and tension might be affecting me. Reading that essay for my group caused a visceral reaction in my body. Could inherited generational trauma manifest itself in chronic pain and illness? My mother and father had both experienced abandonment and attachment traumas and had both endured long seasons of chronic body pain, brain fog, and extreme fatigue. My daughter was beginning to experience it too. Would walking back through the history of our lives provide answers or at least clues? If so, could it heal us?

One fall evening, after giving a reading at a literary festival, I slipped in to see a panel discussion my sister was moderating nearby. Justin Perry, a local therapist, was speaking on generational trauma and explained it this way: "The same way you're passing food in utero, you're also passing through a lot of other experiences as well, so generational trauma makes sense. But we think about trauma in terms of what we can actually see. If I can see that plane flying into those towers on

9/11, then I can see it being traumatic. What you don't see is that person who is pregnant and going from the moment of being so happy that they're pregnant to being terrified of what kind of world they are bringing their child into." An audience member raised her hand and asked what we can do to heal inherited trauma. His response was swift.

"We can't undo what has already been done. What we can do is start to recognize it, talk about it out loud, and shed light on it. And then we can help our next generation start a little further ahead than we did." What resonated with me here was the idea that talking about it, and writing about it, could lead to healing.

After that night, I began my research in earnest. In his book, *When the Body Says No*[1], Dr. Gabor Maté explains how stress puts into motion a biochemical response to powerful emotional stimuli. "Physiologically, emotions are themselves electrical, chemical, and hormonal discharges of the human nervous system." A common coping mechanism for stressful situations is repression of emotions. In some extreme cases this is a survival technique. He explains that repression inhibits and breaks down the body's ability to defend against illness. He goes on to explain how these emotional experiences influence the function of our body's organs and our

---

1. Maté, Gabor. *When the Body Says No.* Hoboken, New Jersey: John Wiley & Sons, 2011.

immune systems, purporting that our immune systems are affected by our daily experiences.

He gives the example of how immune function in healthy medical students has been shown to be repressed under the pressure of final exams. He goes on to say, "The pressure of exams is obvious and short term, but many people unwittingly spend their entire lives as if under the gaze of a powerful and judgmental examiner whom they must please at all costs." This feels unequivocally true to me. But who is this examiner in my life? God? My husband? My parents? My boss? I think this "cat on a hot tin roof" version of me, shaped by unprocessed traumas, is at odds with my true, free-spirit nature, or my "God self." Could this idea of a powerful and judgmental examiner be the reason we try to shapeshift and wedge ourselves into places we don't belong?

I'd gone as far down the alternative medical road as our resources would allow. I'd tried so many different therapies: medications, dietary plans, coffee enemas, supplements, teas, meditations, bodywork modalities, and mantras. Twice a week for six weeks, a nurse removed my blood from my body, bag by bag, as we watched it pass under a UVB light to cleanse it of bacteria and viruses before closing the loop and returning to my body. I'd had numerous IV treatments and one subsequent ER trip from adverse reactions to them. I'd swallowed mega doses of vitamin C and lysine and regularly gave myself a prescription dose of glutathione compounded in an out-of-state pharmacy, delivered to my door and popped right up my butt each night.

I was sinking deeper into depression. The work of trying to get well and working for my income was not sustainable. I wasn't doing well at either of them in any consistent way. Recently, I'd stuffed my carry-on suitcase with everything I needed for a two-night work commitment on the opposite coast. Its contents illustrated my life at the time. Heating pad, topical pain relief cream, topical pain relief oil, magnesium supplements, massage balls, and snacks for nausea that were compliant with the anti-inflammatory diet I'd been prescribed to lower pain levels. I'd learned to get creative with my wardrobe choices, since there was little room left for clothing. The solution to these trips: one pair of black yoga pants, two sweaters, and a pair of boots comfortable enough for the redeye flight and dressy enough for my work meetings. Controlling my chronic body pain and managing my fatigue had taken first place among the priorities of my daily life.

As the days passed, I continued to reflect on that night at Kelly's when I'd read aloud that piece of my writing and the pain that had wrapped its tentacles around me, breaking through the medication meant to make my nerves numb. I continued to think about the possibility of healing my body through an evaluation and recollection of the events of my life so far. I thought about how past experiences taught me how to feel about myself, told me I was an unwanted inconvenience, that I didn't belong. How hypervigilance was the best protection from further harm. I thought about it while I washed dishes, my neck and shoulders in a chronic clench of anxiety. I mulled it over while I folded clean sheets and towels and placed them in the linen closet, my mind constantly trying to predict what horrible shoe might drop next. If repressed emotions could uncoil from my body and be released, then perhaps it's possible to heal. I envisioned my tissue as a white-knuckled fist holding all the negative emotions and experiences I was too young or too disassociated to process and wondered, *what if that fist let go?*

Uncertainty, fear, anxiety, self-doubt, abandonment, and sexual traumas all loitered inside me. They were like the monsters in the beloved children's book, *Where the Wild Things Are*[2], and they were dancing around on my tender tissues, stomping their feet, wailing their primal screams, demanding to be heard. My body had finally gotten my attention. The time for reckoning had come.

---

2. Sendak, Maurice. *Where the Wild Things Are*. Harper Collins, 1963.

Author's Note

There was a time when I believed the in the doctrine of the Christian church. When our daughter came out as gay, I quickly learned that feeling of belonging I had longed for so desperately was conditional. I regret that it took a personal experience to help me understand the hurt and harm this has caused many in the LGBTQ+ community and those who were born into other beautiful religions of the world.

While I no longer believe Jesus is the only way to heaven, I do believe in his message to love the downtrodden and not just a select few who meet predetermined criteria. Exclusionary faith has no place in our society today. So when I speak of God, I mean the divine creator accessible to us all. If I could distill the teachings of Jesus into one idea, it would be this: everyone thrives when you pour more love on them.

Once We Were a Family

Childhood is what you spend the rest of your life trying to overcome. That's what Momma always says. She says that beginnings are scary, endings are usually sad, but it's the middle that counts the most. Try to remember that when you find yourself at a new beginning. Just give hope a chance to float up. And it will . . .
—Hope Floats

Streaks of orange, yellow, and pink lit up the sky above the lake in our backyard. A spectacular lightning storm had knocked out the power, and thunder shook the ground outside where, just moments earlier, I'd been practicing my clumsy cartwheels till I was red-faced and dizzy. My scrawny wrists always gave out on me and sent me crashing to the ground. But now, safe and cozy inside, we were playing a game I'd mastered: hide and seek. My tiny, spirited mom scaled the kitchen cabinets and pulled me up on top of the refrigerator behind her. Our lives were not yet complicated. Back then, she was fun and I was a fearless five-year-old. She sat crisscross applesauce and I sat inside the circle of her legs. We huddled and tried not to giggle while Dad and my older sister, Angie, searched the house for our hiding spot. This is my earliest memory. My parents each carried a heavy load of familial trauma with which they didn't have the skills to cope—no one did back then. When they got together it was like a cataclysmic collision of stars, and later, when they parted, my sister and I fell from the sky like burning embers.

When I was a little girl, I relished playing alone because that meant no one could disrupt my imagined worlds. Inside my bedroom closet, I would line up all my shoes and stuffed animals like little soldiers and play there for hours at a time. I wrote my first stories in those closets: *There's a snake in the bathtub. Somebody call the police!* If anyone had been in my room, I knew it. After an aggravating day doing schoolwork with instructions I couldn't seem to follow, I'd run upstairs to my room and pace from end to end, sizing it up like a detective. *Hmm, this stuffed animal lives here, but I came home to find it there.* With little fists balled up by my sides, I'd interrogate my family. I would later learn a neighborhood friend often came by with her young daughter and my mom allowed her to play in my room. Mom says this infuriated me beyond reason for a child my age, but this particularity over my space is still very much a part of who I am. My dad says he enjoyed my independence, but it frustrated my mom who desperately wanted to mother me. I refused help with eating, bathing, and using the potty, and I did not like to be held—especially by men.

In the living room downstairs, I sat in a beloved tan suede bucket chair on a swivel base with one leg curled under me, touching my toes to the gold shag carpet with the other leg. Then I'd make it spin and spin until everything went kaleidoscopic because in that trippy kaleidoscope of light and sounds, my thoughts could be quiet, suspended in midair.

There was a coffee table made from a thick, curvy lacquered hunk of tree, where sometimes adults would visit and pass around joints or bowls of weed made of toilet paper rolls and aluminum foil. The furniture in our bedrooms was light and airy: a sweet canopy bed for my sister and a curved, white wrought iron antique for me. The furniture in Mom and Dad's room was heavy and dark, as if it meant to anchor them in this one spot. But we were anchored to nothing.

I remember the day my father left. I was sitting at the breakfast bar in our kitchen eating peanut butter Capt'n Crunch cereal and drinking OJ out of a Smurf glass from Hardees. My five-year-old feet were stuffed into my signature blue-and-white Nikes, and I used them for leverage against the wall of the counter as I twisted the barstool from side to side. Though the cereal shredded the roof of my mouth and the OJ stung the rawness as I drank it, I enjoyed the discomfort of it. Dad sat down beside me. He was handsome with olive skin, dark hair, dark eyes, and thick muscles on a compact frame. Back in those days, his buddies called him The Tasmanian Devil because of his muscular build. When

Dad's magnetic smile peeked out from under his Sam Elliot-esque mustache, it made you feel like the light of heaven had shone upon you. He is a man that makes people instinctively want to please and impress him.

In lieu of domestic life, he preferred fishing for sharks whiskey drunk with a gaff and gun on the outer banks of the Atlantic at night with his gang of wild-ass but fiercely loyal friends. He fenced competitively and trained middle to heavyweight boxers in the ring. When I was a kid, he trained a boxer that I came to love, his lifelong friend Henry "Bulldog" Patterson. Back then, Mack Trucks sponsored Bulldog, so a T-shirt was made that read *Built Like a Mack Truck*, and I wore it till the threads gave way. One time while at one of Bulldog's matches, I asked Dad if it was over because he and the other boxer were hugging. He tried to convince me the boxers were resting, not hugging. I loved the excitement of attending these fights, so on this point I chose to stay in denial. *Aw, see Dad, they were fighting but now they're hugging!*

When Dad turned his focus on you it was like a rush of adrenaline. What would happen next? Groundhog hunting on my belly with a rifle? I did this while silently praying that no groundhog would ever surface because there was no way in hell I'd ever shoot at one. A ride in his Lotus or Alfa Romeo at a speed so fast I couldn't lift my head from the back of the seat? Or, my favorite, squasharini time. Angie and I would often spend the afternoons after school upstairs in our bedrooms.

She would be listening to eight-track tapes and doing homework while I played with my electric racetrack. Dad would announce his homecoming like this: "I'm on the first step. I'm on the second step. I'm on the third step." By that time, I was squealing in my room, feigning fear but ridiculously excited for his attention. Once he got to the top of the steps near our bedrooms, he would spring forth into the hallway and yell, "Squasharini time!" He'd find us, paralyze us with his body weight and then tickle the ever-living shit out of us. Afterward, my sister (who loved and hated it when he did that to her) would often focus her attention on me. I think she liked overpowering me the way Dad had just done to her. She would sit on me and hold my arms over my head. My underarms were so ticklish that she didn't even have to touch me. Just force my arms over my head and I'd laugh so hard I'd nearly pee. This was way more fun for her than me, but I absolutely lived for the attention.

On this particular morning he told me he was going away for a while and that our beloved German shepherd, Sox, was going with him. He said I would see them both again real soon. "Like a vacation?" I asked. He shrugged. "Yeah, sort of." I don't remember being sad necessarily, but this must've been the moment I learned that life as I knew it could change in an instant. That I could wake up one morning to a different life with some people missing from it. Or perhaps this churning anxiety already existed, dormant, enmeshed in my design, encoded in the strands of my DNA, only to be awakened at this moment. I took another spoonful of cereal followed by another stinging sip of OJ.

My parents' separation was a trial separation until a neighbor saw Dad at the mall with his arms wrapped around a girl with long dark hair and a body shaped like a boy and reported back to my mom. It strikes me now that this description was the complete opposite of my blonde, curvy mother, and I wonder if she saw it that way too. When their split became finalized, my parents sold our brown house by the lake. My first-grade teacher and her husband purchased it. I had memories of living in that odd, boxy brown house by the lake with my family and living in the apartment that followed it but had no recollection of the move.

Decades later, when I went back to college to pursue my writing degree at age thirty-nine, I was assigned a short essay on the subject of home. This led me to ask my mom how I handled that move, or for that matter, any of the twelve moves we would later make together. I was stunned to find out that when my dad moved to Hickory, the next town over, and my mom and sister moved to an apartment forty-five minutes away in Charlotte, I'd stayed behind in our old house by the lake with my teacher and her family to finish out my first-grade school year. I remember her, but only from the classroom. My six-year-old impression of her is still with me today. She was smart, blonde, pretty, and no-nonsense. How exactly did that arrangement work? My friend Debbie once mused aloud, "Imagine the real estate listing: house comes with child." I wonder if I sat on the gold shag-carpeted stairs and watched as our belongings were whisked away and strange new furniture rolled in to take their place.

Maybe tiny, stubborn me thought that if I stayed there, my presence, like a rare earth magnet, would draw the family back home. I am certain I was not given a choice in this matter. Mom had become a single, working mother. The more likely scenario would be that it was easier to move and get settled in a new place without me. Angie was old enough to make herself something to eat and stay home alone. She didn't have an overabundance of big emotional needs and endless, exhausting questions the way I did.

Those questions persist. Did my lifelong fear of abandonment and feeling out of place, like a burden, originate from this distance from my family at such a formative age? Maybe some of us are just born this way, full of the inheritance of ancestral trauma. While I don't remember living with my teacher or anything about her family, perhaps more alarmingly, I don't remember a single thing about the entire year following it. I have no recollection of second grade or even which school I attended that year. No one in my family can say for sure how long I stayed with my teacher and her family. My dad said he had no idea any of that had happened at all. My stepfather, whom we would meet the year after I returned home to live with my mother, also never knew of it, but said, jokingly, that it sure explained a lot.

I'm fascinated that while our lives were turned upside down by their divorce and the sale of our home, my parents thought it acceptable to leave me behind to work out the details of this new life on my own. Maybe the simple answer is that, whatever the reasons may be, the baby boomer generation was on the search to find themselves, earning their reputation for being the least nurturing generation of parents. Perhaps they thought my youth protected me from understanding what was happening or feeling sad about this new arrangement. Something my Aunt Carmen had once casually mentioned came to mind: "Your parents were always looking for someone to ship you off to." When I was a kid, I sometimes spent weekends with Aunt Carmen and her live-in girlfriend, Vicky. When I was sick, which was often, and had to stay home from school, my mom would take me to my Aunt Karen's dog grooming shop because she couldn't miss work. The hum of the hair dryers would lull me to sleep, and once I felt better, she'd paint each of my nails a different color before sending me home. When Mom enrolled me in the Big Sisters Big Brothers program, I spent several evenings with my new Big Sister and her husband at the park or having dinner together until she got pregnant with a baby of her own.

At the time, I immediately dismissed Aunt Carmen's idea for two reasons: one, because being an inconvenience was a soul-deep feeling that had always been with me, and two, because I understood that my parents just didn't have the tools to be who I needed them to be and figured nothing good could come of dwelling on that. Curious about her comment, I asked my mom what I was like as a kid. Her blue eyes twinkled under her blonde bangs. She put down her latte and paused for a moment. "If you had been born first, I would have never had another one. You were a difficult child and I didn't know what to do with you!" I repeated her sentiment to my dad a few days later. He paused a moment longer, poker-faced, before cracking that million-dollar smile. "I completely agree with that." This wasn't upsetting to me the way it would have been years before, because I'd always felt I was too much for both of them, and at the same time, not enough. The "rub some dirt on it" generation of parents just didn't grasp the idea little kids had feelings and could sense the energetic shifts regardless of what facts their parents withheld from them. What I understand now is this: I was a lot of work—more than most six-year-olds—and that didn't fit with young, working parents and a sister independent enough not to drain them.

After that period in my life, I never stayed away from home without my family again—at least not without tears and a good fight. Whenever I attempted a sleepover with friends, I would inevitably call home and ask to be retrieved. My friends seemed so at ease, nestled into their beds or sleeping bags, while I'd become panic-stricken in the quiet stillness, overcome by a profound loneliness and stricken with anxiety. On weekends when Mom wanted to go out and dance the two-step, her friend Steven, a young restauranter, would take me to his friend's restaurants where we wandered through their kitchens sneaking fries and hanging out at the bar talking to the patrons and bartenders. When the sugar rush from unlimited Shirley Temples wore off, so did the novelty of being in a new, adult environment. When the sun set and the sky darkened, homesickness paralyzed me like a lead blanket. I felt unmoored. Like I was floating away from everyone and everything. Once when I was three or four years old, my family went camping on the Green River in the mountains of Western North Carolina. While tubing down the river, my parents lost hold of my inner tube and I got away from them. I floated down the river alone on that tube while my parents and their friends put it into hyper speed trying to regain a hold of me, which they eventually did. They say it's our earliest memories, the things that happen to and around us until age five, that shape our view of the world and of ourselves. I don't know if I remember floating away from them that day on the river or if the memory is mine because it was told to me. Either way, I have carried with me the sensation of floating past the reach of safety's arm.

I'd always sensed I was "too much" and yet at the same time lacking some quality that kept me from being happy, carefree, and childlike—the way I saw other kids. I was weighed down by something. I was no longer that independent little soul, born in Virgo season and with no use at all for men. Could this heaviness have been an inborn quality that would have surfaced regardless of life experience? Perhaps. Abandonment had worn deep ruts on both sides of my lineage, so the probability of inherited ancestral trauma was high.

A fear of abrupt change and rejection still haunts me today. Dad's affair with the boy-shaped girl was a core memory that left me with a certainty that I would eventually be traded out for a new friend or lover. That was the energy I brought to every relationship I'd have as a young person and into adulthood. I regularly have dreams of friends suddenly turning on me, discarding me like an old sock. I often have dreams in which my husband decides out of the blue that he doesn't love me anymore. A switch is flipped and the relationship always abruptly ends, without explanation, a cold turn of the shoulder, and I am unmoored. The first twinkling of the dream is illuminated with love that inexplicably turns dark as pitch, devoid of warmth and love.

In my dreams, I watch him change his mind about me, his face visibly darkening, pulling further away, morphing into a stranger right before my eyes. In every variation of this dream, he always chooses someone else, and she's always the opposite of me. She is comfortable in her own skin, and the way she looks at me says she knows that I am not. Though I don't see her family in the dream, I feel a strong sense that she is valued and imbued with their love. When I wake up, my cheeks are still hot with shame, and the feeling of being unwanted lingers. It takes hours to shake off the devastation.

Sometimes, I wake up angry at my husband. This took some adjusting to at first, but he learned not to take it personally and to reassure me. Some mornings when I wake and tell him I had bad dreams, he says, "Oh my God, I'm such a jerk! What did I do this time?" His ability to understand my deeply rooted fear of abandonment and his willingness to put aside his instinct to defend himself have saved me, time and time again. I was a heap of broken pieces and my jagged edges nicked him every time he opened his arms to catch me.

The Lost Year

The sky was electric blue and dotted with bright white clouds so puffy it looked like God had sculpted it all from Play-Doh. I was driving my kids to my dad and stepmom's house to play in the pool with my sister and her kids. My daughter had the iTunes dialed in and the sunroof was open. There was a kind of lightness to the air. The song "Little Jeannie" by Elton John came on the radio, and the second I heard those opening notes, an inscrutable sadness took my breath. My eyes burned with salty tears and I sobbed—hard. My reaction to this song was confounding to me and I couldn't remember the last time I'd heard it. The tinker of the Rhodes piano traveled across time and space like a musical umbilical cord, punching me in the gut, the place where the ghost of memories live, the memories we can feel, but can't consciously remember.

I could associate no specific memory with this song, and yet, here I was, ugly crying my way down the highway on a beautiful Carolina day, swiping at my face so I could see the road. "What's wrong, Mama?" my daughter asked.

"I don't know. I haven't heard this song since I was a kid. I have no idea why I'm crying."

A sick feeling fluttered in my belly and I felt a longing for something I couldn't identify. The way the lyrics of the chorus caused a physical ache in my bones made me feel exposed. I could not, and still can't, parse out the vague sadness associated with the song from the way those lyrics perfectly narrated my own coming-of-age story because I, too, was always someone's fool. When the song was over, I restarted it, hoping to fan this spark of a memory into flames. We pulled into my dad's driveway, and I filed it away to be examined at a later time. Later turned into years.

At the acupuncturist recently, I hopped up on the table, eager to be stuck like a pincushion in all the right places in hopes of relief from chronic back pain. Once the needles were in place, and not without me wincing and offering much commentary about how each pin hurt like hell, my acupuncturist, Stephen, turned down the lights and left the room. For the next twenty minutes, I drifted in and out of a tranquil state that's as out-of-body as anything I've ever known. I think it's called relaxation. When he returned, he removed the needles and began to perform some energy work on me. It's not as hoodoo voodoo as it sounds. He placed his hands under my lower back and gently manipulated my spinal fluid, you know, energetically. That's when my right shoulder began to twitch. As is my habit, I apologized for being weird.

"Don't be sorry. That's a grief point releasing. You're releasing grief."

This continued to happen for the next few minutes. It felt as though coils were unwinding inside of me as my right side jerked involuntarily. Twitch, jerk, twitch. In an almost trance-like voice, I proposed a possible theory on the source of this grief.

"I learned, not too many years ago, that I had been left behind to live with my first-grade teacher in our home that we had just sold to her and her husband, while my newly divorced parents and sister moved on to separate apartments in different towns. I was in my forties when Mom casually revealed this news to me, but I had no memory of it. She said she wasn't sure how long I was there, and Dad said that was the first he'd heard of it. Apparently, the arrangement had been made so that I could finish out my first-grade school year. My sister, six years older, was also school-aged, so I never could understand why I required this accommodation and she was allowed to move to our new apartment with our mom. I felt this could be a good explanation for why I can't remember anything about the following school year. I have always referred to it as The Lost Year." I let out a sigh, still twitching on the table.

"Wow, your voice changed while you were telling me this," he said.

"How can I grieve something I can't remember?"

"Abandonment," he said. "Your grief is about abandonment." The session ended and I got in my car to go home.

The next day was Easter Sunday. I was preparing two kinds of mashed potatoes, because we are a family divided. One half needs butter and cream, and the other half is lactose intolerant. I switched on the iTunes and "Little Jeannie" began to play. I hadn't thought about the song since that day in the car all those years ago, and I was immediately overcome by a groundswell of emotion. As if on cue, the tears poured forth from some deep, hidden place. *Grief*, I thought. *Elton and I are like Proust and his madeleine.*

In *Remembrance of Things Past*[3], author Marcel Proust describes the exquisite pleasure that unexpectedly invaded his senses at the taste of a madeleine cake dipped in tea, and though he could not connect it to a conscious memory, he felt it was a remembrance of an experience of the past. We know we can be transported in time by a flavor, a scent, a song, but can a song call forth subconscious connections to a past experience? I put down the potato masher and grabbed my laptop to see if Rabbi Google could explicate this oddity. Dr. Nikki Rickard, a music psychologist, explained it this way: "An event, an emotion, and a song get bound together in a part of the brain called the medial prefrontal cortex. When someone hears that music later

---
3. Proust, Marcel. *Remembrance of Things Past*. Grasset, 1913.

on, it's like the tip of the tongue effect. The memory is there; the sound helps bring it front of mind."

Hearing this song moved me so deeply, though the reason remains veiled. The melody and lyrics drape over the past like a scarf dampening the lamplight. Nostalgic and curious, I decided to look up the year the song came out. Turns out it was released in May 1980. Some quick math revealed that was the spring I would have been living with my teacher and the summer before my second-grade year, The Lost Year. "Little Jeannie" became Elton John's fifth number-one hit that summer and still to this day evokes in me a longing for something I just can't name.

An Urban Cowboy

The summer before I turned seven, I made the transition from our old house with my teacher to the apartment in the city with my mom and sister. I was a cute little kid with sandy-blonde hair and a little potbelly that my T-shirts strained to cover. I didn't wear dresses. My standard uniform was a pair of faded bell-bottom jeans and a T-shirt. My favorite one read, in prismatic letters, *Never Underestimate the Power of a Kid*. I was an entertainer and belted out off-key songs and choreographed sock-slide dances in my baggy sweatpants. I majored in telling dirty jokes: "Why did the flea fall off the dog's leg? He got pissed off!" My mom taught me all the best ones. "What do you call the world's largest condom? A condominium!" I practiced my comedic timing and delivered my punch lines whenever there was an opportunity. I was most often in the company of adults or my older sister and cousins. I craved their short flashes of attention. Their praise and interaction were like gold to me. I remember feeling starved for it and yet could never get enough, which I imagine made me tiresome to be around. The moment my insatiable need to be seen and heard had exhausted those around me, I panicked, certain I'd made an irrevocable mistake. I was afraid their temporary distance would soon become an ever-growing chasm between us. Mostly, I feared being alone.

Sometimes my sister Angie and I spent weekends with our dad. Some weekend nights when Mom had us, she and my Aunt Karen would go to a nightclub called the Country Underground to blow off steam. They were young and newly single, working full time and exhausted from trying to hold together all the pieces of their lives. With a guarded neighborhood entrance and an alarm system in the apartment, Mom felt we were safe, but my sister and I didn't. My sister, thirteen years old at the time, was unable to sleep and would sit at the top of the stairs with her back to the wall and fling herself into bed the moment she heard Mom's key in the door, pretending to be asleep and unafraid. I spent those nights hunkered down in my own bed with thirty or so of my closest companions. Shrouded in a blanket of stuffed animals, I was comforted by the knowledge that if someone broke in and managed to get past my big sister on watch duty, they would think my room was unoccupied. Upon close inspection, an intruder may have been able to make out a large brown teddy bear, a red stuffed dog with white ears, or a yellow dog-bear hybrid in denim overalls, but wouldn't see much more of me than my eyeballs. I was hiding, but from what?

My meticulous nature had morphed into a kind of OCD. I could never, ever sleep in the dark or with my back to the door. Every single night, without exception, I methodically arranged my stuffed friends in a formation around me, two deep in circular fashion, until I was surrounded by a plush wall of protection. The shape of the circle was critical because each one had to have a friend on both sides. This was as much for their safety as for mine. I could not rest if any of us had an exposed side. My mom always joked that she had a hard time finding me when she came to kiss me goodnight. I felt safer this way, but I didn't feel at ease there or anywhere. I had this habit of holding my blanket to my nose and mouth while I slept. Mom always worried I would suffocate, but I had to sleep this way. I constantly felt the need to cover, to hunker, and pull up my blanket until I disappeared underneath. I felt like a body with no skin on. For decades, I slept in a blanket cocoon, with an extra blanket twisted up around me under the covers. My husband would later grow adept in finding me and fishing me out. I was, and still am, a constant seeker of comfort with fuzzy blankets, warm drinks, slippers, pillows, and heating pads always within reach. After the stuffed animal ritual, I would say my prayers, being sure to cover everyone and everything. I didn't know to whom exactly I was praying. The majestic receiver of prayers in the sky? God was good if you pleased him, mean if you didn't. *Now I lay me down to sleep . . .*

It was the era of *Urban Cowboy*, my favorite movie when I was a kid. It had everything a kid growing up in the seventies and eighties could expect in a movie: domestic violence, drinking, sex, bad language, good ole bar fights, and even a mechanical bull ride. Don't judge my mom though. It was rated PG in 1980. I liked *My Little Pony* and *Sesame Street*, but mostly I dreamed of riding that bull like Sissy did. I wanted to slow dance with a handsome, dark, and moody cowboy and be loved in the fucked-up way Bud loved Sissy. More than anything, I wanted to look like Sissy, with her lithe body, flat chest, and raspy Southern twang. Spoiler alert: I would later sprout the largest boobs in the sixth-grade class, which is to say the *only* boobs in the sixth-grade class.

Mom was petite, whip smart, and gorgeous. She turned heads with her big, bright smile and frosted hair that feathered out on the sides. Her looks were an amalgamation of Barbara Mandrell and Goldie Hawn. In my mind's eye, she pulled on her brown felt hat and tan broken-in Frye boots and headed out to Country Underground where she found us an urban cowboy of our own. His name was Ken, and he came to court the three of us in a shiny El Camino. He was tall, lanky, and bearded and reminded me of Kenny Rogers. Rogers and Sam Elliot, who had the same smiling, twinkly eyes and dark mustache as my dad, were my childhood heroes. For all I knew, Kenny Rogers could have majored in drugs, alcohol, and breaking hearts, but his songs made him sound like a man who cared about the right things. He seemed like a human teddy bear to me and his thick head of hair and full beard made him resemble one. Besides, he had the penultimate endorsement: he was good enough for Dolly Parton. Back then I assumed they were a couple since I heard them profess they were islands in the stream multiple times a day on the radio. His proximity to her made him good enough for me.

When they first met, Mom's new boyfriend Ken made floor lamps out of scrap brass and sold them in a tiny storefront called Yesteryear Lighting. He fell in love with Mom and became smitten with us girls. Rumor had it he had called off an engagement to another woman to be with my mom, but I have never asked for clarification on this. He lived life by his own rules, which were something along the lines of "if you can dream it, you can do it" and "do what you want as long as it feels good." This kind of early-eighties carelessness was framed as fun by his "there's humor in everything if you look for it" approach to life. Soon after they started dating, Ken started a bathtub refinishing business. There was an article about him in the local paper with a headline that read, "This Guy Spends All Day in the Bathtub" and a photo of him, handsome and young, standing in a bathtub.

One day he announced that Louisville, Kentucky, was a great place to grow a small business, and it wasn't long before we packed up the apartment and headed for the Bluegrass State. This would be the first of eight moves we would make over the next seven years. We loaded our things into a U-Haul and made our way through the winding mountain roads of West Virginia and into Kentucky. I sat up front with my mom for a while and kept her company as she drove. My sister Angie and Ken were in the back, goofing off. There was a tap at the window that separated the cab from the cargo area where they were riding. They were both laughing hysterically as they had tied the power cord of my sister's hair rollers around the neck of my stuffed Smurf and were swinging him in front of the window for me to see, turning their heads to the side and sticking out their tongues to cruelly mock his death. I wish I'd found that funny then, but I didn't. Know your audience, people. By this time, I had what my parents referred to as a chip on my shoulder, which I understood to be literal not figurative, leading me to wonder, *how did it get there?* My shoulders did feel heavy. I felt misunderstood, like the things I liked and the things I worried over were dumb in the eyes of the older people I was always surrounded by, and the emotions I had were too much to make me tolerable. I felt silly for loving the stupid stuffed animal, which was totally age appropriate. As we crossed the state lines, leaving behind everyone and everything we knew, the Smurf and all his stuffed buddies were a steadfast source of comfort.

It occurs to me now, with young parents and a much older sibling, not much of our family life was oriented toward anything childlike. Doesn't every seven-year-old give their mom knitted nipple covers with dangling tassels from Spencer's Gifts for her birthday? While my mom always made sure Santa, the Easter Bunny, and the Tooth Fairy came to visit us and made every Valentine's Day sweet, being a child with lots of emotional needs made me feel like the outlier among my adult-oriented, rather impatient family members.

When we settled in Kentucky, Mom and Ken set up the chemical spray booth in the garage and continued to build their bathtub refinishing business. Ken seemed to know how to do everything. That year he taught me how to chemically etch glass for an elementary school science fair project. My sister and I would still make our way back to North Carolina to visit my dad in the summers. He'd moved from the bachelor apartment, where we spent all day at the swimming pool, to an A-frame house in the middle of a golf course. Angie, who was dark-haired, wide-eyed, and looked like a movie star, would hunker down on the sofa and watch soap operas while Dad was at work, sometimes practicing her cheer routines in front of the TV. This allowed me to wander the golf course unattended. I'd slide on my signature Nikes, red-and-black striped skort and matching top—because, you know, spontaneous cartwheel practice—and head out to inspect all the ball washing stations for forgotten balls. The neon green, orange, and yellow ones were a particularly exciting score. After that, I'd wander down to the tennis courts and hit balls against the backboard with Dad's spare racket. Like everything athletic I tried, I wasn't any good at it, but I practiced in case Dad wanted to hit some balls with me after work. I wanted to impress him with my skills. He was so good at all the things, and so far, exactly none of that skill or natural talent had shown up in me like it had in my sister. I know now that I carried shame and embarrassment about that.

Sometimes I ended the day with a walk over to the clubhouse to order a hamburger—Carolina-style with chili, slaw, onions, and mustard—and charge it to Dad, please. I'd sit out on the green and eat it out of a cardboard container, juices from the slaw dribbling down my chin and onto my shirt. I was comforted by ritual and routine so I created my own, and of course, it revolved around food. Mornings began with chocolate frosted Pop Tarts or sugary cereal, and TV shows were incomplete without chips, crackers, or popcorn. On one particular visit, we received a letter from Mom back home. She told us she missed us bunches and caught us up on everything going on with her and Ken before asking, "How are you girls doing with your weight?" I was ten and my sister was sixteen, and as petite girls growing up in a world of women who were getting thinner and thinner, she foresaw the struggle ahead of us. Some might criticize a mother for this, but I'm grateful she taught me to understand my relationship with food and how to be mindful of it. She also knew what I was soon to learn, that according to *Cosmopolitan* magazine, MTV, and Calvin Klein ads, the valuation of a woman was based on the slimness and sensuality of her body.

The year I started sixth grade, my mom's father came to stay with us. Pawpaw was a mostly deaf Navy veteran who had also been a long-haul truck driver, and he had the mudflap girl tattooed on both forearms. He mostly nodded and smiled. When I was small and we still lived in Charlotte, he'd bestowed upon us nicknames. My sister's nickname was Pineapple, which I'd assumed was on account of our last name being Pyne. Mine was Crabapple and required no explanation. He mostly kept to himself by staying busy working on the rolling hills of our park-like yard and going to bed by six p.m. every night. Once when Mom and Ken went away on vacation, Pawpaw fried potatoes and onions in bacon fat and served it to me for dinner every night. He didn't like me walking to school as I normally did, so he drove me, eliminating my means of exercise. When they returned after a week away, my face was rounder and my parachute pants tighter than was appropriate. I was put on a diet and lost the weight pretty quickly just by not eating fried potatoes every night and walking to school again. Later on, there would be the cabbage soup diet, the grapefruit diet, and the food combining diets, all with varying degrees of temporary success.

Back at our rented home in Kentucky, I tried to settle in and make new friends. One fall morning I was mesmerized by the "Video Killed the Radio Star" video on the brand-new phenomenon known as MTV when I should have been raking the leaves. My mom called the house phone. I answered it and stretched the long brown coiled cord back to my spot in front of the TV. "Shellie, have you raked the leaves like I asked you to?" she inquired. "Yep. Sure did," I lied easily. "Okay. We'll be home soon," was her cryptic reply. Deciding I should make good on that declaration, I switched off the TV and grabbed the rake. I'd been raking only about twenty minutes or so when I managed to cut my leg on a ragged piece of gutter. How in the world I had managed this I have no idea. In my intensely dramatic fashion, I dragged the wounded leg behind me into the house, howling and in tears as I called for my big sister. Angie cleaned my leg in the bathroom sink, and when I was all fixed up, I walked out of the back door and right into my mom and Ken.

Mom was so angry when she realized the raking wasn't complete and that I had lied. The cut was all but ignored. She sent me to my room and came in a short while later with a notebook. She had written "SHELLIE" in all caps across the cover. She announced, "You will write 'I will not lie' one thousand times in this notebook." As a fourth grader with a short attention span and terrible penmanship, I declared this a cruel and unusual punishment. I argued that I had *intended* to do the raking, and that was basically the same thing, but she wasn't buying it. When I had completed the task, she wrote my name again in the back of the notebook and circled "LIE" at the end of my name. I had been branded a liar and now there was shame associated with my name. The moment I realized there were other spellings for my nickname, I chose "Shelley" and never looked back. My given name was Rachelle, though it was only spoken by my mother if I was in trouble and unknown to my friends.

Not too long after that, Mom discovered Ken was having an affair with their secretary. My usually chipper mom was irate and distraught as she slammed her belongings into her overnight bag. Angry and heartbroken, her blonde curls bounced as she told my sister and me to gather our things for a trip. I packed a shiny purple swimsuit, my teddy bear, my favorite white pillow with red trim, a nighty, and a pair of shorts into my duffle bag and waited at the back door. We drove out of town and through the Eastern Kentucky countryside. We finally stopped after what seemed like hours, but probably wasn't, and checked in to a Holiday Inn. I walked over to a park across the street and found the swing set while mom sat in the hotel room on the phone with Ken. Once it got dark, we came in and turned the TV to *Gilligan's Island*.

Just before bed, Mom shut off the TV and packed us back into the car. We went right back home and life resumed as normal as far as I could tell. That Christmas, Mom and Ken surprised me with a beautiful, blond-haired, brown-eyed cocker spaniel puppy. The very first time I ever had a dog of my own. On Christmas Eve, they had told me there was a mouse in the garage to explain away the strange noises this puppy was making in his crate. On Christmas morning, they handed me a squirming duffle bag with my name embroidered on it, spelled *SHELLIE*, of course. I just knew that mouse had gotten into the bag, so I was too terrified to touch it. Mom and Ken finally insisted I open it. When a golden-headed puppy wearing a red Santa hat popped out of the bag, my chest filled with a feeling I didn't remember ever having had before. The blood running through my body felt warm, and I had butterflies. It felt like true joy. To put it simply, I felt like a kid. I named him Kelly so it would rhyme with my name. I was obsessed with him and he followed me everywhere.

A few years (and another house) later, when I would walk to school in the sixth and seventh grades, Kelly would follow my scent through the neighborhood the moment he was let out in the morning. Sitting in class, I could hear him howling outside the window. A peek through the blinds would reveal that silky, golden-haired dog with the big brown eyes sitting in the parking lot with his head thrown back, a deep howl calling out for me from his barrel chest. The principal would have to call my parents to come get him. One time when I went to North Carolina to visit Dad, I had to leave Kelly behind with Mom and Ken. Kelly fell down the exterior set of concrete steps that led from the patio to the basement and broke his leg. It was storming that night and my parents were convinced he'd gone looking for me. He wore a cast for weeks and it rubbed his little nuggets raw, which made Ken pity him and give him extra treats. Kelly was always loving and protective of me, except when he had to be crated. My sweet, loyal companion would growl, snarl, and become unrecognizable if I so much as looked at him while he was in the crate. I remember being so mad at him for the betrayal that I would sometimes retaliate with a slap on the top of the crate when he did it. Horrible of me, I know, but the rejection stung.

One day when Kelly was five years old, Ken raised his hand at me while reprimanding me for something I can't recall, probably for being a smartass, and Kelly, perceiving that as a threat, lunged and bit him on the hand. That was it for Kelly. My parents returned him to the breeder's farm from which he came, and he lived out the rest of his days as a stud. Ken tried to convince me he was living his best life, and he probably was, but the sudden loss of him reopened the pit of loneliness in me.

Barreling through like a Storm

Obviously, I can't remember my birth, but I'm certain that one glimpse of life outside the womb was all it took for me to understand I was an alien in this world. As a child, I was always squirmy while in the arms of others, desperately trying *not* to be held, and later, as a disassociated adult, I longed for arms to encircle and protect me. I didn't want anyone to see the tender parts of me until one day I did, and then that became all I thought about, the thing I wanted most in the world: to be loved consistently, exclusively in a way that felt like I'd finally arrived home. I felt as though the love of someone else could bring me back to my body and make me feel real, like the Velveteen Rabbit.

When I was a kid, a family friend looked our mom in the eye with an odd intensity and asked, "When are you going to tell her she has 'the gift'?" Apparently, he saw some clairvoyance in me. I wish I knew what I'd said or done to give him this certainty. My mom simply nodded in agreement, as if it were the most natural thing to say about her five-year-old child. She was always ahead of her time in matters like the supernatural. I never saw myself as gifted, but I did feel different from everyone else. I understood little about what was going on inside me and around me, yet I had a keen sense of the undercurrents of energy from people. I learned to read their faces and body language for signs of impending rejection and abandonment.

I have often heard some people referred to as "old souls." I know very few things for certain, but I do know this: my soul is brand new here, as clueless as a bare-assed baby. This is definitely my first time here on Earth. Later, when I had a daughter of my own, she would be a twenty-one-year-old college student when she confessed to me that she just now felt like a teenager. I immediately confessed that, at nearly fifty years old, I just now felt like I'd make a good parent. I think Mom's friend caught on to one right thing about me. I did and do have a knowing, a sixth sense, a deep intuition. It's a shame it would be decades before I'd be confident enough to trust it.

There's a photo of my dad, my sister, and me stuck on the mirror in front of my writing desk. My dad is kneeling, dukes up, on a green grassy lawn facing my sister, who was about thirteen at the time. She is playing along with a big grin and her fists are up too. I'm running up behind my dad with both hands out, about to push him hard with all my seven-year-old might. Once the image was snapped, I came barreling through, like a storm, destroying an otherwise perfect day. I wanted some of that attention. I wanted to play too, but their reaction was one of annoyance because I didn't understand the rules of engagement. My dad had taught Angie how to protect her face, how to throw a punch, how to let his mood determine her level of interaction with him. She was confidently showing him her form and skill. They had a history together. He had been present and had taught her things for many years, and they'd grown close before I arrived in their world. She was cool and collected like him. I was a deep well of unmet needs, a human question mark.

I would spend many decades trying to quiet those needs and learning to hide the constant questions that looped over and over in my mind: *Do you love me? Do I belong here? Am I broken? Are you going to leave me? What does everyone else know about this moment or that thing I'd somehow managed to miss?* That photo is a snapshot of how I felt the entirety of my childhood and adolescence: as though I was imposing myself upon people who'd prefer I wasn't there at all. What I recall the most about childhood is always doing things wrong, being farmed out to the care of others, and feeling like a tremendous inconvenience and a failure. I have come to understand that for me, it wasn't the trauma of having been left behind, no matter how temporary it may have been; farmed out to friends and family; or the sense that I was too much to deal with, but the subsequent narrative it created within my psyche. I saw myself through this cracked lens of unworthiness.

Take, for example, the family trip to Reno we took when I was thirteen years old. I woke up in our motel room at the bottom of the mountain near the popular Lake Tahoe ski resort, Heavenly. On our first night in town, we'd gone to Caesar's Palace in Reno to gamble. When we arrived, we were told I wasn't old enough to enter, so I had to stay in the arcade while Mom, Ken, and Ang were in the casino. Had they not known that I was too young to join them on this outing? No matter, I had the entire place to myself and spent my whole wad of money on the stuffed-animal-filled claw machine. I played like a girl possessed. I plucked animal after animal out of the glass boxes, pumping my fist in the air, rejoicing in my solitary victory. Toward the end of the night, a member of the staff happened by and a smile broke over her face when she saw the growing mountain of stuffed animals on the floor beside me. She helped me pack my haul into two large trash bags. It was a glorious victory.

The next night, the four of us saw comedian Kevin Nealon of *Saturday Night Live* open for The Pointer Sisters at Caesar's Palace. Another exclusively adult evening, but this time I was admitted entry. My lips were stained maraschino red from cherries and grenadine. I was wired from bottomless Shirley Temples, the energy of the performances, the lights, the roar of the audience, and the edgy content of the comedy set. The following morning, I awakened to the whir of hair dryers and the sound of the news blaring from the TV. I slid out of bed, got dressed and ready for adventure. I sat on the edge of the bed, watching my mom and sister fluff their hair and apply their makeup. Ken told me to walk over to the McDonald's across the parking lot and get us breakfast. *May as well*, I thought with an attitude. I had given up on my campaign to switch the news to cartoons. I was to get four biscuits, four hash browns, an orange juice, three coffees, and a specific number of creamers and sugar packets. I was distracted and annoyed at being the errand girl, especially fetching coffee for my older sister who had, just the day before, been allowed to drink cocktails and gamble with our parents while they set up a date for her with some dude at the bar. I was dressed in a putty-gray ski bib looking like an Oompa Loompa while Angie and Mom wore sparkly ski sweaters and sexy black ski pants designed to fit like the stirrup pants trend of the time.

I tucked the greasy bag under my arm and balanced the foam drink carrier piled with what I would soon learn was the incorrect number of creamers and sugars. Irritated with me, mostly because it was pre-coffee and post-too-many Chivas Regals, Ken admonished me and sent me back three more times until I was in tears with frustration and embarrassment and finally had something close to the correct number of creamers and sugars—a number I was convinced had changed every time he sent me out the door.

I pouted through breakfast, but by the time we got to the powdery white slopes of Heavenly at Lake Tahoe, I'd forgotten my recent humiliation and couldn't care less what I was wearing. High up on the ski lift, where you could see snow on one cliff side and desert on the other, I wasn't afraid. It was one of those rare times when I didn't have intrusive thoughts and felt a sense of belonging. We were all skiing together, having the same experience—no need to leave me with a teacher, send me to the arcade, find me a sitter, or send me on a solo mission to fetch everyone a meal. When the lift dropped us off at the top of the run, Ken, handsome as ever, dressed in a red ski bib pantsuit like mine, waved me over with a conspiratorial grin and said, "Come on!" So, the two of us glided down the intimidating black diamond run together, communicating only through the swish of our skis as they cut through the powder. We were together, so I wasn't afraid, and he was proud of that.

We Were the Trees

While enrolled in middle school at St. Leonard's Catholic School, I began to study other students in an attempt to create an identity for myself. Comparison was my habit so when I noticed the beautiful handwriting of my classmate, I deemed my own bordered on illegible. So as with most areas in which I found myself lacking, I attempted to imitate the flowing script and cute doodles of my classmate, Lizzie. She drew delightful, puffy, rounded versions of stick people that she would sketch in her notebook with uplifting titles such as "Happy Spring!" that she'd draw in bubble letters. The joy-filled, balloon-like characters, which I studied over her shoulder long enough to replicate, were not as well matched to the attitude of my autobiographical-inspired drawings based on the nickname given me by Ken and Mom: "Shit Breath Says Happy Winter!" And my own balloon characters looked more like bowling pins with faces than people, waves of green emanating from their word bubbles illustrating their bad breath.

The new neighborhood was full of traditional families, which confirmed my suspicions that we were square pegs in an ocean of round holes. There was Cassie with her

L.L. Bean tote bag embroidered with her monogram in pink and green, obviously to match the floral wallpaper and the comforter of her bedroom. And Lizzie, with her big brown doe eyes, perfectly smooth chestnut hair, and that spectacular handwriting that I still to this day try to imitate. She came across as being put together, cared for, and confident, while I felt shaggy and sure that nothing about me was special. I saw her handwriting and ability to draw as her thing. I wanted a thing.

I couldn't penetrate the cliques of the preppy, well-adjusted kids. I found a few friendships among the outliers and made fast friends with any wayward kid that didn't have a tribe. I just didn't know how to be myself. Being cool was an act, and it came across as disjointed and not authentic. I was wound tight as a tick and completely out of touch with my body. I was anxious, unsure of every move, and weighed down by that giant chip on my shoulder—which was really just the weight of feeling like I didn't belong at school or in my family. After years of constant change and no outlet to process the emotions surrounding it, I had become disengaged from myself.

A double perm and bi-level haircut topped the list of ways I tried too hard. In a show of the chronic pissed-offness my parents were ill-equipped to understand, I gave them, and everyone else, the middle finger, literally and figuratively. Shame made me feel as though I had to hide the deeper parts of me that felt broken so I was impossibly hard to reach. I didn't know how to communicate my feelings with words so

I flipped the bird and mooned anyone and everyone every chance I got. On the outside, I was defensive and unsure of myself. On the inside, I was a little girl with her hair on fire, a cat on a hot tin roof waiting for the next rejection, ready to yank her pants down and show her ass to the world.

The neighborhood families seemed to have deep roots in the community, and they had religion. I'm sure not all of them were Catholic, but most were. Once a month, the whole neighborhood would participate in a fish fry, replete with beer and bingo. I was a regular winner, often taking home six-packs of Budweiser, two-liters of Coke, bags of flavored popcorn, and giant candy bars. On my first day at the neighborhood Catholic school, the teacher, Mrs. V, introduced me to my new sixth-grade classmates. "We have a new student joining us today." And then she asked me in front of everyone, "What religion are you?" My father's side of the family is ethnically Jewish and since that is also a religion, I proudly pronounced myself Jewish to a classroom full of Catholic kids. The teacher didn't hide her surprise. I'd labeled myself an outlier. From that moment on I knew, instinctively, it was best to act like I didn't care about fitting in. I spent the entire school year making up words as I attempted to recite their holy prayers. I acted my way through every school day and every social event. I hid away my tender self and watched others to see how I should behave in any given circumstance. I connected with no one and there were a few kids who absolutely lived to terrorize me.

That fall, my parents gave me the money to host a baby shower for my teacher, Mrs. V, in the rectory. Unfortunately, I discovered at an early age that if you give everything of yourself, if you open a vein and bleed out, you might just get a teeny morsel of acceptance in return. That day I belonged. I may have just as well run around that rectory shouting, "Do you love me now?" Every petit four I placed on the doily-lined tray was a question. "Am I one of you now? Do you accept me?"

Mom and Ken installed a giant hot tub on the back porch of our new house. They were still unmarried, and this fact drew the attention of the conservative neighbors and my Catholic school faculty, but their unconventional lifestyle quickly found them kinship with another "good time" family that lived behind us. My fast friendship with their son, Matt Maple, was life-saving. I felt as though our last names, mine Pyne and his Maple, had destined us to be friends. We were the trees. When a bad thunderstorm would come and our parents were at work, he'd bravely run over full-speed from his house and sit with me in my basement until it passed. I was terrified of storms.

We were both small in stature, artsy, and tortured, both from broken and hastily rebuilt families. He had a killer smile, breakdance moves, and parachute pants, and I lived in purple-and-black flannel, had an accidental double perm—thanks to the first one that didn't completely take—braces, and an awkward interpretation of Michael Jackson's moonwalk. Matt was the only hope I had of being cool. He liked me and accepted me more than anyone I knew, boy or girl. I acted like myself around him and he knew me better than anyone. It should have been a lesson to me: the one person that liked me the most was the one person I acted like myself around. Aside from Matt, I had no other friends at St. Leonard, only the aforementioned Lizzie and Cassie. They were nice because they were raised that way, but unwilling to truly be my friend and risk angering The Evil Trio, the mean girls of the school. Awkward and perpetually the new kid, I was an easy target and these three mean girls hated me immediately and immensely. Their teasing was relentless. As a defense, I had curated an arsenal of smart-assery. Also not helpful in making friends with these girls were the oversized boobs I'd grown the summer before. Oh, how I wish I'd understood their powers.

In gym class, we often had to play basketball. I was short and not even a little bit athletically skilled. Becky, Tory, and Mary Katherine would point and laugh at me. "You're an idiot. Go home, loser!" they'd say. While this was textbook bullying, I was not innocent. I'd come to this school full of hope that this one might be different and I would find a sense of belonging. When it was clear that was not going to happen and that I would be the butt of their jokes and target for all their snarky barbs, I became a real asshole and gave it right back to them. I was outnumbered and that felt unfair. The boys, whose attention they sought constantly, were so nice to me. They laughed at my jokes and hung out with me when the girls didn't. Finding easy friendships with guys would continue throughout my youth and into my young adult years.

A deep well of loneliness and the dread of what antics awaited me at school churned inside me, rattling me awake with nausea and nervousness each morning. I slipped out of bed and into Mom and Ken's room, hovering over them as they slept. When one of them would crack an eyelid, I would declare myself unwell and unable to go to school that day. I said the same few words, "I don't feel good." I never said, "I'm sick" because in our family that was already code for, "Do *not* go in there," referring to the bathroom from which we had just exited.

This was different. I was panic-stricken by the thought of going to school every single morning. I had the Sunday scaries every night of the school week. No one suspected anxiety was behind this daily ritual. We didn't talk about any of that back then. If a child was anxious, it read as difficult and was treated as a discipline issue. Truth was, I hated school because I just couldn't fit in and I was bullied relentlessly. There was a sharp undercurrent of energy at home that I just couldn't put my finger on, but it felt like every man for himself. My father wasn't a regular presence in my life and when he was, the conversation was usually about whatever discord was taking place between him and my mom and Ken. I was deeply insecure and full of self-loathing and anxiety. I masked it with a sharp, bitter attitude, so I may as well have had a target on my back.

Anxiety, shame, and the feeling of not belonging left me chronically sick to my stomach and exhausted. They had to have known something was up, because one day I found a book on my bed entitled, *How to Survive Catholic School.* My parents chose to send me to St. Leonard's because it was in the neighborhood and therefore walking distance. They worked long days, so I needed to get myself to and from school and be self-sufficient until dinnertime. One day at school, I noticed dissention among the mean-girl ranks. The Evil Trio was bickering about a boy and ignoring me for once. My case of morning nerves, combined with a breakfast of cereal and milk, had caused a concerning gurgling in my gut. I let go of a giant, silent fart as I quietly slipped behind them, unnoticed, and watched from the other side of the court as they waved their hands furiously and pointed fingers at one another. I'd caused division among them and celebrated this small victory.

Morning after morning, my parents were startled awake by my creepy stare. One such morning, out of desperation, Ken instructed my mom to call the doctor. "Stick her with every needle you can," I imagine he directed. "Run every test you have so we can be sure she is healthy." Wink, wink. I was an anxiety-ridden kid as it was, so adding needles to the situation sent me right over the hairy edge. I was more stubborn than scared, so game on.

I resolved to take those needles while I silently prayed for something to be wrong with me—something that would allow me to be homeschooled, but not result in disfigurement or death. Clammy, shaking, and about ready to yarf, I set my jaw and laid my arm out for the nurse. She brandished a two-pronged needle that looked like a little white sombrero that she used to create a bubble under my skin. This was a tuberculosis test. Then she gave me a tetanus booster and finished with a blood test.

Once they declared me healthy, Ken rewarded me with warm, salty fries and a chocolate milkshake from the drive-thru and then dropped me off at school. I arrived just in time for the weekly mass. I made my way down the aisle to the pew where I sat by myself every Thursday, aching to be welcomed inside this world of incense and ritual, protection and belonging. Instead, I watched as those students, the ones I understood were acceptable to God, stood in line for their wafer and wine.

Stone-Cold Sober, but Also Kind of Drunk

When we lived in Kentucky, we would sometimes meet up with my dad's parents, Nana and Bobo, at a hotel close to where they lived in Cincinnati. The most exciting thing about this hotel was the indoor pool. It wasn't just any pool. Designed to feel as if you're in a cavern, it was surrounded by rocks with little waterfalls spilling over and into the pool. The restaurant had a five-star rating and the best burger I'd ever eaten. Or maybe food always tastes that good when you're waterlogged from a day of swimming, bone-tired with fingers and toes shriveled up like raisins.

Years later, when I was thirteen, Ken was hired as the general manager of this hotel and we would sometimes go to visit him there for the weekend. On one memorable trip, Spuds McKenzie, the Bud Light dog, was scheduled to make an appearance at the pool party on Saturday. I spent Friday afternoon swimming in the rock pool and had dinner in the restaurant. For the rest of the evening, I sat at a table in the bar reading Judy

Blume and VC Andrews, occasionally laughing out loud at a copy of *MAD* magazine, while Mom and Ken talked and drank at the bar with some employees. At some point in the night, Ken wandered off, and the employees were just drunk enough to feel comfortable telling my mom how much of an asshole he was as a boss. I think she probably looked around and noticed he was missing because soon she was charging down the hallway with great purpose, a few servers and bartenders following her. "Come on, Shellie!" she called out over her shoulder. Flustered and trying to catch up, I gathered my books and my Walkman and hauled ass after her. They protested to my mother. "Miss Libby, come back and sit down. You're drunk."

"I am stone-cold sober," my mom repeated over and over like a mantra, as though if she said it enough it would be true.

Mom eventually found Ken passed-out drunk and facedown on the lawn near the outdoor pool where we would sit in the sun as a family the next day and watch the famous dog entertain the guests.

There is a photo of me taken either that night or the next morning. I am sleeping on the sofa in their hotel room with a fuzzy gold blanket twisted up in my fist and pulled up to my nose. The roundness of my cheeks is in sharp contrast with the bi-level punk haircut of my early teen years. I remember wondering what possessed them to take this photo of me. I was sleeping peacefully as though my nervous system hadn't been short-circuited again and my parents hadn't been comically drunk and arguing. What I wanted was for my pain to be seen and for it to matter how these things affected me. I wanted them to put an end to the nuclear-level arguments and outsized reactions. I didn't think about what this might mean for my mom's sense of well-being or of what pain my stepdad was self-medicating, because I saw them as parents, not people who were once neglected and abused children, carrying shame they tried to outrun with busyness, asserting control over what they thought they could and drinking away the rest. How could I have known when they themselves didn't know? I was a kid who could only wish for stability and a sense of belonging, for no more moves or new schools where I'd once again feel like the outlier. My bones ached to feel settled in my body, my mind longed for stasis. Unfortunately, another big move was just around the corner.

Teenage Musicians Are Jerks

By the time I was seventeen, I'd moved twelve times and never attended the same school more than two consecutive years. Every other year I was the new girl in class, always flying in a solo orbit, a weirdo circling just outside tightly wound circles of friends. These friends had a shared history, years of dance classes, Sunday school lessons, and soccer at the Y. I'd never fit in with the children of conventional homes like the families in the neighborhoods where we lived. Their faces would change from school to school, but the fact that I couldn't assimilate didn't.

With my hands in my lap in class, I repeatedly cracked my knuckles hard, and then press my fingers backward until the skin there would dry out, crack, and bleed. Eczema, the doctor said. It was an outwardly visible sign of my invisible pain. I liked the concern on my mom's face when she examined my hands, so I went along with it. Too squeamish to do myself any real harm, I'd jam one fingernail underneath, peel back the skin until the blood came and the damaged skin underneath turned black—a habit I still revert to when anxiety threatens to overwhelm me. Though I gave up biting my nails decades ago, back then, I'd bite off a piece of fingernail and wedge it between my teeth, painfully, making my gums sting and bleed. I'd keep it there for hours while in class until eventually the pain would ease. It was gross, distracting, and self-inflicted. A smokescreen for the ever-present pain I could not name.

When my high school science teacher (his name was Pete Moss; I swear, it's true) revealed to our ninth-grade class that he had this very same habit, I thought to myself, *He is my people!* I examined him closely, searching for the gap in his teeth. Later, in my late teens or early twenties, this hurts-so-good torture took place two teeth over from the front, and eventually created a gap in my gums that my sister affectionately referred to as my "pepper tooth." The space in the gums I'd created looked like a piece of pepper perpetually stuck between my teeth. She'd point to her mouth and say, "You got a little something . . . oh, it's just your pepper tooth." Pepper tooth was mild in comparison to my nickname: Shit Breath. Occasionally, if my sinuses were really bad, which was almost always, my nickname was upgraded to Death Breath. Oh, how many times I wished to inhale and exhale deeply and take someone out like a sniper. My pepper tooth and bad breath were just two more things to feel self-conscious about.

When I was a freshman in high school, we moved into a townhome in a golf course community while my parents built a house a few streets over in the fancier, less transient part of the neighborhood. Once again, I spent hours hunting golf balls, but this time I made money doing it. The country club paid us kids for any recovered balls we collected. This age-appropriate activity was in stark contrast to the other activities I'd eventually engage in with the neighborhood kids. Back then, we'd walk to a nearby wooded creek that had a rope swing made accessible by several two-by-fours nailed to the trunk. Then we'd grab the rope, swing out over the creek, and drop into the water below. Sitting on the rocks alongside the water in my ruffled, strapless pink one-piece that looked like a two-piece but was connected on one side, we stole puffs of a cigarette while we dried off in the hot Kentucky sun. Some older kids made out, but no boys showed interested in me. I wore my insecurity like a forehead tattoo.

I thought my luck was changing when the cool new girl in school moved into the condo right next door to us. Her name was Crystal Rose. She was mysterious, confident, and had wild, tousled dark hair like Jami Gertz in the movie *Less Than Zero*. One night she invited me to come with her to a friend's house for a small get-together. I hopped into the passenger seat of her 240zx and slid a homemade cassette of all my favorite Led Zeppelin songs into the tape player. We sang along to "Kashmir" and "Going to California" on the short drive there. We made our way down the steep driveway and knocked on the back door of the house that opened to a rec room in the basement. I sucked in my breath when I saw Bobby Banks, an eighteen-year-old guitar-playing senior and a dead ringer for U2's front man, Bono, and three other guys standing around a pool table. Crystal was as cool as I was awkward. Beers were passed around the room and I sipped my first taste of alcohol. Bobby announced the stakes of the evening's pool game. "We'll play for sexual favors." Everyone laughed but me. Sexual favors? I had zero idea what this meant and felt nervous for one million reasons. They were seniors and I was a freshman and I'd never played pool in my life.

I cannot recall how the game went, but I do remember being on the bathroom floor, the room spinning as Bobby hovered over me, scrunched uncomfortably with my torso half up the wall and my lower half naked on the cold tile floor as he tried repeatedly to "make sex happen" between us. I had no idea what to do with him. I'd never even been properly kissed, much less fantasized about this moment in any anatomically correct way. At fourteen years old, I had not the slightest idea what my responsibility was in this act between girl and boy. After a confusing few minutes of trying, he gave up, leaving me with my Benetton sweatshirt pushed up to my chin, sobering up on the bathroom floor. I pulled myself together and walked back to the pool table only to find it empty. I spotted a spiral staircase and heard murmurs coming from above. I walked up the stairs and into the kitchen to find Bobby hunched over a bowl of SpaghettiOs. A guy I didn't recognize was seated at the table with him. He smiled and his face lit up when he saw me. "Who's your friend, Bobby?" In between spoonfuls he mumbled with his mouth full, "That's Shelley. She ain't worth a dime." In that moment, his rejection of me and summation of my worth weaved itself into my DNA.

Embarrassment flooded every cell of my body, and my face was hot and pink with shame. What had been the last private piece of my burgeoning womanhood and previously unknown to anyone else was now branded worthless. I couldn't get out of there fast enough. Crystal and I walked up the steep driveway, my body weighed down with a thousand pounds of humiliation. When the speakers pounded out Led Zeppelin's "Black Dog," the coincidence of the lyrics was not lost on me.

The next day my family told me I'd cried out several times in my sleep, "I'm pregnant! I'm pregnant!" They laughed about it and chalked it up to the recent onslaught of after-school specials about teen pregnancy that played on TV in the afternoon hours. Not knowing the exact mechanics of this "parts-touching and making-a-baby business" I just hoped I wasn't, in fact, pregnant. That year I would see him in the halls at school with his willowy blonde slip of girlfriend, Sloane, on his arm. He would never look at me or speak to me again. On the last day of school, I found a once red rose, now dried to a deathly black, in my locker, a gift from a sweet boy named Steve with floppy long hair and a sexy, boyish smile who was happy just to kiss my neck at the St. X high school dance. Being with Steve was easy and lacked challenge, so like every other train wreck of a girl, I didn't know what to do with him. I stuck that dead and rotting rose between the vents of Bobby's locker and wished him the very worst life had to offer.

Turns Out, Surfers Are Jerks Too

After spending seven years in Kentucky, Mom and Ken decided it was time to move back east to North Carolina. My heart fluttered with excitement. The idea of living in the same state as my dad gave me butterflies. I imagined Friday afternoons when he would roll up to the school and pick me up in his red Ferrari 308 GTSI, just like the one Tom Selleck drove in *Magnum PI*. Did I mention they also had the same hair color and mustache? I just knew all the kids would think he was so smooth.

It was the summer before my junior year and we had just finished building a giant brick home with a second-floor catwalk and soaring ceilings in the same golf course community as the rental where we'd been staying. I think the house immediately felt too big because my older sister, Angela, who had dropped her nickname when she graduated from college, had headed to Myrtle Beach, South Carolina, to try out adult life. Mom, Ken, and I took a road trip to scope out housing, tracing our path backward from that trip we'd made in the U-Haul truck all those years before.

Two weeks before we moved from Louisville to Wilmington, I'd finally met a decent boy who I liked and actually liked me back for once instead of the usual one-sided love bombs of my past. Derek was so handsome in a clean-cut, preppy, traditional way. Given what was attractive to me, it was likely that lurking just underneath was a dark side, something I seemed to gravitate toward. If he didn't have that edge somewhere in there, then I wasn't interested. For better or worse, we'll never know. I didn't get to stay around long enough to find out. As we crossed through Kentucky and the grassy hills of West Virginia, I moped in the car the whole ride, immersing myself in misery over the lost chance at love and listening to sad songs, specifically the hit song "Into the Night" by Benny Mardones. "She's just sixteen years old . . ." I made sure it was a long and tragic car ride.

We drove all day and night until we arrived in a small town surrounded by backwater neighborhoods on the North Carolina coast. The night sky was black as ink and revealed nothing of our surroundings as we pulled into the parking lot of the Waterway Inn. The next morning, I slid out of bed and pulled back the curtains to see a crayon-blue sky, the intracoastal waterway, and dozens of cars stopped on the road in front of the hotel. People were standing around chatting outside their station wagons and VW buses, most of which had surfboards strapped to the top. Time itself seemed to have stopped alongside the traffic. There was no rush and everyone seemed okay with it. Ken pointed to the drawbridge that was up and showed me the barge that was about to pass under it. There was a lightness in the air. Negative ions or something like that. The place made my shoulders relax.

My mom had forbidden me to tell my dad about our upcoming move to North Carolina. She believed that this information would lessen her chances of winning her lawsuit against my dad for more child support for me. The cost of living was on the rise and his payment hadn't changed in years. Eager to hear how excited he would be at the prospect of seeing me more and being a part of my life, I decided to tell him my news anyway and make him promise not to tell. After all, we'd get to see each other regularly, and I just knew he'd be equally excited about that. That would be more important to him than winning in court, right?

We'd been living in Wilmington for at least a few weeks by the time they went to court. We drove to the outskirts of Charlotte to stay with my mom's sister, Aunt Karen, and her husband Jim while my parents had their court date. At the end of the day, my mom came flying through the door in a rage. She'd lost the case and wasn't granted more child support. She said it was because I'd told my dad about the move. She was heartbroken that I'd betrayed her. Her reasoning had been that the court knows it costs money to move, so she was denied the increase in child support. I called my dad in tears, demanding to know why he would betray my confidence like that, and he said that he did not tell his lawyer, but that the judge knew because our new Wilmington address was on the court paperwork. This seemed like a gross oversight on my mom's part, which was unlike her. She didn't miss details like that. One of them was lying to me, but which one of my parents couldn't I trust? I only wanted to make them both happy, and as all children of contentious divorce know, that was impossible. I can see now how badly my betrayal had hurt her. I was desperate for my dad's attention while she was always there, doing the hard work of raising me. I felt both misunderstood and mistreated that I was incapable of empathy for her at the time. Then Dad added salt to the wound.

"Sorry, kiddo," Dad said. "I was going to buy you this sweet little red convertible for your sixteenth birthday coming up, but when your mom sued me for more child support, I had to hire a lawyer and spent all my money on that."

My punishment for trying to get close to my dad was losing a sweet ride and my punishment for betraying my mom's confidence was that now I wasn't allowed to take driver's ed classes, which were mandatory in the state of North Carolina in order to get a driver's license. Mom and Ken withheld that from me for a few months until they felt I had done my time. Then they bought me a cute little white Honda Civic hatchback so I could get to work and school. I should have been more grateful, but instead I was fixated on the ongoing struggle of trying to fit in my new environment while trying to manage the unprocessed grief I carried around with me.

There were many battles, and I threatened to go live with Dad. My mom would say my dad wouldn't have me, that he was too selfish to spend time caring for a child. He had remarried and my stepmother did not want children of her own, so why would she want any living in her house? I was not invited to their wedding, a fact that didn't hurt too bad until I found out, much later in life, that they'd had a church wedding with all her family present. I was his child, but not important enough in his life to be at their wedding. One time when I was visiting them, they had just gotten a new black lab puppy. She joked, "Al, a dog and a kid in the same week? What are you trying to do to me?" But if I was unwelcome, she never let on. She always made sure I ate well and that we did fun things when I visited, but back then, she firmly stood behind my dad and his wishes. I remember Mom telling me that she was just doing her job as his wife and maybe my resemblance to my mother didn't help much. My stepmom, Bobbette, really enjoyed beating me at Connect Four, a game she played with me over and over until I was tired enough to go to bed. We had a joke between us back then. I called her my step-monster, and we both thought it was the funniest thing because she was petite and pretty.

One night at our new home in the beach town, Ken and Dad argued on the phone about something regarding me, and my grandmother who was visiting picked up the phone and heard them threatening to kick each other's asses if one of them should come to the other's town. She was livid about it for reasons I don't understand. My hard-scrabble, West Virginian grandmother, Helen, wasn't warm or kind. She had never been nurturing toward my mother or any of us for that matter. When any of us grandkids stayed over, she would make us bathe every night. She would come in, grab a washcloth that felt like steel wool, and scrub our skin till it was angry and red, like she was trying to wash the sin off of us. She was all hellfire and brimstone with flecks of tobacco from her unfiltered Chesterfields stuck to her pink lipsticked mouth. Grandmother slipped me cigs to smoke and forbade us grandkids to call her Granny. We called her Grandmother, a deceptively formal title for such an informal family. The fighting in the house that night was epic and awful. And while fighting is not abuse, it was hell on my nervous system. That night, dramatic and desperately in pain, I ingested whatever was left in a bottle of Tylenol and had to be rushed to the doctor. They ran some lab tests that revealed the only thing I managed to do was damage my liver. I was so miserably depressed, though it would be a few more years before Mom figured that out. Soon afterward, we went about life business as usual, but we never talked about what I'd done or why.

The next day, Ken took me waterskiing on the intracoastal waterway with one of his buddies who was also named Ken. The great thing about Ken is that he always loved to spend time with me, even if I didn't appreciate it then. The sun was warm and I was ready to have some fun. When Ken number two got off the skis, I jumped in the water and he tossed them to me one at a time. When I caught the second one, his considerable weight had caused the metal trim to pull away from the ski and it sliced through my fingers. I treaded water with blood running crimson down my arm. I was bleeding in the water and panic-stricken because one word kept echoing in my head: SHARK! My Ken jumped in and helped me get to the boat. He wrapped my hand in a towel and we headed home. They bandaged my hand, and, after making sure I could shift gears with two fingers taped together, they tossed me the keys to the BMW and let me go out for the evening. An olive branch had been extended.

I finally started making some friends in the new beach town. I spent a lot of time with Laney, an athletic brunette who was involved in the local theater and could pull off red lipstick like no one else our age. I met a surfer boy with messy, sun-bleached hair and a year-round tan. Bodhi reminded me of James Spader's sexy but asshole-ish character Steff in the movie *Pretty in Pink*. I wore his black tie-dyed Rip Curl T-shirt, the scent of his Obsession cologne reminding me, in intermittent wafts, of steamy kisses and possibilities unknown. I wasn't having sex yet, but I was pretty sure he was. We cruised the beach roads with the wholly inappropriate, explicit rap music by Too Short blaring from the sunroof. He lived with his dad on Carolina Beach and I was so into him. He possessed the two characteristics that seemed to draw me to a guy: emotional unavailability and a carelessness with drugs and alcohol. When I met Bodhi, I threw myself headfirst into the possibility of him.

One Friday night after we'd been dating a few months (an absolute eternity on a teenager's calendar), Laney and I met up with Bodhi and one of his friends named Scotty. Scotty was another cute blond surfer from Carolina Beach. He was the teenage host of a local reggae radio show. Like Bodhi and most of the beach kids I would meet, he'd already dropped out of high school. When they picked us up from my house that night, in a dizzying turn of events, Laney jumped in the car with Bodhi and I found myself in the car with Scotty. *Why are we driving two cars? Why is she with him? What are they talking about?* By the time we got to Bodhi's house, I began to understand that he was trading me out for my friend Laney. Compared to the dark-haired, confident theater chick with strong dancer's legs, I knew I had no chance. My despair was beginning to show. I wasn't able to participate in the banter. My confidence and my smile were gone. The abandonment switch in me had been tripped. I was distraught.

I cornered Laney in the surf shack's one bathroom and quizzed her. "You don't like him, do you? Is he flirting with you? I feel like he is and I'm embarrassed." She assured me they had been good friends long before I'd even moved here and that I was reading it wrong. By the time Scotty drove me home to meet my midnight curfew, I had figured out that I had indeed been replaced when he leaned over to kiss me and asked if I wanted to hang tomorrow. I knew he wouldn't do that to his best friend if Bodhi had really liked me. The next morning when I woke up, Laney's station wagon was still parked outside my house. The girl with the dancer's legs and no curfew had spent the night with my boyfriend. And that was the end of that. The message was clear. I was disposable. Abandonment wound triggered.

Something took root inside me then. It became obvious to me that sex is what it took to be loved and desired. It wasn't that I didn't want to. I thought there would come a time when love and closeness would grow and lead to sex. But Bobby and Bodhi showed me that sex was more transactional than romantic. I would spend many years using my body as currency for love and hoping to feel valued. In my distorted thoughts, being desired meant I had value. I was ready and willing because I liked the focused attention and the feeling of connection in the moment. I craved being held. With arms around me and a body on top of me, I wouldn't float away.

Unlike the moment on the bathroom floor with the Bono wannabe, I came to understand what was expected of me. What I loathed was the minutes and hours afterward, when it was clear I had given them what they wanted and they offered me nothing in return. Meaningless encounters would continue to chip away tiny fragments of my wholeness. Death by a million tiny cuts. Just when I didn't think it was possible to feel hollower, I'd feel scooped out, disposable, worthless. Giving guys access to that part of me never resulted in the magical love and acceptance I hoped for. I only felt lonelier. That childhood sensation returned. I was without skin. I had no covering for my tissue and bones.

A Lullaby for the Reckless

My first long-term boyfriend, Ash, stood beside the bed, strumming his guitar in the dark. His eyes were uncharacteristically serious. This serenade was a rare display of genuine affection and vulnerability between two seventeen-year-olds. This tender gesture made me think he was terrified that he'd successfully convinced me to leave home just a few weeks before. It wasn't long before we found out his parents weren't okay with me staying at their house for more than the occasional weekend night. On weekends, we would hang out in their garage or backyard, coming and going from their hall bathroom and kitchen while his parents drank and partied inside with their friends. During the week, they drew a hard line.

In a sense, he was right about my home life. It *was* bullshit. In a lot of ways, so was his—along with the home lives of most of our friends from working-class families. Instead of focusing on connecting with their kids and creating secure families, many boomer parents, mine among them, just did their own thing most of the time, doling out punishments and gas money when necessary. Understandably, parents of this generation and social class rejected the boring, traditional lives of their parents they saw as oppressive. The free-love and partying lifestyle they'd experienced in their youth, for fun and as a way to cope with volatile parents, became a habit that lingered long after the novelty wore off. I squeezed my eyes tighter so no tears could slip through.

I'd met Ash and the guys one Saturday night at a party just a year earlier. I'd walked out to my car Friday after school to see a hand-drawn flier tucked under my windshield. There was a sketch of a Marshall guitar amp, a bottle of Jim Beam and PARTYTIME written in big block letters. I walked into that party alone knowing Shawn, the host, but not knowing him well, and connected with Ash right away. We played Journey albums all night and sang along to every song. I was smitten by his boyish charm, longish light-brown curls, and his bell-bottom jeans. He wasn't too tall and had caramel eyes that were both warm and dangerous. I could tell he liked me, but also caught glimpses of something that looked like trouble. I remember him holding my chin and kissing me that night. With an impish grin he said, "This could end badly," and once he had completely swept me off my feet with a combo of charm and mind-fuckery, the balance of power was solely in his hands. In an ongoing cycle of "conceal and reveal," he would act cold and aloof, as though it was a game to see how mean he could be without actually pushing me away for good. I kept coming back for more and, in quiet retaliation, I slept with one of his closest friends.

Most of Ash's friends had become mine too. If he minded, he never said so. David, Greg, Brian, Randy, Ben, Jason, and Alan all lived in or close to Tanglewood, Ash's neighborhood. If no one's parents were out of town, we'd spend Friday nights on a deeply wooded dirt road that connected Tanglewood with another nearby neighborhood. Amid the smoke of bonfires and weed, we passed around fifths of cheap whiskey or a jar of homemade moonshine swiped from somebody's daddy. Along with the booze and pot, music was a constant wherever we were. In the woods, we kept it at a level loud enough to set the mood without alerting the nearby homes of our presence. Together, we built up high tolerances for substances, puked, passed out, lost our minds on acid, argued, and regularly made fools of ourselves. These dirt road stories would become our shared history, expanded upon and sometimes weaponized if the need to cut someone down arose—and it always did. The guys talked about their musical heroes and ribbed each other for being drunk and slurring, while the few girls that inevitably joined us made moves on the guys they hoped to hook up with late night. Sometimes the police would patrol the dirt road for a while after we'd had a good rager, so we'd move the party over to a spot on the intracoastal waterway we called The Point. Surrounded by water on three sides, roots reggae or Rush playing on someone's car stereo, we partied till one of us stumbled too close to the water's edge; then we knew it was time to go home. If we could stand up, walk to our car, get in and crank it up without issue, we considered ourselves sober enough to drive home.

Most of the guys were talented musicians, so on Saturday nights about twenty-five of us would cram into Ash's garage, already packed with amps, guitars, and a full drum kit. Covers of Van Halen, the Stones, Led Zeppelin, Steely Dan, Rush, and Jimi Hendrix songs blasted through Marshall full-stacks, getting louder as we swiftly transitioned from buzzed to full-blown fucked up. We drank cheap brown liquor and passed joints until the wee hours of the morning.

I tried in vain to sleep in a bed that was not my own, in a house that was not my home. My friend Billy had kindly offered me his room for the night, and tucked me in before rejoining the party in the living room. Billy was a few years older than us, and the first of our friends to have his own place. The yard out front was mostly sand, spotted with a few clumps of dead grass. Inside, the walls were dark with paneled wood. The coffee table was a sea of red Solo cups, the white bottoms obscured by the last dregs of Jim Beam or a Sun Drop chaser. Billy lived there with his older brother, Steve. They worked long days and partied at the house most nights. As usual, Ash hadn't paid much attention to me that night, but had apparently noticed my absence when I went to bed.

I closed my eyes and prayed the morbid prayer:

Now I lay me down to sleep
I pray the Lord my soul to keep
If I shall die before I awake
I pray the Lord my soul to take.

Though this dark prayer is actually a nursery rhyme first printed in a New England primer in the 1700s, it was the only prayer I felt was rightfully my own. My mom, raised to believe in hellfire and damnation deep in the coal-dusted hollers of West Virginia, taught it to me and always reminded me to say it if I was frightened or a bad dream startled me awake. Afterward, I would ask God to protect everyone in my family, and would panic if I left out anyone, believing my negligence meant their imminent death. I prayed this ritual prayer as a matter of duty, but I didn't understand the true concept of faith: the decision to believe my prayers were heard and to allow myself to be comforted by that knowledge. What I did not understand was that prayers, whether prayed to God or a tree, meant laying down your fears and trusting you will be cared for, sheltered from danger. Reciting the prayer was more of a safety check, a requirement if one wanted to stay in God's good graces than it was an act of communing with a higher power whom I did not yet know.

The God I prayed to back then would bless you if you made the right choices and if you were a very good girl and smite you if you weren't. I was not a good girl. I knew the Lord's Prayer by heart, thanks to those years at Catholic school, but just like the communion I wasn't allowed to taste, this prayer seemed as though it were for someone else, someone who had all their shit in one sock. Maybe a girl with a neat and tidy life who came from a family that felt blessed to have her instead of inconvenienced by the care she required. Maybe it belonged to anyone but Shit Breath. Maybe it was the rightful prayer of Lizzie with her beautiful block handwriting, or Cassie with her wallpaper and monogrammed L.L. Bean bag, but it was a prayer that didn't belong to a girl as messy as me.

Still playing guitar at my bedside, Ash picked out the familiar notes of Kansas's "Dust in the Wind." For at least the hundredth time, my thoughts found their way back to the night I left home. Home. Where had I ever felt at home? No four walls had ever held me for any length of time before they expanded, contracted, and heaved me out the door and down the road. I searched my heart for a correlating emotion. I searched my mind for an image and recalled the houses I drew as a child: blockish, always with a chimney chuffing up white smoke and a green tree with a brown trunk in the front yard. Growing up, I had unpacked my bags in a new house about every two years of my life, but not one ever looked like the houses I sketched out on paper. To me, the idea of home was a place you came from and a place you could return to in order to remember who you are and where you belong. I imagined home to be a sheltering place, physically and psychologically. People in my life changed from year to year, as did my home, and we didn't live near our extended family. I longed to return to a place where my nervous system could regulate, to awake in the morning to consistency, reliability, and a sense of belonging with no take backs.

My parents were hippies-turned-hard-working-entrepreneurs. It seemed we were forever seeking a place in which we could realize the American dream. Once we did, we sought to multiply it a million times over. My stepfather worked relentlessly and Mom kept their remodeling business running like a machine. Mom grew up in the Appalachian coal-mining town of Welch, West Virginia (also home to *The Glass Castle* author Jeanette Walls), where poverty and parental abandonment bred in her a relentless work ethic. Going back home to her dysfunctional parents was never an option. Ken was determined to prove wrong his heavy-drinking, often abusive father who told him he would never amount to anything. Ken always meant well during his long tenure with my mom, my sister, and me, and we knew he loved us, though his moods were extreme. When the dark clouds of his anger formed, we all felt it, and when sunshine shone from his smile, we couldn't help but feel happy too.

He loved to laugh and that laughter was contagious. When we were young, Angie and I had the weekly chore of first sweeping the hardwood floors of our old house in Kentucky, then mopping them before applying lemon oil with a dust mop. This made the floors slick and a source of great entertainment. We would get the dogs running in circles through the dining room, kitchen, and living room so they would slide around the corners and through the large, arched doorways. They would Scooby Doo around the turns and lose traction. The look of determination to stay upright would have us howling in laughter. The dogs seemed to love it too because they never failed to participate.

My sister and I resented this chore, particularly having to repeat this process on the wooden staircase, which made it extra sweet one day when Ken was in a bad mood and in a hurry. He was leaving town for a work trip and running late. From our perch in the oversized peach-cushioned papasan chairs in the living room, we could hear him grumbling and storming around upstairs. We knew to stay out of the way. A moment later we heard a ruckus. Man-sized grunts accompanied by loud thumping sounds boomed from the stairwell behind us. I ran to my sister's chair, positioned closest to the stairs, and half hid behind it. Consumed with schadenfreude, modeled for us by our dear stepfather, we turned toward the foyer and braced for hilarity. First, the suitcase tumbled down the stairs and across the foyer, slamming hard into the front door. Then Ken quickly followed, head over ass in a mess of arms and legs and cuss words. We nearly died from laughter, and, so many decades later, it's one of our favorite stories to retell when we gather together.

I had seismic meltdowns at home, but have only vague memories of them. The infuriating agony of feeling unseen, invalidated, and misunderstood by Mom and Ken overwhelmed me as my emotions were continually dismissed. Born to members of the silent generation, none of my parents knew how to regulate their emotions. But now they were adults and their repressed anger seemed to simmer just below the surface, a hair trigger away from erupting. The infuriating thing was how their anger was permitted while mine was not. My sadness and anxiety spiraled into a coil of anger ready to whip loose and wreak havoc at any hint of criticism. I would have big, loud feelings about something to which Ken would reply, "I am the adult. You are the child. You have no words." This silencing suffocated my spirit as my unspoken words knotted into fury in my throat. I did not know how to name what I was feeling because I was repeatedly dismissed, never encouraged to try to understand what I was feeling, only to tamp it down, rein it in. On the surface, it was a battle of the wills, but underlying was some great wound no one, including myself, could understand. A kind of trance overcame me during these fights that I have since learned is a nervous system response. I can't recall the subject matter or causes of most of the fights and arguments, but it lingers in my muscles, tissues, and bones, suspended within my anatomy like a fly in amber. I know now that he could not deal with what I call my shadow pain, because he had not dealt with his own. Shutting me down like that infuriated me. My parents had no tools other than punishments with which to help me, and I refused to be controlled.

I had no emotional regulation, therefore sobbed uncontrollably in frustration during these fights. A decade of loneliness, pain, and confusion rose up in me, and my parents just couldn't see any of their part in it. To them it was just who I was, a character flaw that had no deeper, underlying cause or anything to do with the great emotional pain I felt. Every time the crying meltdown happened, Mom called the doctor and he would call Ativan into the pharmacy to calm me down. Maybe, looking through the larger lens, I shouldn't have let it feel so catastrophic that horrible last night before I left. Truth was, I already had one foot out the door, and as I would soon find out, so did Ken. My family was dissolving again. We all needed to find our way, and it wasn't going to be together.

What had caused the nuclear fallout between us that night was my smoking habit. Ken detested smoking, and I think he felt helpless in his efforts to keep me from it. He'd once tried to make me smoke a whole pack before I turned green and ran to my bedroom to puke for half an hour, horrifying my Aunt Karen and Uncle Jim who were visiting from Charlotte at the time. His fear of what smoking could cost me had much to do with losing his mother to cancer and she'd been a smoker.

My mom had been out of town and before my friend Patricia and I left the house one evening, Ken handed us a bottle of tequila. A point of bonding between us had taken place earlier that year when, at our kitchen table, he showed one of his friends how his youngest daughter could "hold her own" with the Cuervo Gold. And I did. That was the night I learned that putting one foot on the floor would stop the bed spins.

Like him, I had dark moods and was completely disconnected from myself. I gave him hell, but I would stop at nothing to win his approval, and trying to prove myself with the tequila was proof of that. Not much for drinking on a school night, Pat and I only opened the bottle to share with the guys. Smoking was our biggest crime that night. After that fight, I felt so confused, angry, and alone.

In her book, *Mystery and Manners*[4], Flannery O'Connor wrote, "Anybody who has survived his childhood has enough information about life to last him the rest of his days. If you can't make something out of a little experience, you probably won't be able to make it out of a lot." The most important "something" I gleaned from my childhood is that people are rarely one dimensional and bring both good and bad to the stories of our lives. Later on in my life, long after their divorce, Ken would be the one to come to my rescue many times just when I needed him. Their split was imminent, but before he left, he made sure I filled out the college applications

---

4. O'Connor, Flannery. *Mystery and Manners*. Farrar, Straus and Giroux, 1969.

to schools he determined might accept my mediocre grades. He taught me to ride a bike when I was seven, how to drive a five-speed when I was sixteen, and how to hold my liquor when I was seventeen. He made sure I knew that just because I'd slept with Ash didn't mean I had to stay with him. I saw him as both parent and enemy, and because of that our fights were explosive.

I packed up my favorite things and walked away from my home, my family, and my car. I knew that if things got any worse between my parents and me, it would reach a point of no return. I needed relief. Now, I can see how desperate a move it was to leave. Not knowing where I was going to sleep or where my next meal would come from seemed to me the easier option than staying. I put all my hope in a teenage boyfriend and a handful of aimless but relatively faithful friends.

I tossed and turned in the borrowed bed as Ash continued to play me lullabies. We'd been seeing each other for more than a year. I'd been captivated when he'd slung his electric guitar behind his head and flawlessly played Jimi Hendrix's rendition of the "Star-Spangled Banner," I'd been transfixed by the guitar solos he played with his teeth, by how he made me laugh, by how hard he was to hold. Although I was still attending high school at this time, I had little concern for my future.

I don't recall my parents ever telling me to think about what I wanted out of life or how to get there, short of the admonishment to make good grades. Maybe they did, but I only wanted to escape my pain by partying in places I probably shouldn't have been, desperately seeking a place to belong and a sense of identity. Trauma had caused me to disassociate from myself, to think only of this moment and then maybe the next, but not any further. I spent years with Ash; he floated in and out of my days and nights as he pleased, leaving me to wonder where he was and where we stood. Like my mom had found in both of my dads, I'd found what would become an unrequited love, and it was like holy water to me. I was determined to drown myself in it. It never occurred to me to think about what I wanted in this relationship, or any of the relationships that would follow. I never thought about whether I truly wanted to be with any of the men I dated or considered how their treatment of me made me feel. I wanted to avoid rejection at all costs. I wanted to love and be loved, to keep someone and to be kept. My desires and feelings were foreign to me. I was not taught to trust them and expressing myself always seems to come at a price. I can see now that my mom was haunted by the same ghost. The following few nights at Billy's, I brushed off Doritos crumbs and slept on the sagging sofa. The following few months, I moved from house to house and stayed with friends until the welcome wore off.

I spent a few nights at my friend Brandy's empty house. Her family had moved back to Texas where they were from, and she was determined not to leave her friends behind again. She'd run away, back to North Carolina, and was squatting in their two-story home that was still on the market. With her golden-blonde curls and impish smile, her energy was electric. She made you feel like anything was possible and she made everything infinitely more fun. We invited all the guys over to drink our signature Jim Beam with a Sun Drop chaser. By the end of the first night, we found a blanket in the linen closet and fashioned a sled by folding it in half lengthwise, sitting on it at the top of the stairs and pulling the second half up over our bodies like a sled with reins. We teetered on the edge of the top step until someone else gave us a violent push and we went sailing down the stairs. This went on for a while before we heard the knock at the door.

After a few weeks, Ken somehow found me at Brandy's and tried to convince me to come home. But I didn't want to go back to a place where I constantly felt on edge, disconnected, and lonely. The stubborn child in me, the one that was told she had no words, was going to do anything except what she was told. My mom was so upset I didn't go with him that the next time I talked to her, she let me know coming home was no longer an option. They changed the locks and sold my car. Once we were discovered at Brandy's house, we took up residence at Laney's house, the same Laney with the dancer's legs and red lipstick. A few weeks later, Brandy finally went back to Texas and soon, I'd be moving on too.

Mama, He's a Bad, Bad Man

When Laney's parents had had enough of me, I went to stay with my friend Shorty and her family. Her mom was a hair stylist with an abusive drunk of a boyfriend who was often away on long benders. Shorty had a little sister that I adored—Amy. They were both petite, blonde replicas of their gorgeous mother. I shared a bed with Shorty, though I remember being alone in it most nights since she often stayed with her surfer boyfriend Fettuccini—a nickname, of course. There were few, if any, rules in that house. I had a bedtime ritual of putting Pink Floyd's *The Wall* album on the record player and falling asleep to it. It soothed me. It was the one record I had packed with me when I left home. To this day, any song from that album can take me right back to the most vulnerable time in my life—a time when I felt so alone in the world. I would sometimes hear Ash's mustang idling outside the window. He wanted sex and fun, but I wanted love and protection. The record player spun, "Hey you . . ." as I tried to calm myself enough to sleep. Sometimes I went with Ash and pretended it was an act of love between us, as it would later become, but some nights I turned over and tried to sleep.

I got a job working at an amusement park on Pleasure Island that spring. The management hired only the best-looking girls and a few guys, but rarely any young, attractive ones. Of the two male owners, one appeared to be in an open marriage and the other was single. I shall call that one Turd. Turd was handsome with electric-blue eyes, dark hair, and serious swagger. He drove a dark-green Jaguar, giving off the vibe that he had a lot of money. Several of us girls worked the frozen lemonade stand, the waterslide, and the gift shop in rotation while the few guys they'd hired operated the rides. We had fun after the park closed. Ripping off our uniforms of khaki shorts and T-shirts, stripping down to our bikinis, we took turns flying down the waterslide with the tunes turned up over the loudspeaker while the owners counted the day's cash in the office nearby.

Turd made his way through several female employees each week. He took them as his date to parties at his house and on his boat in a gated community nearby, and rumor had it he regularly slept with the more experienced girls. Looking back on it now, I think we somehow felt chosen if he threw a glance our way and rejected if he didn't. I wanted to be invited to these parties, so when Turd finally turned his attention toward me, I was game. I was good enough to be the date of an older, successful man in his thirties, though part of me understood I was arm candy. Being my employer, he understood I was not yet eighteen.

After a short conversation with the other male owner, Turd and I left the park in his Jag and made our way off the island and onto the beach road. After work, I had changed into my favorite Billabong dress and flip-flops, my tan legs crossed at the ankles in his passenger seat. He was still dressed in his pressed khaki shorts and short-sleeved button-down from work. He rested his hand on my thigh, which at the time seemed normal and very grown up.

I was still seeing Ash, though I wasn't sure how to define it. If Facebook had been around back then, our relationship status would have been "it's complicated." I knew he cared about me, but he had recently broken my heart by sending flowers to another girl and flirting publicly with yet another, even as he continued to idle his Mustang loudly outside of Shorty's bedroom window in the middle of the night. I was good enough for sex, but not for flowers. My dedication to him over the years had been steadfast, though he continued the game of conceal and reveal in our relationship. As close as our friend group was, no one knew our status from day to day. Some nights I felt like I was being good to myself, empowered even, by rolling over to sleep instead of going out to be used by him.

As we rolled through the electric gate of Turd's neighborhood, he slowed to a stop, held up a finger without saying a word, and hopped out. He retrieved something from a bench behind the hedge. He got back in the car with two heavy, cut-crystal highball glasses and handed one to me.

"Cocktails!" he said.

It looked like vodka with fresh ice and smelled like nothing, but mine had a lime wheel on the side. I felt sophisticated. I felt grown up. I felt wanted. Where did the drinks come from? Why hadn't I asked that? I remember thinking his partner likely had something to do with it.

"You want to see the boat before we go to the party?" he asked.

"Sure. Sounds good."

We clinked glasses as he pulled back onto the road. He nodded toward the drink and tipped his head back as if to say, drink up. I remember walking into the cabin of the large boat docked at the end of the neighborhood's main street. I had never seen anything like this before. The bed was messy, as if he'd just leaped out of it, and the biggest thing in the room. That's the last thing I remember about that night. I woke up in that bed the next morning and I remember the room had a sour smell. I played it cool when he finally woke up and offered me a glass of water. I pulled on my dress and flip-flops and walked out onto the bow of the boat. The sun hurt my eyes, and I felt really sick. One drink had never done this to me before. Many a night I had shared a fifth of rot-gut whiskey with Ash and the guys and chased it with fluorescent-yellow Sun Drop and never had I felt this bad.

We drove the short distance to Shorty's house in silence, and I climbed out of his car without saying a word to him. Most nights I was scared to go to sleep there because they never locked the door, but on this early morning I was so grateful I could slip in without anyone noticing. Shorty was sleeping peacefully when I came in, her long blonde hair a tangled, partially dreaded mess on the pillow. I was suddenly so homesick. I was comforted by the familiar room. The Rastafarian flag hanging over the bed had Bob Marley's face on it and a scarf was draped over a lamp, making the room feel cozy. I shut the lamp off and crawled into bed next to her.

I felt confused. I thought, *This is what adults do? This feels awful*. I felt ashamed, but why? *Was that what they call a one-night stand? Why don't I remember any of it? Did we go to a party? Why did I assume I would be safe with Turd solely because he was an adult? Is this the treatment all men thought I deserved?* I never went back to work at the amusement park, but I would run into Turd around town in the years to come. The hatred I had for him paled in comparison to the hot, murderous rage my mother instinctively felt toward him, though I never told her the whole story. Thinking it was somehow my fault, a result of yet another poor decision I'd made, I told no one. This secret settled deep into my bones until that feeling of worthlessness became me.

Leaving Shorty's

Things between Shorty and her mom got loud and messy, so she took off with Fettuccini to follow the Grateful Dead around the country. I felt uneasy there in her absence, so I headed to Austin's house. Austin had been my boyfriend just after Bodhi but before Ash, and we were still good friends. He was tall with blond hair, a square jawline, and a perpetual golden tan from surfing whenever he found a spare moment. I loved his family. He was kind and easy to be with. Is it any wonder we didn't last? I didn't know what to do with that. I only knew chaos and struggle. He had a brother close in age, and they shared a large room above the garage. The other three bedrooms were downstairs. His parents were in one, his little sister in another, and I was in the third bedroom. They made me feel at home there, and I stayed for a while. We started hooking up again and eventually it became hard for me to determine what my living there meant for us. Were we back together, and if so, were we "living together"? He was easy to love, but I was in survival mode and, though he hadn't proposed, I took off like a runaway bride.

Before long, I moved on to my next temporary home, which was a sofa on the porch at my friend Annie's house. She lived with her mom, and their house was a regular hangout for most of the neighborhood teenagers. She was petite like me, had adorably messy blonde hair with brown roots, and chronically stoned eyes. The best part about her was her crooked, mischievous smile. We drank her mom's sloe gin fizz, smoked a lot of pot, and listened to Peter Tosh and Black Uhuru on her porch. She was pretty good to me for letting me stay there, and when she ate, I ate. When she had cigarettes, I had cigarettes.

Regrettably, I'd slept with her boyfriend the month before I moved in with her. To this day, it is shocking to me that I never considered how this might make her feel. What kind of person only seeks to comfort themselves at the expense of others? Me. Horrible, disassociated me. She eventually found out about it, thanks to a coke-dealing, wave-chasing Spicoli wannabe who had a big crush on her and saw this as his opportunity to wreck her relationship. She took all of my clothes and divided them up among her friends and threw the discards into the front yard. That night, word got around that she'd found out and that my belongings were now strewn about her front yard. Bad news traveled fast in this small beach town, and just before midnight, it managed to make its way to the trailer at the beach where I was hanging out.

This ended my season of couch surfing, and in the wee hours of the morning, with as much of my dew-drenched clothing as I could stuff in my bag, I walked to Ash's house and tapped on his window. He'd already heard that I slept with someone else. It had blindsided him because he'd thought my love for him was so steadfast that I would patiently wait it out until he was ready to fully interlock his heart with mine. He slipped out of the house and drove me to the nearest gas station where I called my mom from a pay phone. She'd agreed I could come home and pulled into the parking lot to get me just as the sun was rising.

Eventually, Annie hunted me down at my parents' museum-like house of bright whites and worldly art and gave me that hair grab and smack in the face I had coming. I managed to close the glass front door before any real damage was done. Even after returning home, dark circles of anemia and restless sleep ringed my eyes. There is always an ever-present unrest that comes with living in the midst of marital conflict and moods that shift with the cycle of excessive drinking and hangovers, especially if she is your dear mother and a man you love like a father. We lived a rollercoaster life of high and low emotions none of us knew how to manage. My mom didn't have many coping skills, and both her and Ken's moods were often volatile. It was her deepest desire to be loved and treasured unlike she'd ever been before and to keep her family together despite the gnawing truth that it was doomed. I'd become an impenetrable brick wall through which no reasoning could pass. We were three lost souls, my mom, Ken, and me—rooted to nothing. They sometimes tried with lectures and angry threats, but they couldn't help me find my way.

I longed for tenderness, understanding, and stability. I needed them to shoulder some of the responsibility of how my life had turned out so far. So little thought had been invested in what I needed. What I needed was to process the shadow pain of everything that had transpired in my life up to this point. But I wasn't warm, and no one responds with compassion to a cold, aloof teenage asshole and they weren't healed enough for that anyway. Would I have even accepted tenderness and guidance? In my mind I knew everything. I would later learn that Ken already had a new relationship brewing. For years afterward, the timing of it all would leave me to believe my leaving home was the reason their marriage fell apart. Even if that wasn't the case, I'm sure the stress of it didn't help.

Fear of Sharks

My father was emotionally distant in his younger years, a polar opposite of me, his overly emotive, second-born child. He no doubt learned this coping mechanism as a way to survive a heartbreaking childhood that included being abandoned at an orphanage by his father after his narcissistic mother left him for reasons unknown. He and his brother were placed in a foster home before being retrieved by his mom at the insistence of his new stepfather. After that, he would forever feel unloved by his emotional train wreck of a mother who added insult to injury by always making it clear that his brother was her favorite. He would later find out through genetic testing at the age of seventy-seven that his brother was only his half brother, sharing only their mother's DNA.

I'd always fantasized that my sense of self and identity might be found in a fairytale relationship with my dad. I thought that if I were prettier, smarter, wittier, a better shot with a rifle, or had a better golf swing, then he would want me to be a part of his world. My dad was good at everything. I was good at nothing. When I went to a therapist a few times in middle school, the doctor told my mom that I put my dad on a pedestal and there wasn't much she could do to change that. Later, I would think about how it must have felt to be the parent dealing with the daily work of raising us kids and how thankless it was that I held the absent parent in such high regard. It wasn't Dad's fault we moved away, yet I surmised, since I didn't see him much, that he just didn't care. When I was little, he wrote me letters and I felt so important thinking about him taking the time to sit down—I imagined at his desk at work—and try to think of something to say to a child he hardly knew. When he neared the bottom of the card he'd write, *Oops, I'm running out of room! Love you, Dad.*

I thought I would miraculously start to feel like the other girls if he deemed me valuable: worthy of protection and worthy of his time, and therefore instantaneously desirable to all the boys in a way I had not been. If I could just be good enough to matter to him, I, too, would understand how the world worked instead of being perpetually lost in it. He would pull me aside and whisper in my ear some magical words that would transform me into something of value instead of someone "not a worth a dime" as Bobby had pronounced me to a room full of guys. Only in my forties did I discover my feelings of unworthiness were likely tied to my fear of abandonment—by the divorce, by being left behind, and by not feeling accepted by my peers and like I didn't belong in my adult-centered family. I was a confounding mix of tender, tough, and angry, while it seemed everyone around me was confident, well adjusted, and self-sufficient. Dad got the blame because he was absent and that was convenient. I just didn't know how to process a single emotion on my own. I only knew how to feel angry and hurt, but couldn't begin to parse out or express the reasons why.

A white-hot grief and piercing loneliness overcome my spirit when I think about that time away from home, living in survival mode at such a critical time in my young life. Why wasn't my mom outraged at Ken when I told her about the epic fight the last night before I left home? Where were my protectors? CPS had come out to the house and promptly left after the assertion was made that I was just a teenager acting out. Why didn't my dad ask me to come live with him and encourage me to finish out the last few months of school? How did he sleep at night all those months knowing I was out there, vulnerable and unguarded from the darkness lurking both in the shadows and in the corners of my own mind? Instead, he mailed me a $25 check each week to the address of whichever sofa I was sleeping on at the time. One day on the phone, he reckoned aloud that the street smarts I would get from living on my own at such an early age would serve me well in the business world one day. Though it was but a morsel of affirmation, I took it to heart.

Maybe the abandonment wound from such an early age made his ongoing absence loom large. Or maybe I unfairly fixated on his absence because his absence was an obvious deficit when I couldn't see my own culpability in the mess my life had become. I was too close to the fighting and the chaos in my home, making it impossible to clearly see its dysfunction. I could not articulate the pain of having lived in an ongoing, disquieting chasm opening between my mom and Ken, between them and me. It was easy to wag a finger at my father. The sin of neglect he had committed was in plain sight, while it was harder to pinpoint the harms under the current state of the union. When we quarreled or my parents raged, something within my mind and heart clouded over, like I'd woven my own temporary skin for protection, and all I could do was survive.

The adults in my life took no accountability for how their choices had led to the mess I was in. Only now is it obvious that this was also the case for them and their parents, a cycle repeating itself. We were all just trying to make it through the days and nights, trying to calm the feeling of desperation and manage the unworthiness we had all been taught to feel. Our souls sang the same song, *love me, love me, love me, and please don't leave me*, but we went after it in different ways. A few boys had taken advantage of this deep need to be held, especially Ash. Had I learned this behavior from my mom? When she was eleven years old, her mother, who possessed the warmth of a stone, packed up the car and headed from West Virginia to Charlotte under the ruse of going on vacation. When they arrived in town, my grandmother announced that they had just moved to Charlotte. This was no vacation, but a permanent move. She then dropped my mother off at the home of my grandmother's sister, Hazel—who made no bones about letting my mom know she didn't like her being there—before my grandmother headed to another sister's house with the rest of the children. My mom stayed there several months and my grandmother didn't come to visit even once. Had Mom been full of too many questions and big emotions the way I had been as a child? Was it just easier to abandon her to the care of someone else the same way it was less emotionally taxing to tell her four children they were going on vacation than to tell them they had to say goodbye to their neighborhood friends, schoolteachers, and classmates? My mother had an early abandonment wound too. Was this a generational curse? What we wouldn't know for many years to come was that my grandmother had just learned of her husband's affair, one that had produced a child that looked as though he'd been spit right out of my grandfather's mouth. My grandmother was running from the public humiliation of this scandal, thinking only of herself and not how it would affect her children.

Earlier that year, before I left home, my depression had been at its worst. My mom recognized in me the same sadness that weighed on her and insisted I go to the doctor. I was prescribed Prozac, the newest solution to every problem. Walking into an oyster roast and keg party in our friend Kyle's garage one night, Ash slipped his arm around my disappearing waist and declared, "I think you're skinny enough to be my girlfriend now." The Prozac had caused me to lose about five pounds of baby fat. On my four-foot-eleven frame, this loss appeared substantial. The message was clear: the more my body disappeared, the more I was loved.

I eventually quit going to school. Although I had been just a few short months away from graduating, not having a car or a regular place to sleep had made it nearly impossible to attend regular school hours. In the beach town where we lived, the dropout rate of high school students was nearly 40 percent. Eventually, my friend Allen started going to night school and since I could ride with him, I enrolled and finished up my senior year on my own that summer. I received my high school diploma, without ceremony, in the riverfront office of the local community college. I remember the redheaded secretary that handed it to me and the jangle of her bracelets as she patted me on the back with a sad smile. When I got home that day, my mom met me in the driveway, face beaming with pride, holding a velvet box with a heart-shaped diamond-and-sapphire necklace and matching earrings nestled inside. That night after dinner, I sat at the kitchen table with Ken and filled out the college applications he'd prepared for me.

Though life at home was now relatively calm and uneventful, Ash was a disrupter. One stormy night, a few months after I'd moved back home, I left Ash's apartment in the enormous '85 Buick Regal my dad had bought me. It always overheated, so I kept gallons of water in the cavernous trunk. Ash checked the water level in my radiator, poured a gallon of water in, and asked that I call to let him know I made it home. When I got there, the phone lines were down due to the storm. When he didn't hear from me, he drove across town, scanning the sides of the roads for my car. My stepdad heard his Mustang idling on the street corner nearest my bedroom windows. I could just make out the sound of Steely Dan coming from his car stereo, faintly floating across the side yard. I went to the window to take a look. Shirtless, with a chest carpeted like a bear, Ken flung the front door open and started yelling. "You leaving again? You gonna run off with him again?" Ash was walking up to my window to check on me. I tried to explain to Ken that he was just looking out for me, but the hate he felt for Ash and his fear of losing me again resulted in a deaf ear and was communicated in anger. Teary-eyed and triggered, I thanked Ash for coming to check on me, loud enough that my parents could hear, told him I loved him and would call him tomorrow. Ken had always blamed Ash for my leaving home, and Ash thought my stepdad's alpha-dog existence had been reason enough to leave.

Earlier that summer, a bunch of us camped out on Masonboro Island, which was just a short skiff ride across the waterway. We brought over borrowed tents and sleeping bags and set up camp. With squares of acid on our tongues and nothing in our heads, we ran about the island chasing ghost crabs in the dark. Their translucent bodies seemed to hover just above the sand, reflecting the light of a few low-hanging stars. In ripped up denim cutoffs and someone else's T-shirt, I felt free for the moment. I sought relief from the anxious heart that always pounded hammer-like in the hollow of my chest. I'd always been afraid of the dark, of being alone, of being unprotected, yet there I was, foolishly exposed to real and present dangers. Late that night a storm raged overhead. On this uninhabited island, we had no shelter save for our tents. A light show flashed in the sky and the booming thunder competed with the sound of the waves that crashed around us.

The next morning, we woke up in rain-soaked tents on the seaside of the island. My friend Kenny lay directly on the sand, zipped up to his head in a sleeping bag, like a cocoon. I breathed a sigh of relief when he began to squirm and wiggle. He would die too young and break our hearts, but not that day. The hot July sun scorched the island from its place in a cloudless blue sky. When the heat began to suffocate us, we sprang from our tents and ran for the water.

The ocean was a tranquil lake, calm after the storm. Floating on my back, the salt water covered my ears and silenced the noise around me. It cooled the perpetual summer sunburn on my face. I wondered where Ash had spent the night, with whom, and if he'd thought about me at all. Floating on my back there in the ocean, I was suddenly overcome with fear. It wasn't the dangerous drugs I'd done or how vulnerable I'd been, exposed on an island in a terrible storm, or the education I'd nearly thrown away. I didn't think of the past or fear what the future might hold for me. A clear perception began to form, pulling from the darkened corners of my mind. Home had always been a moving target. There was no eternal flame of hope, or safety, or the dependability of unconditional love to return to. My family had never had it, so how could they possibly give it to me? This was our inheritance, the one commonality among us all. Panic continued to rise within me. I felt vulnerable as I scanned the horizon for sharks. Panic gave way to terror and sent me scrambling onto my friend Randy's back. We floated this way, him treading water, me clinging to the breadth of his back, praying no sharks would get me.

Dorm Rooms and Teddy Bears

Her sleek black BMW zipped along the mountain road while my toes cramped on the floored accelerator of my old blue Honda. Mom was just about out of eyesight when that familiar fearfulness began to rise in my chest. While it's true that panic was my default state of being for as long as I could remember, in this moment it was justified. I was following her to my new college campus, and I would be completely lost in the mountains far from home if I lagged too far behind. Compounding the worry of being left behind, my father had insisted I take the Highway 40 route to school so I could drop by his house for my tuition check. When I told my mom, she flat out refused. "I'm not going the long way just because *he* wants me to." We were living at the beach at the time, and after a few semesters at the community college, I was headed off to a university in the mountains to start the spring semester. The car radio, a reliable omniscient narrator of my life at the time, played "It Keeps You Running" by the Doobie Brothers while my home receded into the distance.

The university was four hundred miles away from home and a seven-hour drive. It was no small trip and the distance was deliberate. Ken had gathered college applications from any in-state college that might possibly accept me. He couldn't stand my boyfriend, Ash, and, if you'd asked Ash, the feeling was mutual. He had been my one big high school love, but our relationship was tumultuous at best. I didn't know any better. Adversarial relationships were the only kind familiar to me. In my family, whenever there was fear over losing ground in a relationship, I saw false bravado emerge; when there were wounds inflicted, threats were made and walls were erected. We practiced the art of the freeze-out and were quick to enact nuclear-bomb-level options. We stormed out with attitude. What I never witnessed was taking a true account of one's feelings and the courage and self-assuredness it takes to be vulnerable. Vulnerability was scary for people like me, a girl who seemed to possess the very most number of feelings of any person to ever walk the Earth. I would open my mouth to say how I was feeling and out poured a flood of angry tears instead. Feelings were something to hide, conceal, deny. Feelings and emotions were thought of as inherently weak and seen as dramatic rather than part of the human. Problems required strategies or flat-out denial, not vulnerability and careful listening. This made every confrontation and conversation feel charged with the possibility of abandonment.

My concerns about Mom leaving me in the dust were not unfounded. For the past couple months, her presence had been ghostlike, her mind occupied with the fears and facts of her uncertain future. It was like she was sleepwalking, partially because she slept a lot. Since Ken had been gone, she was around, but only physically, functional only enough to go through the motions. A deep loneliness and aching quiet had shrouded our home, the life force extinguished. It was possible she could forget entirely that I was trailing behind her.

My mind was full of unease about being left alone in the mountains where I knew no one, and my stomach lurched with butterflies. My little blue car played the little engine that could, and I eventually caught up with her. It was late afternoon when we finally rolled up to my new dorm room, only to find that the fall semester tenant had yet to vacate. She greeted us with an apology and a promise to be completely moved out by morning. *Don't leave*, I thought. *You could be the one person I know!*

The business my mom and Ken owned was under contract to remodel a hotel about forty miles away in Asheville. Mom decided we'd just head there because we could stay overnight for free and then come back to the school in the morning. When we arrived, Ken's work truck was there, but his boxy gold BMW wasn't. It was Friday, so Mom figured aloud that he was probably at his family's lake house for the weekend. The lack of communication between them certainly wasn't due to an absence of cell phones. They were a new invention, bulky and expensive, but they each had one. Mom had recently received a jaw-dropping bill for over $700. She looked it over and decided to call the one number she saw repeatedly on the itemized bill. A woman answered and Mom explained she was just trying to figure out if her husband had run up the phone bill or if it had been their daughter. This woman told Mom she'd been doing some work for Ken, thereby necessitating frequent phone calls between them. And besides, she added, Ken doesn't even have any kids.

Mom didn't hide this from me. It fell like a stone, heavy from her lips, straight to the pit of my stomach. Already suspecting he was having another affair, she had changed the locks that winter and forbidden him from coming home for Christmas. I got a ton of presents from all my parental figures that Christmas. Children of divorce are opportunists by nature. Ken sent me a Christmas card with my presents, and inside the card was a pencil sketch of a teddy bear. The bear looked exactly like the one I'd clung to since the day I'd met him when I was seven years old. He wrote, "Shellie, this bear reminds me of you. This bear was a part of my life too. I miss you." Tears burned my eyes. I don't remember any of the gifts from that Christmas, but I will never forget that card. His grief was more than I had the skill to process. I wanted to reach out. I wanted to talk to him, but I didn't know what to say so I stuffed it. I smoked, drank, tripped, partied, had meaningless sexual encounters, repeat.

Back at the hotel, Mom and I had decided to change clothes and head to the local Applebee's for dinner. As soon as we walked through the door, Mom stopped dead in her tracks. In a calm voice that belied the scene before us, she said, "There's your dad and his new girlfriend." I looked over at the bar to see Ken facing the bartender, his back to me and his strong, confident arm around the waist of this strange young woman with short brown hair. Mom asked the hostess for a booth. Stunned, I walked right over to the bar and tapped him on the shoulder. He turned to me and said, "Oh, Shellie, I was so upset about not being able to take you to school." His eyes scanned the room. "Where's your mom?" I could only point toward the booth where she sat staring straight ahead at the empty booth across the table, her hands folded in her lap. She'd been in this position before, too many times than seemed even remotely fair. That's when the woman turned to me and said, "Well, aren't you a cute little thing? This must be your daughter." All the pain, all the hurt I'd ever felt up until that point in my life unleashed a rage in me that almost felt out-of-body. I lunged at her, but Ken wedged himself between us and she quickly made her way out the door.

Ken and I headed for the booth where Mom sat waiting. My parents tried unsuccessfully to order a shot of whiskey to calm my nerves. Having witnessed the scene we'd already caused at the bar, it seemed the staff was hesitant to serve me without a valid ID. Probably wise since I was underage.

Somehow, we made it through dinner, but I could sense the ground splitting beneath me again, threatening to swallow up life as I knew it, another shift in the fault planes. I suddenly, desperately wanted to talk to my boyfriend, Ash, the only person that I could count on to agree with me that this was bullshit. My parents were cordial to one another as we picked at our meals.

After dinner, I walked with them through a last-minute shopping trip to the local Walmart for rubber flip-flops to wear in the shower and a few forgotten items for my dorm room. By the time we arrived back at the hotel, Mom decided I needed a Xanax. I gladly swallowed it and passed out while they went to Ken's room for the night—I'm sure to hash it all out. I have to give them credit for not doing that in front of me.

As we headed back to the university the next morning, traveling in three separate cars, it felt like we were moving through molasses. We carried my belongings inside the dorm building where I met my roommate, petite like me, with a deep country accent and bleached-blonde hair. While the two of us headed to orientation, Mom made up my bed and neatly put away my clothes and toiletries, and Ken set up my cable TV. It was late afternoon when we said our goodbyes. Everything felt surreal.

Loneliness, heavier than I'd ever felt, settled deep into my bones. My roommate had left for her boyfriend's house, where she informed me that she planned to sleep most nights. In fact, she ended up only returning one more time to move all her things to his place. I lit a stick of lavender incense and sat down on the edge of the bed. The fragrant smoke cut white curls through the air like an SOS signal. Whatever excitement I had formerly possessed had completely given way to anxiety. I had no idea what was happening to my family, a family that seemed to always teeter on the edge of existence. Feeling utterly alone, I picked up the phone and called my father. I greeted him with the news that I had made it safely to school and was all moved in. He greeted me very pissed off that I hadn't taken the route he'd requested. He told me that I could figure out how the hell to pay for school, so I worried over that for a few days, but he'd called the school and arranged for payment of the bill soon after classes started. How could I tell him about what had just happened to us at Applebee's? He had no interest in or compassion for his ex-wife and her husband and certainly did not understand how sad and unmoored I was feeling about it. How could he? He'd never had an inkling of familial stability, so how could he properly understand its impact on me? This dysfunction and disconnection were our shared inheritance.

Driving always made me feel better, something I learned from Dad. I decided to take a drive and get familiar with my surroundings. It was January and the sun was already behind the mountains. I mostly coasted down the steep highway to the only stoplight in the little valley town. My car's engine sputtered and died, right there in the middle of the intersection of this town, about which I knew nothing and no one. Because of my anxious nature, I both hoped and feared someone would stop to help me. I don't know how long I sat with my forehead on the steering wheel before a policeman knocked gently on the driver-side window. If my tears took him by surprise, he hid it behind kind eyes and a smile as he radioed for a tow truck.

The first sight my fellow dorm mates ever glimpsed of me was when I stepped out of the back of a police cruiser wearing the uniform of the nineties: ripped up jeans, a red flannel shirt, and smudged mascara à la Alicia Silverstone in the Aerosmith videos, and though I didn't yet have the belly ring, it was coming. I had an armful of belongings salvaged from my car that I balanced under my chin. I avoided all contact and looked straight ahead as I walked through the front doors of my dormitory building. I turned the key and the lock slid open. Inside my room, I found a yellow warning slip from the RA on the floor. Offense: Burning of candles and incense not allowed in campus housing.

Mom and Ken officially separated that semester, and when Easter weekend rolled around, my car was still in the shop. Ken was the only person to visit me during my time away at school. He picked me up in his work truck and took me to his grandmother's house to be with his side of the family for Easter weekend. An old song from the early '80s came on the radio.

"If you like piña coladas . . ."

Staring out the window, I searched the shadows for anything that would give me hope for our family, something to hold on to. I told him the song made me think of him and Mom. I blurted out something about how I thought they belonged together, despite all their problems. In a move of childlike desperation, I asked him if he found out he didn't have long to live, wouldn't he want to be with Mom? Darkness had erased everything outside the car window. He took his eyes off the road long enough to look at me and say, "Yes, of course."

Later that semester, I went home to the beach town for spring break. I had no idea it would be the last time, because they would sell the house before the semester ended. At some point during spring break, Ken joined us and slept in the guest room. The phone rang several times that night. It was his girlfriend—the one from the cell phone bill and Applebee's. She was relentless in her efforts to speak to him. Mom, who had had about as much as she could take, marched into his room brandishing her little pearl-handled pistol to let him know she was pissed and hurt and that he needed to leave. I remember him repeating over and over, with his hands in the air signaling surrender, that he came home because wanted to see me and take me to dinner. I don't remember if he left that night and have no recollection of how I got back to school to finish the semester.

A Walking Achy Boo-Boo

I finally started to make some friends by becoming a little sister to a fraternity on campus. I received a letter in the mail from an outraged Ash that read, "You joined a men's group? Maybe I'll join the Girl Scouts!" He was beside himself with heartache. He knew he was losing me. The first night we met, he expressed this could end badly. He feared that the balance of power would tip the scale in my favor and he would be left brokenhearted. It had been his intention to be coy and keep me chasing him all the years we were together. He kept his entire heart just out of reach, always leaving just enough sweetness on my lips to keep me coming back for more. His letters and care packages became bipolar in nature, vacillating in sentiment from "How could you do this to me? You whore!" to "Please consider coming to school here. I'll pay the rent, buy you all the fashion magazines and manicures you could possibly want. I'll work while you go to school!" His letters would always include a thoughtful memento like a cassette tape with a recording of Lynyrd Skynyrd's

"I Need You," or a little nugget of weed, or lines from the Fleetwood Mac song "Gold Dust Woman" carefully written out. With a nod to Steely Dan, one of our favorite bands, he always signed them, *With Pretzel Logic*.

It reminded me of the year before when he made me a homemade book out of a Led Zeppelin album cover. It was an apology for having disappeared with the girlfriend of his best friend and bandmate, David, one Friday night. I'd never find out exactly what happened or didn't happen that night, and to my knowledge neither did his friend who elected not to break up with the offending girlfriend. He'd picked me up the Monday following the night in question and presented me with the book that promised a more sensitive Ash and more quality time together. Each page had a word, phrase, or picture glued to it with a caption he'd written underneath. At the top of one page, a magazine cutout read, "Favorite," and below that it said, "You are my favorite person of all time and space." The next page was a commitment to do whatever it would take to keep us together. A page featuring a photo of Eddie Van Halen passionately playing guitar and a caption that read, "I'm Eddie and you're the guitar," followed this serious sentiment. There was an entire homage to my bad breath, which I took to be the highest level of acceptance possible. Thus came my newest nickname, Halle Tosis. Always about the breath! In a gesture of humility, he added a word bubble declaring that his breath stank too. I flipped through the book while he drove me to the beach in his underwear.

Meanwhile, I experienced extreme enjoyment as the trucks passed by and honked at us on the beach road as they looked down to see his bare legs the same shade of white as his souped-up Mustang. He thought this was a fittingly humiliating act to demonstrate his level of remorse. And just like that, we were back together, spending weekend nights in the band room in the seediest part of our beach town where my parents owned a coin-operated laundromat that I was not allowed to go to without my stepdad. We spent weeknights eating sunflower seeds and watching movies like *Willy Wonka & the Chocolate Factory*.

I made the drive from Western Carolina to see him a few times and he went all out during my visits. We went to dinner and he bought me every fashion and home decor magazine on the shelf. We slept in his twin bed and he always touched me like it might be the last time he got the chance. I felt terrible that only now did he truly understand what I meant to him. I was finding myself and, in the process, discovering that there were other emotionally unavailable men out there that intrigued me. His once unshakable confidence was now eclipsed by mine.

I ended up spending only one semester at the college in the mountains. My parents' separation had scattered us to the four corners of the state, and I longed to be near my people. When summer came around, Ken came to get my things and stashed them in his rented storage building. I headed east to spend a few days with my mom at the beach condo where she was living at the time. Her long-term plan was to move to Charlotte to live with a beloved family friend Liz until she got on her feet. The drive over the bridge into Wrightsville Beach felt like a sigh escaping a long-closed mouth. The feeling was much like it had been years earlier when I'd stepped out onto the balcony of the Waterway Inn, glimpsed the drawbridge, and inhaled the salty air. I unpacked my things and walked out to the pier that jutted out into the intracoastal waterway. I felt lighter than I had in a long time. It had been a dark and dreary winter and a rainy spring in the North Carolina mountains.

Out on the pier, I rolled out my towel and thought about the guy I'd been seeing while away at school. Chris was a KA, prelaw, and attractive to me in every way, but our relationship lacked an emotional connection. He had a foot in both worlds. The world of partying that I'd long inhabited, but also an eye to the future he was actively pursuing. But I wasn't even a whole person yet. I was like an empty vessel yet to be filled with anything substantial. It was my subconscious habit to perform a chameleon transformation in order to suit the people I was with and places I inhabited in the moment. That can be a good skill to have if you have a set point of personality, virtues, and boundaries in your life to ground you. But if you don't, the practice of conforming will leave you feeling adrift and panicky, as if out on open water whenever someone asks what you want, what you like or dislike, and who you really are. I was a walking achy boo-boo trying to find a place to heal, though I didn't know it at the time. When the pain of your life has been with you so long, it becomes what you subconsciously seek; it's pain, but it's also comfort. Struggle is familiar. I thought the love of another person might make me whole and give me a skin to slip into.

That night I talked to Chris on the phone. He was having a blast celebrating his graduation with his fraternity brothers and his family. We made plans for me to come to Raleigh soon to visit. Then I heard that my high school buddies, David and Greg, two of Ash's best friends, were having a party at their parents' house. I pulled on a sundress and hopped into the champagne-colored, four-door BMW with navy leather interior my parents had recently passed down to me. My little blue Honda never made it out of the repair shop where it had been since that first night it broke down on me in the little mountain town. It wasn't worth repairing.

I wasn't sure what to expect when I got there, but all my old friends were welcoming. Ash hardly spoke to me and it was still awkward to be around the girl he'd disappeared with that one night the year before. She and David were still together, so why did I feel it was necessary to hold a grudge? After having a beer and catching up with a few friends, I decided to head back to my mom's. My keys were nowhere to be found. I couldn't leave. I was totally panicked. The peace and ease I had felt only for a short time evaporated instantly. The entire party searched for them to no avail. I called my mom to come get me, so she put on her clothes and drove across town. The phone woke me the next morning.

"Morning sunshine." Mom was calling from work to say she'd just received a flower arrangement from Ash. The card read, "I'm sorry for all the trouble I've caused over the years and last night. I love your daughter very much. Losing her hurts." Within the hour he had returned my car keys. Despite the bright sky, that goodbye left me with a heavy heart. For so long I had chased him and his love that he'd kept out of reach, dangling just beyond my reach. It felt like a gut punch to both of us, as young love often does, but I had moved on.

Chris lived in a suburb outside of Raleigh, and having just graduated that semester, he had returned home for the summer. I would visit him off and on throughout the next year. After that week at the beach with my mom, I moved to Charlotte to live in my sister's condo. She slept at her boyfriend's every night, so she was rarely home. Before I met Chris, I'd reconnected with a friend from the beach town. I'd heard Jake had been living in Charlotte and we'd gone out on a few dates the summer before I headed to school in the mountains. One of his roommates had a family home in the nearby town of Cashiers, so they had made the trip up there and I drove over the mountain to stay the night with them. I adored quiet Jake with his good looks and kind brown eyes and fell even harder for his roommates, who would quickly become my best buddies.

A Walking Achy Boo-Boo

While living in my sister's condo, I got in touch with the Rob, Nate, and Sam and they hooked me up with a job hosting at the restaurant where they all worked as servers. Though it never went anywhere with Jake and me, these guys became my closest friends. They took me out to a bar the night before my birthday, and when the clock struck midnight, they each ordered me very different shots. While Bob Marley played on the jukebox, I tried a lemon drop, something that tastes like cough medicine, then rounded it out with some tequila shots.

In the giant wooden booth, surrounded by these guys that were never more than friends, there was no expectation of sex. There was no exchange needed for their friendship and affection. An older drunk woman slid into the booth next to me and began to chat us up. I didn't think anything of it until she started talking to the guys about me, in front of me, as though I wasn't there. It became clear she wanted to take me home with her. At first the guys were charmed by this idea, but then declared me done for the night and ready to go home.

I vaguely remember hugging the toilet back at their apartment, yarfing up a stomach-churning potpourri of alcohol and a poorly timed grilled cheese sandwich made in an attempt to sober me up. Mostly, I remember waking up in Sam's bed with the front section of my hair pulled back with a twisted pipe cleaner that was fresh and had not yet been used to clean the bong—no doubt Sam's work. My contacts were in bowls of saline on the counter and labeled left and right on a torn sheet of notebook paper—absolutely Rob's doing. I loved these men like brothers. Rob's bed was in what should have been the dining room and we often jumped on it like kids when we were excited about having spaghetti for dinner or just happy to see each other on a night off from the restaurant where we all worked.

That next morning was my birthday proper. My gold BMW flew through the small towns between Charlotte and Raleigh. I was on my way to meet up with Chris for the weekend, and then head up to Richmond for Horde Fest. The music festival was being hosted by Richmond, Virginia, that year, which also happened to be the murder capital of the South at the time. This fact gave me only a moment of pause. We met up with another couple, friends of his, and pregamed with some whiskey in the parking lot. Wearing a giant blue tie-dyed tank dress, a chain of tiny silver bells on my ankle, and my hair pulled into a messy ponytail, I looked the part. I always knew how to look like I belonged, but I never felt like it. We had a great time partying that weekend and several more weekend visits before he finally saw me as the walking achy boo-boo I was, and that I had no more to offer than partying and sex. I had no authentic sense of self. I didn't look past the moment. I had no hobbies or interests at the time. It's hard to evolve as a person while you're in survival mode. It hurt, but he soon moved on, and though reluctantly, and with a broken heart, so did I.

An Inside Job

I spent that summer in Charlotte living out of a suitcase at my sister's condo. Our cousin, Tracy, was her roommate, though they were rarely ever home. Angela spent most nights at her boyfriend's house, and Tracy seemed to work all the time. I waited tables and took a math course at the community college, a condition of my acceptance to UNC-Charlotte. The decision to attend the local university instead of returning to the isolation of college in the mountains was born of the desire to be near my family. A sense of sadness and the feeling of being displaced weighed heavily on me. I was twenty-one, and I wasn't ready to be out on my own with no family home to return to. Despite having been accepted to the college I wished to transfer to, I still felt aimless. My belongings from home were stored in Ken's storage building, along with the contents of our former home that had been sold a few months earlier. One night Ken called and his voice sounded distraught.

"Shel, the police just called. Someone broke into my storage unit. They took a lot of my things . . . things from the house and all of your belongings. I don't understand why."

His voice sounded bewildered and tired. "The police said I should look in the dumpsters for your stuff since none of it had any value, but it's raining. If it's out there then it's ruined by now."

I sat on the floor at the top of the stairs and cried. I felt abandoned, alarmed, and once again, like a rootless tree poised to fall. I thought of the memorabilia from high school, my dorm room decorations I had so carefully picked out, my favorite records, my stuffed animals, my clothes, notes, yearbooks, stuffed animals, letters and cards from high school. I hung up with him and called my mom where she was staying at her friend Liz's house. I told her all my things had been stolen from the storage unit. Her voice was even, her tone was cool. I don't think she had any capacity to feel anything but hurt and betrayal at the time. I can imagine now how she must have seen me as loyal to the man who had broken her heart and broken up our family. I was a traitor. I didn't see him as the man who broke my mother's heart, I saw him as the parent she brought into our lives when I was seven years old. I couldn't help it. I wanted so desperately to feel like I mattered to one of them, and Ken had the capacity to make me feel important when everyone else was too busy trying to find their own way. I wished I'd had the capacity to think of more than just myself, but I didn't.

As summer came to a close, I prepared to move into a campus apartment at UNCC. I started packing up what few belongings I had and taking them across town. I bought a Jim Belushi poster and a Bob Marley tapestry for my dorm room, but I didn't have any bedding and linens now. One day Mom called to say she had some things of mine that I might need for my move and she would drop them off at my sister's house over the next few days. When I opened those boxes, my heart sank as I realized these were my things that had been taken from Ken's storage room that rainy summer night. I called Liz's house for my mother, but Liz intercepted the call. "Shellie, your mom did what she had to do. She had no idea what was going to happen with Ken and was worried that you would lose your things. She was just protecting you."

I was stunned. I couldn't trust anyone. She had let me cry and mourn the loss of the belongings that made up my personal history, the only remaining remnants of home. Why didn't she just tell me when I'd called her that night? Sadly, she probably couldn't trust that I wouldn't tell him. Shortly after my things were returned to me, Ken and I sat at the bar of the restaurant where I worked and drank Goldschläger shots until Sam and Rob finished their shifts and joined us. When it was closing time, he left first. We walked out to the parking lot to find him crying in his truck and writing me a note he planned to leave on the windshield of my car: "I'm sorry for everything that happened to us. I love you." He handed it to me and we sobbed together outside his truck. I was an emotional wreck standing in the parking lot, holding the letter in my hand while I watched him drive away. I turned to see Sam and Rob with their arms outstretched to me. Sam grabbed my keys, drove me home, and tucked me in bed. That feeling was back. I felt like a body with no skin on.

The following semester didn't go well for me. While I was failing my classes, my sister was preparing to get married, and my mom was deeply concerned about her finances and drowning in anger and disappointment over her failed marriage to Ken. She had moved out of Liz's house and into a house she had purchased. She was having difficulty making ends meet and was, understandably, deeply depressed. One day that semester, I stopped by to find her in bed in the middle of the day, tear-stained and distraught, surrounded by paperwork and crumpled tissues. She told me she'd lose the house if Ken didn't pay his alimony right away. So, I called him to ask for it and he agreed to get it to her at once. That problem was solved, for the moment anyway, but when my dad received my abysmal grades at the end of that semester, I had another problem. He refused to pay another dime toward my school.

Sandy the Hippie

When spring break rolled around that semester at UNCC, I couldn't stand the thought of spending it in my depressing campus apartment. I grabbed a backpack and shoved some clothes and a bikini inside and went home to Wilmington with my high school best friend, Ari, who was also attending UNCC, to stay with her family. When we arrived, I went to Ari's room to unpack and she went to shower. When she didn't return after quite some time, I made my way through the spacious house to the game room in the basement to look for her. Her mom met me at the door and told me that Ari needed some rest, some downtime, and that I should find somewhere else to stay. She didn't ask if I had another place to go or thank me for driving her home. In high school, our families had lived just down the road from each other, and she knew my folks had recently divorced and moved away. I had attended church with Ari and her family a few times back when we were in high school. It was the first time I'd been in a church since the Catholic school masses of my middle school years.

This adult had no concern for my well-being. She turned her back to me, tucked the brown blanket around Ari's legs as she lay resting in the recliner, and didn't look back. My friend did not feel the need to explain this rejection. Neither of them spoke another word, so I left. I sat in my car in front of our old house down the street and tried to process what had just happened. Since Ari and I were best friends from high school and were attending the same college, I remember thinking it would have made sense for us to live together instead of rooming with strangers, but rooming with strangers was exactly what we did. Her mom wasn't keen on me, but I never knew why. Did she think of me as a troublemaker? Maybe because my family didn't go to church? In reality, Ari was the wild one. In high school, when her boyfriend would start gnarly fights that scared her, I was brave (or dumb) enough to get in my car, drive over there, and remove her from the situation.

Earlier that semester, at a Grateful Dead show, she somehow lost her ticket somewhere between my parked car and the front door of the coliseum. When she made instant friends with some people sitting outside their VW bus, I made sure I memorized the parking lot row number where it was parked so I could find her later, but at the end of the show, she was nowhere to be found. I waited until there were nearly no cars left in the parking lot. When she still wasn't home the next day, I went looking for her and somehow managed to find her at a hotel with her new friends from the VW bus.

Not too long after that, I took care of her when she tried the drug Special K. I stopped by her apartment on the way home from the convenience store to find her crouched on her toilet in the bathroom with her knees pulled up to her chin in the throes of a full-blown hallucinogenic meltdown. I smoothed her dark-blonde curls, talked her through it, and didn't leave her side until she was completely sober again. Foolishly, I cussed out the guy that gave it to her while he sat on her bed watching as I tried to bring Ari back around. Thankfully, he left without incident.

Now here I was, displaced on spring break, longing for the comfort of home and nowhere to go. Skinless. Unprotected. My own mother was deeply depressed and could only really care for herself at the time. My father was distant. Geography hadn't changed much about his involvement in my life. I felt mostly like an obligation, an expense. We'd not grown closer after the move. He didn't want to think that Mom and Ken's divorce and subsequent fallout had any effect on me, which kept him from understanding the fact that it did.

I drove around town, trying to decide where I should stay for a few nights. I thought of Bill and Sandy, a couple that had lived in the apartment across the street from my high school boyfriend Ash. I knew I could stay there. Bill was nice and entertaining, but became more intense the drunker he got. Sandy was a true hippie, soft and wise in the ways of being a woman. She lovingly tended to a monstrous aloe plant and tinkered in the kitchen when all of us teenagers would hang out at their place. She rolled us joints and listened more than she talked, though she told great stories when you could get her to open up. She would play peacemaker and shoo us out the door when, inevitably, Bill would get drunk and weird and start some heated argument with one of the teenage boys. I always wondered if he turned that on her after we left.

Bill was a trucker and he was on the road that week, but to my great relief, Sandy was home and threw the door and her arms wide open to me. Sandy the hippie and I sat at the kitchen table while we caught up on my life since leaving Wilmington. As I talked, she doodled potential tattoos for me. We'd decided that if the world was gonna insist on my independence, I would give polite society the middle finger by getting tattooed on this trip. This tattoo would be like a rite of passage. It was 1993, and it was not common to see a tattoo on a young lady at the time.

The guest room was lean, modest, and comfortable. Nothing fancy. I know Sandy saved me when I had nowhere to go and I was grateful. Yet, that skinless, unprotected feeling haunted my sleep. Sandy fed me. She let me come and go while I dropped in on a few friends and tucked my toes in the sand at the beach while she worked. On the last day of the trip, we headed to the tattoo shop and I handed the guy Sandy's drawing. "You sober?" he asked.

"Uh, yeah," I lied. It was eleven in the morning. I wasn't drunk, but I was high. He tattooed a small laughing half-moon in blues and purples on the center of my lower back while Sandy watched from the other side of the glass window that separated the waiting room, fist pumping in the air whenever we locked eyes. Afterward, we headed to the beach, my new tattoo all bandaged and requiring the cover of a tank top. I still have a photo of Sandy from that day, looking beautiful and peaceful with long blonde hair pulled over to one side and spilling down one shoulder, the contrast of the black one-piece suit stark on her smooth, pale skin. I never saw her again. We lost touch.

Ari and I eventually met up again at the end of spring break and I drove us both back to school. I didn't have the words to articulate how I felt, so I just didn't, and she offered no apology that I can recall. She was so dear to me and after any time apart, we always picked right back up where we left off. She did seem more rested. We eventually did become roommates a year later. Her parents had moved to Florida and she'd started dating an older guy. Upon meeting him, the father of our other roommate, Shana, declared he had the eyes of a murderer. Shana and I both agreed something felt off and hoped we were wrong. He'd told Ari that he was infertile. As smart as she was, she believed him, so the pregnancy was a huge surprise. They decided marriage was the only way to make this right in the eyes of God, so she asked me to drive them to the home of a minister in the middle of nowhere to elope. So, I did. I was the sole witness to their marriage in the living room of this ranch home in a tiny South Carolina town. A few months later, I let her squeeze my hand while she squatted in a hospital bed, trying valiantly to bring a giant baby boy into the world. He would eventually emerge from her body like an alien, weighing a whopping ten pounds. She was exhausted. Sweat-soaked curls clung to her forehead and down her back. I left there in a daze. I'd never seen anything like it.

This marriage and this precious baby would be the beginning of the end of Ari and me. Her husband would do what most abusive husbands do and isolate her by moving her hours away from family and friends where his brutality would go unseen. He made it clear to her that he did not care for me. She eventually slipped through my fingers like water. We wrote to each other regularly and called infrequently. They went on to have another child, another boy, and she worked as a certified nursing assistant.

In her last note to me, after updating me on the kids and the weather down in Florida, she cryptically wrote, "As for other things and how they're going, you just wouldn't believe. You just wouldn't believe." Not too long after that, I was able to reach her by phone and she told me they had finally separated. She didn't provide much in the way of details, but she gave me the address of the apartment where she had moved with her two sons without their father. A few months later, my letters to her were returned to me with "not at this address" stamped across the front. To this day I cannot find her. I wonder if he changed, if he softened as the years passed. I wonder what pain life had shown him that made him act so harshly toward her and exact judgment on those of us he tried to remove from her life. Mostly, I want to know, where was her protection? Where was Ari's rescuer? Where was her Sandy the hippie?

Your Corporate Barbie

When you're an anxious person, you're always looking for cracks in the vessel, scanning the ship for places water could get in. As an anxious person, this can become a quest to seek and destroy any potential issues that make you feel threatened. In my early twenties, my boyfriend of two years, Maddy, admitted to flirting with his coworker at the bar when I questioned him about it. I knew in my gut that something was going on. They worked the nightlife scene together—cool, fun, and age appropriate—while I worked in tech support in the home office of a fast fashion retail chain, a very grown-up job for an immature twenty-two-year-old. I felt him pulling away from me. The opposite schedules didn't help us much. I felt like a boring adult while his life as a bartender and college senior seemed more fun in comparison.

I had a terrible semester at UNCC. My mom had been deeply sad, and for a moment, despair turned her thoughts suicidal. My grades suffered because my only relief from myself and everything going on around me was to find new friends and numb out with pot and alcohol. When I mostly failed that semester, Dad told me I could figure out how to pay for it myself, so I gave it a shot by taking this job. I worked three twelve-hour shifts on the weekends and dragged myself to class during the week. About a year into that, I was promoted to assistant buyer, and dropped out of college altogether.

During this time, Maddy would come back to my place around two thirty or three a.m. after working his bar shift. He'd call to ask me to disarm the alarm to the condo owned by my sister that I now shared with my best friend, Shana. I'd answer in a sleepy voice that he claimed to adore and looked forward to hearing every night. When I'd leave early the next morning for work, dressed for my professional job, he'd wake up long enough for a kiss. "Have a great day, my little corporate Barbie," he'd say.

One night we worked a concert together, me as a beer girl and Maddy and his flirty coworker as bartenders. Her name was Andi. She was a brown-haired, brown-eyed, all-American girl next door that seemed like she would be the cherished little sister to several protective brothers. In the office as we waited for payout, he'd leaned his crotch against her hand as she grasped the back of the metal folding chair in which she was sitting sideways. Some other onlooker could have seen this as subtle or accidental, or not even noticed this at all, but I had been told at a young age that I had a strong innate intuition, and it went on high alert. A familiar red-hot heat climbed up my neck and face and then I felt it in my stomach. How did I know the signs of infidelity long before the time came when it involved me? Maybe it wasn't the cheating that alerted my Spidey senses, but the gnawing feeling of impending abandonment and the realization that people are often not who we think they are. One minute you're eating Capt'n Crunch in your tiny Nikes, and the next thing you know someone is missing from your life and your sense of value disappears with them.

Later I asked him if they flirted with each other at work. He hemmed and hawed and finally admitted they did in fact flirt. I was unmoored. I cried rivers. I cussed and ranted about how I had trusted him and he'd humiliated me. My reaction was so over the top that he broke up with me. In a matter of days, they were a couple and I lost it. I didn't even try to play it cool. I had zero emotional control. I'd been abandoned again, a reminder of my less than zero worth. Marooned on an island of unworthiness. Every vulnerability I possessed was triggered. I felt panicked at the thought of being alone again. I was unloved, unprotected, skinless. A month later he left for the cross-country post-graduation trip he'd long planned with a buddy of his, while I nursed a broken heart.

In my utter grief, I left the city and headed back to the beach town for the weekend. My friend Cammie's dad, a high school physics teacher, had built a floating house on the marshlands, and Ari, Cammie, Cammie's boyfriend, and I jumped in a fishing boat stocked with whiskey and headed over to the floating house for a sleepover. On the ride over, manta rays covered the sea floor, overlapping like a sandy carpet. The floating house had four walls, a few built-in bunks, and a deck for sunning and fishing.

I cried, burying my face in Maddy's flannel until at last, dehydrated, the well of tears had run dry. I had worn this flannel over my bikini all day and later tied it at my waist while we sat around a campfire on the ocean side of Masonboro Island. I'd been sleeping with it, my face pressed to it like the woobie of my childhood. The release of my grief and the adventure of the past few days left me exhilarated as we shuttled back to the floating house from the island in the dark. These kids had grown up exploring these islands and marshlands and could make their way in the dark, even when the way was further obscured by pot and whiskey. Ari was dancing in her purple one-piece on the sundeck of the floating house the next morning as the sun came up, a T-shirt wrapped around her head like a scarf. This levity and the expanse of the surrounding sky gave me the sensation of having been flung into a new reality, one that hinted at the possibility of life after Maddy.

Back home in Charlotte, I made out with a friend on another friend's couch, just because I could. I cashed out my 401(k) and bought the tallest, most badass steel-toed Doc Marten boots I could find, denim overalls, and a pair of Birkenstocks. I painted my toes green and earned the nickname Sprout. I repeatedly ran out of clean underwear and decided to ditch them altogether. I started working at an Irish pub. I started seeing Mark again, a musician I'd met while at college in the mountains and later dated off and on when I moved to Charlotte. After a night of drinking beer and taking shots at a bar downtown, I asked my friend BK to drop me off at Mark's instead of my house. He was happy to see me and we hung out for a while. The next thing I remember I was in his bed. I let go an eternally echoing beer-fueled fart that *woke me up* from a dead sleep. I was mortified and paralyzed with embarrassment, but also feeling lighter than I had felt in months. Mark had his back to me, so if he was awake, then I suppose he pretended not to hear it. When I got back to the apartment, I called my sister to tell her about it. She said, "You blamed it on him, right?" She's a damn genius. Why didn't I think of that? Since we have remained friends over the years, I wanted to say something to him about it, clear the air if you will, but the timing was never right. I was trying to move on, and that night, I was able to catch a glimpse of levity sparking a once dark horizon.

Somehow, as broken as I was, I managed not to pick up the smoking habit I'd kicked just a few months before. I ran three miles a day and went to the gym instead. I got drunk and acted out in public. When I saw Maddy and the girl together one night, the one with whom he had cheated, I drunkenly yelled at them for having the nerve to come to Amos's, the bar where I had hung out with my friends on Sunday nights for years. It was my turf and although I had been the one to cause the scene, every member of the band playing that night was a dear friend of mine. Eric, Timmy, Jeff, Leebo, and Chuck all rallied around me to convince the management to let me stay and make Maddy and his girl leave. For the first time in ages, I felt protected and not alone. In this community, a new skin was beginning to grow, a covering for my skin and bones.

A few months later, my heartache was starting to heal, so naturally, Maddy called me while on the last leg of the trip after three weeks on the road. I'd been out at a bar called Fat City with a musician friend from the local band, Sound of Mine. My roommate, Shana, left me a note that he had called the house phone, but since the ceiling fan had blown it off my pillow, I'd gone to bed without seeing it. He called again while I was sleeping. I answered the phone in the half-awake voice he found so endearing. I hadn't seen him since that night awful at Amos's.

"Mmm, hello?"

"Oh my God, I missed that voice."

"Maddy? Is that you?"

For months I'd waited, full of hope that he might call. When he finally did, I was barely awake and not at all prepared.

"Yes, it's me. I just called to say I miss you so much. The trip has been great, but at every stop along the way, I have thought about you and how it all feels meaningless without you by my side."

"I've missed you too. When do you get home?"

"In two days. Would you pick me up at the airport?"

At the baggage claim, I saw him walking toward me with that crooked grin and those long, dark curls. His arms were opened wide. I greeted him in overalls and Birkenstocks, an outfit I was sure he'd love. I drove him to his parents' house, where he uncharacteristically and confidently pulled me up onto the kitchen counter and kissed me. I remember how it felt like kissing a stranger. This wasn't the man or the kiss I remembered. This was more passionate, more confident. I shook off the feeling and let it go.

He was home for exactly two days before I found him back at that coworker's apartment, naked on her living room floor, music blaring, their fun interrupted by my knock. When I'd arrived there, I noticed his car half in the grass and half in the parking space, as though he didn't notice the curb he'd driven over while trying to park. When he hadn't shown up to my place after work as he promised, I had a sickening certainty that he was with Andi, so I asked my roommate Shana and her boyfriend Joey to drive me over there. It was as though I knew it in my body before I even saw it for myself.

On the way out the door, Joey said, "He's not gonna be over there, but if he is, he's screwing her."

I was destroyed. He later told mutual friends of ours that he had been ready to give me a ring. We always figured we would marry after he graduated. But it was a conversation with his dad he'd recounted to me back when we first broke up that stuck with me. He told his dad there were things that we argued about and that we had issues. He said, "Son, an adversarial relationship is no kind of relationship to have." If there was another kind of relationship, I sure hadn't known it.

That familiar feeling of abandonment sent panic like a rocket to my throat. I fell apart again, after I'd spent so long building myself back up. The rejection was a memory in my body as well as my mind, triggered without warning, a reaction in full motion without my permission. A reminder that I was disposable, unworthy of love, and tossed aside. Abandoned again. It wasn't a fierce love I felt for him; I was too broken a person to be capable of that. It was the sense of loss and the familiar feeling of being unlovable, unwanted. A feeling of being passed over for someone else.

Reeling, I left my roommate a note that said something like "please take care of Bones (my cat) because I am going away for a while." I hit the road to Greensboro and met up with an on-again-off-again snowboarder/surfer boyfriend who had always held space for me. He was a temporary bandage for a deep gash. He was familiar and safe and reminded me that I had a life before Maddy and besides, he always wanted me. I stayed until I felt like my broken pieces were somewhat contained.

When I finally returned home, Shana was livid. Blonde, pretty, and always composed, she had the wrinkle of anger between her brows and was doing this thing with her thumbs that she does when she's really pissed. It had never been directed at me so it was startling. I had worried her with my cryptic note because I couldn't articulate the deep, suck-holey pain I felt. It was more than just a breakup as it appeared on the surface. I felt it to my core. I'd had enough of life. She was furious because she cared about me. She came from a traditional, loving, intact family, so she had no frame of reference for my dysfunctional life, but she was empathetic and knew enough to feel all the pain with me if I had only let her.

When I got back to town, my parents, my sister, and I gathered at a therapist's office I had just begun to see a few short weeks earlier. It was an intervention of sorts. The details are vague, more like snapshots than memories. My mom cried a lot, my dad patted her leg to console her. All I could think was, *I'm in pain. I'm hurting. And somehow, yet again, no one sees this. They only see my behavior as a problem.* I would later come to understand how my mother's pain eclipsed her ability to see or soothe mine. I had so much anger inside me and I felt they'd all abandoned me now.

A Gravitational Pull

A few months later, when word had gotten around that Maddy and I had broken up and it was clear we weren't getting back together, two friends of Maddy's called me on the same night. One at a respectable hour and the other in the middle of the night. The two guys were roommates, best friends from their small hometown in New England.

I ended up dating Kasey, the one that called me first and at a decent hour. He was good looking in a deceptive, clean-cut Northeastern way. The crowd he hung around with was a little dangerous. He was very charming, really smart, and very good to me. Our lives at the time were defined by partying like most twenty-three-year-olds. He was a professional in a starched white button-down, tie, and khakis by day and a flirtatious, unpredictable party boy by night. One time a friend of his stuck his head in the passenger-side window of Kasey's car where I was sitting. He pretended he was going to kiss me, just to get a rise out of Kasey. His cocaine-fueled reaction was to stomp on the gas. Thankfully, the guy jumped away from the car in time to avoid injury.

After we'd been dating about a year, my mom took me on a work trip with her to Puerto Rico. The company she worked for had taken us on a tour of the rainforest where they had a huge Indiana Jones-style stage set with a faux volcano and tiki torches. The next day we were to go into town for some shopping. We got on the bus and before it even moved from the circular drive at the front of the resort, I suddenly felt sick. Mom said I was green. I knew I was going to yarf. In some rapid-fire exchange, it was decided that a male counterpart of my mom's would take me back to our room and sit with me and get me ginger ale and make sure I didn't die while my mom went into town for the shopping excursion as planned.

In a fever fog, I limped to the bathroom several times to vomit. This man waited for me to return to the bed and swiped a cold cloth across my forehead and propped me up to make sure I didn't choke on my own vomit. Yet another angel placed in my life at just the right time. I will never forget his gentle kindness.

My mother and I had a wonderful time of reconnection on that trip, so much so that when my lease was running out shortly after our return, she said I could move in with her. We had fun preparing for the move. When we couldn't get my hand-me-down sofa past the landing in the angular stairwell of my apartment, together we heaved it off the second-floor balcony, our cheeks flushed from effort and laughter. The high mood and closeness wouldn't last long. Not too long after I got there, it was crumbs I repeatedly left on the counter that would do us in. She wrote me a letter explaining how living with me was like living with Ken all over again and that she just couldn't do it anymore. I was inconsiderate and disrespectful of her home and her feelings. She loved me and she wished me the best of luck, but it was time for me to go.

She never spoke to me about it. When things got hard and she felt threatened, she hit the nuclear switch. I wasn't her problem; I wasn't anyone's problem or responsibility. I was displaced again, weighed down with the grief of abandonment and a bone-deep loneliness I could not name. She couldn't talk to me and the pain of our past kept me in such a state of defensiveness that I couldn't listen to her. That chip on my shoulder was easily called up by any sense of being slighted or rejected. I was twenty-three years old and had moved a total of twenty-four times by this point. The idea of home had always been ephemeral, forever slipping through my fingers. What made me so inherently unlovable that even my mother couldn't tolerate me? I triggered something in her that I didn't yet understand.

Kasey and I lived together for two years. I attended massage therapy school and worked part time at a retail skincare shop at the airport while he worked full time and paid the bills. I don't know how I would have survived that time without his help and the willingness of his best friend to let me live with them. They looked out for me. I was protected when they were around and will always be grateful for them.

Not too long after, the three of us moved from their apartment near the university to a condo downtown. Kasey took me home to meet his family in New England. Maine was gorgeous and magical: the coast, the mountains, the lobster we bought from the lobsterman on the side of the road, the wild blueberries his mom and I picked off the bushes up the hill from the house and made into a cobbler for dinner. Taking me home to meet his mom and stepdad, who unfortunately for me drank too much and left the door to the hall bath open while he took a middle-of-the-night dump, was meant to take our relationship to the next level. But when we returned home, life continued as we knew it, with him on the club scene and me at home with a growing sense of unease. I started to feel an emptiness inside of me and a lack of true connection with him and an overwhelming sense that he wasn't being faithful, or maybe just a nagging feeling that I wasn't secure in the relationship. I felt he was two people: a loving boyfriend who doted on me and adored his mother, but also a man battling demons, a man I couldn't entirely trust.

The previous summer, we'd gone to a swanky party at the home of a friend of my sister's. My sister was there with her husband, Paul, and several of our family friends. This was not a pool party, but the pool shone brightly in the moonlight as Kasey and I chatted with the others and had far too much to drink. I don't know what possessed him to do it, but at some point in the evening, he shoved Paul into the pool. I was horrified.

Or maybe I am now, but back then didn't get how mortified I should have been. What I did understand at the moment was the chasm between our lifestyle and that of Paul and my sister. Paul, wearing the Italian leather shoes he had purchased on their honeymoon, popped up out of the water, enraged, but somehow collected himself and did not escalate the situation. He handled it better than anyone I could possibly imagine in that position. From that moment on I knew how my family felt about Kasey and that wouldn't do. I understood then that my sister and I were at different places in our lives and that perhaps my partner had a drinking problem. I keenly felt both safe and uncertain in the familiarity that comes with alcoholic behaviors and the insecure, wobbly sensation that comes when you can't trust the judgment of the drunk people around you.

Lying in bed one of the many nights Kasey went to the nightclubs down the street and I stayed home trying to feel some semblance of a stable life, I had this overwhelming sense that I couldn't trust him. I felt this desperation to live on my own and create my own space. I'd begun to feel a longing, a gravitational pull toward some greater meaning in my life, a search for something I had yet to experience, but I couldn't say what it was exactly. God? A sense of purpose? A deeper, spiritual connection to the man in my life? I had almost always had a boyfriend or been pining over one, and had never lived by myself. I had just finished massage therapy school, but did not have a steady paycheck since I had no regular clients yet. I called my dad and asked him for the money for a first month's rent and deposit on the first place I would live alone. He responded quickly and kindly.

This would be my twenty-sixth move. I had borrowed the money for massage therapy school from Ken. Borrowing money for school from a parent made me feel sad. They'd paid for my sister's school, but I understood that for me, this was a loan. When I was unable to pay Ken and also pay my rent, he didn't speak to me again until he showed up at my wedding, after first declining the invitation. I had let him down, but in my heart, I knew this was unlike him. We had beaten up one another emotionally over the years, but in the end, unconditional acceptance always brought us back together. Rumor had it his soon-to-be new wife told him regularly that I only wanted him for his money. He had been my family since I was seven years old. We were so much more than that. I was still desperate for parental love, to feel as though I had a home and family to return to. I ached for protection for my skin and bones.

I'm with the Band

I don't know where my fear of the dark came from, but it stayed with me well into adulthood. Living alone for the first time really brought this to light for me. The apartment was on the third floor and sat atop a huge grassy hill, making my bedroom windows higher than three stories off the ground. I loved to have the windows open and feel the cool, dry breeze of fall, but I left the bathroom light on all night. I still twisted myself up in a blanket cocoon every night, but didn't sleep much. I never felt safe. I got most of my sleep once the sun began to rise, as though the daylight brought with it some innate safety.

I can only surmise the seeds of fear and terror were planted at the ripe old age of five when my young father, newly separated from my mom, took my sister and me to see the movie *The Amityville Horror*. I sat on his lap during the famous window scene. The foreboding music was coming to a dramatic crescendo, and just before the camera panned to a set of eyeballs on the ground outside the window, the theater completely silent with anticipation, my dad whispered in my ear, "BOO!" I screamed and the entire theater erupted with laughter.

I really hate to think that this one moment, or even having watched the entire movie, is responsible for the way I feel a fleeting moment of fear when I have my back turned to the kitchen doorway as I whir the blender to make my daily smoothie. *Anyone* could creep up behind me and I wouldn't see or hear them because this blender is so loud! Or for the nineteen times an hour I think of a car running over me or someone abducting me while I'm out for a walk. Intrusive thoughts are a daily, sometimes hourly occurrence for me, and some of them are shit-your-pants scary. My mom has them too. Perhaps we've been cursed with some genetic code for irrational fear.

The new apartment was a great home base between working at the spa and the partying that I thought I had wanted to leave behind. Turns out, all my friends were still young and mostly single, so we still went out most nights of the week. I felt an emerging sense of independence in my little two-bedroom apartment. The stylists in the salon were mostly fun, stylish gay guys that doted on me. They convinced me to cut my blonde hair into a chin-length bob. This was a good look with my tortoise-shell glasses. My massage clients fell for me as hard as I fell for them. I had this great desire to be needed and yearned for the approval of others, and this arrangement made me feel deeply important to their well-being, which I enjoyed but also found exhausting. Caregivers have to be on and bring good energy, so massage therapy can be emotionally and physically draining work. I was pretty good at nurturing and was decent when it came to smoothing out tight, ropey muscles. I thrived in the spa's lavender-infused, low-lit vibe.

After work I would usually head down to one of a few bars where my friends, almost all musicians or music enthusiasts like myself, would hang every night. There was one bar in particular, Loafers, where we often went to see live music. My friends Eric, Jeff, Timmy, Chuck, and Leebo had played in a band together for years, and we were together several nights of the week at one show or another. During the time Kasey and I had been dating, Eric and Chuck had joined a second rock band called Wichita Caravan, and several times they'd invited me to come see them play. I could never seem to make it happen. One night, after a terrible call with Ken regarding the money I couldn't yet pay back, I didn't want to be alone, so I finally agreed to go. The band was playing at Loafers, of course, and even though I was beat from a long week of working at the spa, these friends were my comfort zone. I'd even worked there for a short time before I started massage therapy school. One of my coworker buddies, Rusty, had invited me several times to go see his band, Satchelfoot, play in the college town of Boone in the mountains, but I couldn't do that while dating Kasey, so it never happened. More on that later.

My friend, Shelley, a talented, blonde twinkly eyed musician and singer, was at the bar that night too. I watched her interact with the other patrons so effortlessly, though her life had been anything but easy. Shelley and

I grabbed seats at the bar and had a quick catch-up. I noticed a tall, lanky, brown-haired guy in round black wire-rimmed glasses, a fly seventies button-down with a huge pointy collar, and bell-bottom jeans. He had a confident walk, warm hazel eyes, and I was pretty sure he'd just flashed me a smile. I didn't recognize him, and since I knew most everyone else on this scene, I chalked it up to his age, which appeared to be pretty young. *But he's in a bar*, I rationalized. He walked over to a table and sat with some friends while Shelley told me about her week.

"Okay, what's going on here? Are you even listening to me?"

"Yeah, sorry. I just . . . do you know that guy?" I pointed at him as he sat chatting with friends. She said his name was Jason and he was kind of new in town, but couldn't remember where he was from. When I confessed that I thought he was cute, she lit up. "Oh, you guys should go out!" About that time Eric finished setting up his gear and Shelley went off to mingle.

Eric and I migrated to a high-top cocktail table near the bar. Perfectly comfortable in each other's company, we just sat and sipped our beers for a while and watched the crowd roll in. We had been there for each other through some big life stuff already. He had gone through a separation from his wife, and before my time, had suffered the loss of his father and a brother, and had been to LA and back with a heavy metal band that had been ripe with promise. I had been through tough times with my family, the loss of a job, and that brutal breakup. We didn't recognize it then, but we were in the process of choosing each other as family. We sat there for a while at the table in the middle of the bar before I finally broke the silence by asking him a question that would change my life forever.

"What would you do if a girl asked you out? I mean, does that even happen? And if it does, is it a good thing?"

"Well, it depends on the girl. Would that girl be you?" he asked.

"Suppose it was."

"Well, hell yeah! Who's the guy?"

He knew I'd been unlucky in love as long as I'd been alive. I pointed him out. I felt a magnetic pull toward him in a way I still can't explain. "Oh, that's Jason, my keyboard player!"

Of course. "You're gonna tell him, aren't you?"

"You're damn right I am." Eric had an easy-going nature and a deeply thoughtful mind. I trusted his judgment. We shoved ourselves into clothing that screamed *we are not like you*, costumes of self-expression. I tucked flowers in his hair and he rocked a long floral hippie skirt onstage. I wore tall black combat boots, cut-off jean shorts, and had my belly on full display because I just couldn't give away enough of myself. We drank too much and we smoked too much pot, but sometimes we had the presence of mind to look out for each other. We were all lonely back then, so if there was a romantic scheme brewing, we took it as seriously as we were capable of.

Eric's band took the stage and melted our faces off. The singer, Scott, had this magical presence, thanks in no small part to the primal rock scream he was known for and captivating stage presence that could make you feel like you were flying. Eric and Jason would swap sick electric guitar and keyboard riffs back and forth, and Tom's thumping bass and Chuck's steady drums would make your heart beat in time with the rhythm. Incense was burned, creating a nag champa fog around us. I felt warm from booze and friendship and I was inspired by their self-expression. The experience was transcendent, but when the show was over, my confidence seemed to disappear with the music. I said my goodbyes as the band packed up.

I slid into the driver's seat of my car and cranked it up. Something (God, maybe?) compelled me to turn the car off and go back inside, find Jason, and ask him out. I headed back in and straight to the bathroom to make sure my hair wasn't doing that flippy thing it sometimes did. It seemed the grown-out Rachel bob, à la *Friends*, had muscle memory no matter how I tried to cut it differently. I scanned the bar for him as I headed back toward the patio, which was adjacent to the parking lot. As I walked through the door to the patio, I nearly ran right into him. We exchanged nervous hellos.

"Hi, I'm Shelley."

"I know who you are. I'm Jason."

Warm smile, check! My heart was pounding, but I continued. I remember feeling as though I was on autopilot. Like a force outside myself was taking me by the hand and saying, "This is what you need to do."

"Do you think—? Um, would you want to . . . uh." I looked up from my boots to see him grinning at me and we held each other's gaze long enough to make us both squirmy. Eric was sitting on the half wall behind me, silently cheering me on, possibly laughing and shaking his head with his long, wavy brown hair swinging in time. I remembered his "hell yeah" from earlier and it gave me confidence. "Would you want to go out with me sometime?" I finally choked it out.

"Do you know how old I am?" he asked, catching me off guard. I had fully expected a yes or no, but not a question.

"Yeah," I lied.

"Okay, yes. I would love to go out with you. How's Friday night?" He was twenty years old to my twenty-five, but had a very good fake ID. Though it belonged to his thirty-six-year-old roommate, amazingly, it only failed him once.

"Friday works for me." I gave him my number.

Two days later we had our first date. He picked me up at my apartment in his minivan and took me for tea at a place called La Tea Da's down the street. We sipped from tiny teacups in the beautiful craftsman-style home-turned-teahouse and talked for an hour or so before we headed to see a live band at Tremont, the local music hall. Afterward, determined to do something different this time, I invited him up to my apartment, but not for sex. I wanted to know him and wanted him to know me. I wanted to feel safe, valued, seen, and known for once. We lay in my bed and talked until four in the morning. It was about that time I asked if he was going to kiss me. "I've been wanting to all night." The kiss felt both new and exciting, but also like a homecoming. We fell asleep holding hands, and didn't spend a night apart for months.

I was no longer alone in the dark. He was always with me. Oh, and the significance of my coworker Rusty inviting me to go see his band play in Boone several times the year before this night? Turns out, back then Jason was the keyboard player in Rusty's band too, and though I never managed to get to one of their shows, I see my fate clearly in the way we found each other anyway.

Houses of the Holy

I was desperate for a sense of security, a stabilizing force or guardrails that would guide me toward a peaceful, safe existence. I needed to believe in something bigger than myself, so I was on a mission to find God when I'd met Jason. Although he did not share my desire, he woke up early several Sunday mornings and went along with me. I would later find out that religion of any kind had been something he had sworn off well before meeting me. If you ask us now why he visited those churches with me, I'd wink at you and joke that it was all about the poontang. This gesture of solidarity stoked that all-consuming fire we had between us. We couldn't get enough of each other and couldn't keep our hands off each other. And for the first time, the feeling was reciprocated both physically and emotionally. He saw the wounds of my past and wanted to shelter me. While our troubles were far from over, this twenty-year-old insanely talented rock musician welcomed the chance to be my savior. Life with Jason provided the guardrails I'd longed for, and wherever he was, that became my home.

The first church we visited was the church a coworker at the spa attended with her husband. She was always in great spirits, something she attributed to Sunday sermons filled with Holy Spirit energy and what she described as the persistently hopeful disposition of her church community. I wanted some of that. It was pouring rain that morning, and when we pulled into the already filled parking lot, a little boy about eight or nine years old ran to my side of the car with an umbrella and walked me to the door. This boy and this church already had my heart.

The sermon was powerful and the energy in the chapel was like nothing I had ever felt. After the sermon there was an altar call, a term which I did not know at the time, but have since learned. Wouldn't you know that the preacher looked right through a sea of people and zoomed in on me, seated in a pew very near the back row of the chapel? "I feel the Lord calling to a few of you out there—calling you to step up your faith and be filled with the Spirit! If you feel he is speaking to you, come on up here and let us lay hands on you." It was more of a command than an invitation and was shouted joyfully more than spoken. His passion was contagious. I sat there for a few minutes and tried to read the room. I wanted to understand what was happening, though I was ready to spring from my seat and race to the pastor's open arms. I watched as men and women went to the altar and members of the congregation laid hands on their bodies, loudly imploring the Spirit of God to descend upon them. Then, one by one, they fell on the floor, overcome by the Holy Spirit. They rose, wiping tears of joy, relief and hope showing in their expressions. I wanted some of that.

Jason and I were newly dating at this point, but I didn't even so much as look at him when I finally let go of his hand, got up from my seat, and dashed to the altar, ready to be descended upon and changed into a soul finally at peace, unafraid, devoid of anxiety, once and forevermore. The young male preacher placed his hand on my forehead as the elders surrounded me. They were speaking in tongues and wailing and singing high hallelujahs over me, standing behind me ready to catch me when the old, sinful me fell out on the floor and at the ready to help the new, eternally blessed version of me rise from the blue carpeted holy ground. Only I did not fall. I could not fall. His hand on my head shook and shook with more power and the voices behind me rose and rose and yet I did not feel the earth move. I did not feel overcome. I was so full of hope until the moment I felt him give up on me.

I walked back to the pew and sat down beside Jason, feeling like a failure, a complete heathen. A Jezebel! Jason said something like, "What just happened?"

"Um, nothing, apparently," I said. We left quickly after the service and slid into a booth at McDonald's—the food that fit the tiny budget of a musician and a massage therapist—and just stared at each other, he in disbelief and me in disappointment. He patted my hand. "Don't worry, baby. We'll keep looking till we find the right place."

Sleep like Starfish

"Just let her have a baby, Libby," my grandmother had said to my mom once when I was doubled over in pain. I was eighteen years old, and the doctor had declared my endometriosis so prolific that it was highly unlikely that I could get pregnant. But, he said, if by some miracle I did, it would heal me and the chronic pain I suffered from would be gone. We laughed it off then, but a small part of me believed that my curvy, built-for-babies body was up to the task.

Late one August, Jason and I had gone camping on the New River with our best friends, and because we were tent camping in the dark night of nowhere, my birth control method—running to the bathroom post-sex—was sacrificed in exchange for safety from bears and potential axe murderers. Truth is, I did want a baby. I just didn't know it at the time. But God did, and he sent the unlikeliest of characters to reassure me.

It was a typical day at the spa where I worked, but my coworkers were buzzing with energy. Alice, a fellow massage therapist, approached the desk where I was camped out and asked if I was excited to meet with MaryAnn today.

"Who is MaryAnn?"

Surprised by my cluelessness, she replied, "You haven't met with MaryAnn since you've been working here?"

I shook my head.

She said, "MaryAnn's a psychic. She comes around every couple of months and trades psychic readings for spa services."

Back then I was a "baby Christian," as they called it at church, and the only thing I knew about psychics was that I wasn't supposed to need one if my faith was strong. Never mind the fact that Jason and I were living together in proverbial sin, I was hung up on a verse in the Bible that forbade me to meet with such gifted persons that could potentially illuminate God's will in my life. So, I said, "I think that's against my religion." I was new to having one, so please forgive the ignorance of that statement.

Alice, obviously worldlier than I, just laughed and said, "Well, you're no fun."

No kidding, I thought.

Later that day, when MaryAnn arrived, she made a beeline for me. She told me she'd gotten word that I wouldn't see her on account of my religion. She was not what I expected. There was no flowy caftan or gypsy-like clothing.

She said, "Just so you know, I believe in God too, and when I do a reading, I always open with a prayer. God never reveals anything to me that can be damaging or harmful. He only reveals what he would have you know. But I totally understand if you're not comfortable with that."

Not a woman of many virtues at the time anyway, I agreed to trade services with this psychic and see what she had to say. We met in the relaxation room, where clients lounge in their robes between appointments. I sat down on the leather sofa and she sat facing me, cross-legged, in an overstuffed chair. The first thing to come out of her mouth was, "So . . . you have 'dad issues.'" She made air quotes with her hands.

What the hell? Is it that obvious? How could she know that? Did she also know what a needy girlfriend I'd always been? About my fear of rejection and abandonment? Or how I'd hoped this boy or that boy would make me feel like I mattered in a way that was contrary to the way I felt about myself?

"You need to lie down on your bed in the morning and again at night and extend your arms and legs wide. It's a very vulnerable position." She stuck out her arms and legs, like a starfish, to illustrate. "This is your mantra: 'My father loves me.' When you say this, you are speaking of both your earthly father and your heavenly father." For a quick moment I wondered if that act would somehow alchemize the pain of his absence into something beautiful and new within me. She then tucked some hair behind her ear, closed her eyes, and continued. "You also need to get your hands in the dirt. Gardening will soothe you and ground you in nature. You need to *feel* the earth," she said while extending her hands out in front of her, making grasping motions. It was easy to imagine her hands full of soil. I loved the idea but then thought of meaty, brown earthworms and cringed.

"It will keep all that anxiety at bay," she said as she waved her hands in the air. I imagined she was cleaning my aura.

I certainly had dad issues in that I longed to know him better. I wanted his approval and I wanted to be important to him. I desperately wanted to feel protected and guided by him. It was also true that, just like Pigpen and his cloud of stink, I left a puff of anxiety wherever I went. I wondered if she'd tell me anything I didn't already know. That's when she hit me with the capper.

"You want a family more than you want anything."

"I'm sorry. Say what? I have a family and we are pretty fucked."

"You want a family of your own more than you want anything, and you'll have it within three to six months."

I was a girl who talked straight out of her ass just to shatter any silence and had not yet learned to think before speaking, but now I was speechless. If I had wanted a family, it was definitely news to me. I had honestly thought nothing about that. I'd thought about winning the lottery. I thought about opening my own spa one day, a place where anxiety-ridden folks like me could dunk themselves in lavender essential oils and spend the day in a cocoon of warm blankets. I'd always dreamt about being loved and adored by a man to whom no other woman existed. Remember Bud and Sissy from *Urban Cowboy*? I was pretty certain I'd found him too. I thought about writing, my lifelong passion, while traveling around with my musician boyfriend, Jason, the love of my life, while he toured with various bands. I thought about having Thai food for dinner. I thought about what I was going to wear Friday night. Not once did I think about having a family.

I came home from work that day with a cassette recording of my psychic reading with MaryAnn. I popped it in the stereo the moment Jason walked through the door of our small apartment. He had just come from his shift at the music store. We loved our small apartment. The walls, light switches, and outlets were covered with dozens of layers of off-white paint. We sat there in a haze of incense, under a giant psychedelic Black Crowes wall poster, and listened as this woman predicted our future. We were young and having fun. We were happy that, together, we could afford to pay the rent. We'd given no thought to this family she spoke of, though once, a few weeks earlier, we'd talked briefly about marriage. It was a Sunday afternoon after church. We were washing dishes together, preparing to hunker down for our ritual afternoon nap. I told Jason that whenever I was in the Bible study with the older folks, I felt self-conscious about the fact that we lived together, unmarried.

He grabbed my soapy hand. "You know I want to marry you someday, right?" I didn't know for sure that he did, but I'd hoped we'd always be together. The thought of it felt like warm sunshine.

One Saturday in September, we drove north across the state line and into the mountains of West Virginia to watch Jason's bandmate, Tom, and his fiancée, Jenifer, get married in her parents' backyard. That night I drank champagne with abandon and puffed and passed a joint or two. The next morning, I awoke feeling horribly sick. It was unlike any hangover I'd ever had. This hangover was historic. Just as we finished checking out at the front desk, I was hit with a wave of nausea, and the feeling of warm bubble guts sent me sprinting to the lobby bathroom, which I desecrated, and then speed walked to the car with my head down as to avoid eye contact with any other patrons.

On the drive home, I recalled drunk-fessing to friends that my period was a week late. We stopped by the pharmacy to grab a pack of pregnancy tests on the way home. Sure enough, in our tiny sixties-era bathroom, under a bare lightbulb, we watched as two blue lines formed. It was positive. Just a few weeks after my doctor had confirmed my pregnancy, I was lying on the sofa nursing a severe case of morning sickness when Jason came home clutching a McDonald's bag in his hand. Their salty fries and Coke with that sweet, sharp bite of carbonation were life-giving. He knelt down in front of me and handed me the bag.

Regrettably, I didn't understand the magnitude of the moment and just tore into it, making no effort to look cute in the memory of his mind's eye. Instead of fries, I discovered a blue Tiffany box. My momentary confusion at the absence of fries subsided as he handed me a card with a poem he'd written inside titled, *Just Say Yes*. I sat up, clasped both his hands, a let go a chorus of yes, yes, yes. We were married exactly four months after the day I'd met MaryAnn and our first child would arrive the following May. We were not mentally, emotionally, or financially prepared for what was to come, but we'd become one another's North Star, lighting the way home for each other, time and time again.

The Biggest Damn Handgun

I don't know what possessed Jason to call my dad that night. Maybe I suggested it? I imagine the conversation went something like, "Hey Al, it's Jason. Yeah, um, Shelley and I are getting married." My dad likely responded with something like, "Okay, cool. Why don't y'all come down here and we'll talk about it. Say, dinner Friday night?" On the hour's drive down there, I wasn't really nervous, though I couldn't say the same for my fiancé. The big news wasn't so much that we were getting married, but more so that a baby would arrive in about eight months. As long as we were together, I knew we could handle my parents. My mom was totally on board and so were Jason's parents. Why wouldn't my dad and stepmom be okay with it?

Almost immediately after we arrived, the parents pulled a divide-and-conquer maneuver on us. Dad gave me a hug and asked Jason to go for a walk with him in the pasture. It was understood that I would be staying in the kitchen with my stepmom, Bobbette. When Dad turned his back to the room and headed for the door, I saw he had tucked a giant handgun into the back of his waistband. *Oh shit*, was what I was thinking, but *Good luck, honey*, is what I mouthed at him as he followed Dad out the door. As I recall, Bobbette and I didn't talk about marriage or babies or my relationship with Jason at all while they were gone. We were not yet close back then. While the menfolk were walking the pasture and talking about what a big responsibility I was, we ladies talked about food and the weather. In other words, I let Jason do the dirty work, and to hear him tell it, he waited till the last possible second to spill the baby beans. According to Jason and my dad, here's how it went down.

"Why do you have a gun, Al?" Jason asked.

"In case we run into a snake in the pasture," was my dad's reply. "Do you love her?"

"Yes, sir, I do."

"Well, good."

My father is a man of wisdom so I am certain he imparted some of it to Jason that evening, but whatever else was said has long been forgotten. What remains in our memories is the gun and this: Dad and Jason got back to the house and Jason hadn't yet mentioned I was pregnant. Dad had slipped off his dirty boots and had one hand on the doorknob when Jason bravely blurted out, "Shelley's pregnant!"

My dad's actual words? "Oh, shit."

Dad walked in the door looking like he just heard JFK had been shot all over again and Jason came in behind him looking uncomfortable as hell. My dad turned to my stepmom. "So, I guess you heard the news?"

Bewildered, she replied, "What news?" I guess there was an unspoken agreement that if he was to tell my dad, then I should have told Bobbette, except I did not get the memo.

The rest of the evening wasn't pleasant. Dad said things like, "Your sister and I grew up together. I understand her. I just don't understand you." It was in that moment that I realized the truth that I had long felt but not been able to articulate: he has always been more her father than mine. Their longer history cemented this and would remain like the sun overhead. If I looked at it too long, it would blind me.

I explained to Dad that when I was eighteen years old, the specialists predicted, post-surgery, that conception wouldn't be likely for me due to my extreme case of endometriosis, and how they'd also said if I were to get pregnant, it would likely heal me completely. For the record, it did heal me.

About that endometriosis. . . . The night I started my first period, I was seriously sick with some kind of stomach virus that would not allow me to exit from the family's hall bath for an entire night. I had been there for so long, emptying the contents of my small body, bowl after bowl, thinking how humiliating a death by diarrhea would be. I just kept wiping and wiping and crying and wiping. "I'm not even pooping anymore! Why won't it stop?" I cried from the bathroom.

My stepdad had stayed up with me in the sitting room, wiping my forehead with a cold, damp cloth. He called for my mom when he ran out of ways to try to comfort me from the other side of the bathroom door. She quickly figured out what was happening and got me all sorted and back in the sitting room, where I lay across Ken's knees while he sat up all night so he could wake me to take sips of ginger ale—the only thing I could keep down. I entered no phase of my life without drama, and puberty was no exception.

As a teenager, the pain of the cramps would send me to my knees and—sorry in advance for the gross-out coming your way, but it's necessary to the story—the output was next level. Finally, when I was eighteen, my parents were friends with an OB-GYN who suggested I see a specialist. An exploratory surgery revealed I had an extensive case of endometriosis, and while the work they did inside me helped for a while, medicine had not yet come up with much of a treatment plan. Endometriosis is a disorder in which uterine tissue grows outside the uterus, and in my case, on the ovaries, the colon, and even the bladder. Later on in my twenties, I was referred to Duke Hospital for treatment. I was to self-administer shots of a medicine called Lupron that would stop my periods each month so no more displaced endometrial tissue could grow. This worked somewhat well for a while and is probably the reason I was able to carry two babies to full term.

When I was pregnant with my first child, my doctor realized we had failed to follow up on my last Pap smear that showed abnormal cell growth. He performed a procedure called a colposcopy so he could look more closely at my cervix, and that's when he became concerned. He couldn't perform a biopsy without risking harm to the baby, so he decided that I would have a biopsy six weeks after I gave birth. The biopsy came back as carcinoma in situ of the cervix. My brilliant and beloved doctor suggested we do more surgery to clean up any remaining endometriosis while I was under anesthesia for surgery on my cervix. His work was flawless. Not only did he get my endometriosis under control, he removed the cancerous tissue with a skilled double pass, using the Loop Electrosurgical Excision Procedure (LEEP) on my cervix, leaving me with enough cervical integrity to deliver another baby just two years later.

The pregnancy itself would heal my malfunctioning womb, at least for now, while the baby, her father, and our second baby to come became a forever home for my heart. This family I created would bring hardship and struggle, but also a purpose and meaning I'd never before had in my incongruous life.

Feels like Home

Jason was working at a locally owned music store. It was one of those cool places people stopped in to peruse on dates, and touring musicians dropped in to shop for strings and picks and whatever instrument happened to catch their eye. His position was cashier, so he was the first person you'd see upon entering the store. One day a well-dressed, clean-cut man walked in and made his way straight back to the keyboard room where our friend Kelvin was working. The man told Kelvin he had moved here from Colorado and was looking for a keyboard player for the new church he'd planted in nearby Fort Mill, South Carolina, just a thirty-minute drive across the state line. Kelvin said, "I already have a church gig, but the guy working the register might be interested." Kelvin probably pondered the winged-collared seventies-era shirt and thrifted polyester bell-bottoms my boyfriend sported and wondered how this was gonna go over. "I'm not sure he's a church guy, but he's a hell of a good keyboard player and a really nice kid." The man thanked him and made his way back to the front of the store where Jason was perched on a stool, bespectacled in the expensive Versace glasses he'd bought a few years earlier when his parents sent him with their credit card for an eye exam and new frames. Jason said yes to the church gig.

Pastor Dana, as we would come to know him, later told us that when he walked up to Jason, he was illuminated in light and he heard the words, "This is the one you came here for." We would later wonder and often flatter ourselves thinking Pastor Dana and his wife Dayna (I know, isn't that amazing?) came all this way to find us and save our heathen souls by showing us an unconditionally loving God and becoming our family. We were living together, an unmarried couple—the party girl and her musician boyfriend—sitting every Sunday in fold-up chairs under a neon Bud Light sign in the baseball team's training center, the temporary space of the church at the time. They saw us as children of God and they loved us so hard. I was desperate to belong to someone, and the thought that I was loved no matter how I floundered and failed in the earthly expectations of me was life-changing.

Jason's hands floated across the keys while the small congregation sang songs about the God I had longed to know. After watching him play gigs in music halls and dive bars across the country, friends and fellow musicians would often exclaim, "Jason took us to church tonight!" Now here he was playing the organ with the Spirit so clearly moving through him.

Pastor Dana, his family, and our small congregation embraced us. They took care of us when we were sick. They laughed, cried, and jammed with us. Dana was both a guitar player and a singer, and Ms. Dayna had a killer voice too. After a while, we merged with a more established church and the tone of love they set expanded to hold so many that became dear to us. No one tried to change us. All they did was love us just as we were, broken and flawed. These two joined us for our wedding in a historic home in our neighborhood, not at all offended or in judgment that we did not choose to marry in the church. I was a second-trimester bride, and the seats were filled with family, long-haired musicians, hippies, and childhood friends.

My sister, an event planner, rushed around to check on the champagne she'd arranged to be passed and nodded in approval at the perfect brunch spread that was to be served. To be frugal, she brought over the Thanksgiving flowers from the City Club where she worked, and made my three-tiered wedding cake herself. She did my makeup and took extra flowers from the cake and stuck them in my hair. The La Tea Da catering team, the same company that operated the teahouse from our first date, provided and served the food. Janet, the owner of both the historic home that served as our wedding venue and the catering company, would later become a dear friend and always recalls our wedding as the sweetest she'd ever seen. Jason's best man, Ricky, showed up in a suit and clean work boots, proud as hell to be standing up for Jason while my sister served as my matron of honor. My mom stepped outside and scraped my brand-new shoes on the concrete sidewalk so I wouldn't slide down the slick, polished wood stairs on my ass in front of all who gathered below. That was entirely possible and everyone knew it. The collective sigh of relief confirmed they'd all held their breath until I got to the bottom step. It was an intimate, warm, and emotional ceremony for all of us.

Dana played acoustic guitar as he and Dayna sang a folk-inspired, romantic version of "Draw Me Close" as I descended the narrow staircase where my father waited to take my arm. As we stood in front of the stone fireplace, my dad, not keen on being in front of crowds dressed in a suit, leaned over twice and asked, "Can I go now?" Although we'd practiced the night before, I squeezed his arm closer to my side and reminded him he had to give me away first. After we exchanged vows, we shared Randy Newman's song "Feels Like Home" with our friends and family. While Jason and I stood there crying, and then laughing *because* we were crying, I thought about all the doors God had so painfully closed in my life, the prayers seemingly unanswered, and how many times I had shaken my fists at the sky for not getting what I thought I wanted. I thought of all the hurt and disappointment that had finally led to this moment.

My long-held belief that God's love was meant for only the chosen, only those of a different pedigree who understood the rules and followed them, began to shatter. The God I had finally come to know cracked open my broken heart and interpreted the dreams written inside. This man, this love between us, and the baby on the way were the answer to the deepest longing of my heart: to find purpose and acceptance. I looked at my young husband-to-be and the couple about to marry us whom we'd come to love so dearly. My broken family, not yet united in spirit, but here for me in this moment, all together under one roof. On this day, it was clear to me God had led me to my salvation on Earth, to the love of my life. Trouble wasn't over for me or for us by any stretch of the imagination. We each carried with us the pain and grief of our pasts, and we clung to the dysfunctional security we found in each other. Trauma had bonded us. I would become the repository for all his past hurts and he would become mine. There is a saying that "hurt people hurt people," and that was certainly true in our case, but ultimately, we saved one another's lives because we would no longer walk through this world alone.

Hustling

A few months after we got married, I started interviewing for a job with a local beauty distributor. I had several interviews during the two short months it took my sister, an experienced wedding planner, to throw together a wedding. During this time, my baby belly was beginning to show. I had always been a creative dresser because comfort is my number-one goal, so dressing strategically so as not to reveal the pregnancy was pretty easy. This is no small task, being that I am vertically challenged. That baby weight didn't have many places it could migrate without being seen.

By the time they made me an offer, I had been through two one-on-one interviews, one roundtable interview with the leadership team, and one final interview in which they made me the actual offer. I remember standing up to shake the hand of the young woman who would soon become my boss. I accepted her offer and let her know I would need to take maternity leave in May. I wish that I had a photo of her expression at that moment, but frankly I don't need one because I will never forget it. Second only to the time I ran outside to chase away a huge, scary dog in pursuit of my cat while wearing only a shirt and no pants—Donald

Duck-style—it may have been the ballsiest things I've ever done.

Working as a massage therapist in a high-end spa, I realized I would hit a ceiling of earning potential once I met my five massages per day max. My body just couldn't sustain any more than that. Also, with a baby on the way, we would need a regular paycheck and health insurance.

I researched the benefits of the products I used in the treatment room, as well as the skincare line's few bath and body products. I could find very little information on the product line, which I thought was a major oversight. I contacted the local distributor and told them I thought they were missing a great opportunity by not providing more educational material to the massage and bodywork therapists that used their products. I was transferred a few times and the next thing I knew, I was asked if I was interested in interviewing for a new position called director of spa development. The distributorship needed someone to provide education to their large sales force across the eastern territory. And so I scored a position that provided paid time off and health insurance—just in time to start my new family.

I managed a nine-state territory and met with clients and salespeople to identify their need for skincare products, sundries, and spa equipment. I created service menus and collaborated with the owners on the floor plans. I traveled to major cities from the District of Columbia to New York City and every small town in between. At home, I binge-watched TLC's *A Baby Story*, trying to soak up every anecdotal detail until I was so exhausted and big for my tiny frame, I had to start my maternity leave two weeks early. In my short five months with the company, sales increased more than 30 percent, so they were eager to get me back as soon as possible after I had the baby. So much so, they offered that I could work from home if I needed to, but a few people in the office were bent out of shape over the offer, so they quickly retracted.

Our money ran out pretty quickly, though, which meant my leave ended up being only six weeks long. My friend Summer and I had babies only a few months apart, and she had already found a daycare that she liked, so we chose that one as well. Our babies were together while we worked and would sometimes come home with the other's pacifier. The thought of leaving my baby girl at daycare and driving off to work gutted me, so that was Jason's job. I picked her up on my way home. Daycare was so expensive that it was as though we were paying rent at two places. When my travel schedule picked up again, our mothers would often help him with the baby or Jason and the baby would come along, a situation I would constantly have to defend to my bosses and coworkers.

Eventually, the distributorship would decide to align brands with another independent beauty house, which meant they'd discontinue the skincare line I managed for them. They flew me to Chicago to train on the new product line, and when I returned, they told me the new structure did not have a brand manager position, which meant that I would transition to a sales position.

I always felt I was faking my way, a bad case of imposter syndrome. I faked it till I learned it. At work in a professional environment, I felt like my child-self, still seeking approval while secretly not believing in my worth or abilities at all. However, massage therapy, I eventually came to realize, was a place I thrived because I had a natural, nurturing skill set that was well-suited to the job and the environment had been good for my nervous system. None of this changed the fact that I needed a reliable income and benefits in order to take care of my family.

Word of the coming changes got back to the skincare company I'd been representing for the past two years. They passed along a message to me that I should give them a call. I did and they offered me a brand management position within the new distributorship. This was a larger distributor that was owned by a publicly traded company. I thought this would mean more resources, but that ended up not being the case.

As I continued to travel the same nine-state territory, I found that my expenses quickly added up. The distributorship would owe me thousands of dollars for 60, 90, 120 days at a time. I was frustrated, tired, and inexperienced at advocating for myself. I needed that money for groceries, car payments, and diapers. Soon I would need it for even more diapers. I found out I was pregnant with our second child while on the way home from a trip to Virginia Beach.

Jason picked me up from the airport when I returned, and we stopped for breakfast. I ordered my usual buckwheat pancake breakfast, and only a few bites in, I began to feel very, very sick to my stomach. I knew this feeling. As soon as my mind processed the sensation, I remembered the night it happened! It had been a fun, romantic night after one of Jason's shows. I'll spare you the details, but I looked in pure disbelief at my husband as he hovered over me, smiling.

"Did you mean to do that? I didn't know you were ready for another kid." My immediate thought was that surely if he had done this, had thrown caution to the wind, that meant he so loved being a parent, he wanted to do it again.

"It was just the one time!" Jason had answered. With my health history, all bets were off and he knew it.

"Yes, one time is all it takes!" I said, both excited and terrified at the thought.

Sitting at the IHOP, I replayed that conversation in my head before I spoke a word to Jason. I pushed the pancake bites around on my plate and fussed over our cherub-cheeked daughter in her high chair. I knew this sick feeling in my stomach meant I was pregnant with our second child. When I was visibly green and couldn't conceal my nausea any longer, I told Jason what was going on. We gathered our toddler into the car seat and grabbed a pregnancy test on the way home. In the hall bathroom, we watched as two lines formed to say yes, we were going to have another baby.

I waited a few weeks until I had my regular call with my boss, Lillith. I explained to her that I was expecting another baby. I thought she'd be excited for me. Even if she couldn't care less, I expected her to politely fake it. Instead, she said, "How are you going to do this job with two kids?" I replied without even thinking. "I don't know. You have two kids and you built this international company from the ground up. If you can do that, I can do this. Right?"

I couldn't believe where this voice came from. Who was saying these things to her boss? The survivor in me had risen to the occasion and spoken up for herself and her family. How could this businesswoman and mother of two question how I was going to be a mother and thrive professionally? She sat quietly for a moment and said, "Well, as you get further along, just let us know if you need to pay someone to load your products and displays in and out of the car. Just expense it and we will cover it." Over the years, she and her husband had expressed their parental-like love for me and I could feel her disappointment. The feeling that they approved of me when I was pouring myself empty for the sake of the work and then feeling dismissed or shamed when I didn't perform felt like a familiar parental dynamic. Just like that, I was once again a kid getting the wrong number of coffee creamers and sugars. Just like that, I was having too many big, inconvenient feelings. I was back to making choices no one else seemed to understand. What they thought and felt was valid, while what I thought and felt was not.

Turns out loading the car wasn't a challenge for me at all. I had an able-bodied husband who had quit his job at the music store to stay home with our daughter, Māya Beth. Repeated ear infections and respiratory illnesses combined with the astronomically high cost of daycare deemed it more sensible for Jason to stay home with her. After I had our second child, Brady "Bear" Vance, the challenge would be getting my expenses reimbursed by the distributor in a timely manner. About a year into working with two small children and traveling the East Coast, I put my foot down and told my boss at the distributorship that I was not going back to the DC marketplace until my expenses were paid up to date. That word got back around to Lillith and I know she was not happy about it. There were other issues too. She demanded from the distributorship that her training events be held at finer hotels such as the Ritz Carlton instead of the airport Sheraton. The distributorship's leadership team agreed to this in their meetings with her, but when I presented my plans for these events, they told me to find a lower-budget venue.

In my meetings with Lillith, she said, "The problem is you. They agreed to spend the money that it takes to have a more appropriate venue for our symposiums. You need to make it happen." I didn't feel like a professional that missed the mark. I felt like a scolded, incompetent child.

Once or twice a year, the brand managers across the country would gather at their office in Manhattan for new product education and training. Afterward, we gave a presentation on a new product or treatment in front of Lillith and our peers for her critique. It was excruciating. We were all professional enough to present the material well, so that was never the issue. Instead, we were told our hair was too long for our age, or in my case, that I did not wear enough makeup, but was applauded for making the "safe choice" to wear black on black with a simple strand of pearls, the nicest thing I owned. Not creative, but safe. Oh, and please carry a nicer handbag.

Now, don't get me wrong; Lillith wasn't all hard-nosed business. She was also very dear to me and I am very nostalgic about her even now. Her husband is a lovely, doting and dedicated family man. He was very fatherly to me and I adored him. I think the combination of the personal nature of the relationship with them and the feeling of not measuring up made the rejection sting even more. What I knew for certain was I was the common denominator in both my family and workplace dynamics. I was still tender in places that would inevitably get poked in the workplace. I knew she was difficult because her reputation for it extended well past me. What I didn't know was how to believe in myself and accept her treatment of me at the same time.

A few short months after that training, we were in DC again, and Lillith was particularly cold and unkind to me. She had hired a new brand manager, local to that market, and had introduced her as someone brought on to help me manage the workload. Sidenote: this woman was a gorgeous, stylish train wreck with a high-end retail background that ended up lasting only a few months before her cocaine habit got her in trouble. With fire in her eyes and a sharp tongue, Lillith questioned everything I had done to set up the booth for the show and did so in front of one of my direct reports. I had hired skilled trainers in each of the four corners of my territory and the one working this show owned her own aesthetics school. Lillith ended up being so critical and demeaning to me in front of my trainer as well as the VIP clients that I called my leadership with the distributorship. When it got obviously uncomfortable in the booth, I excused myself and went to speak with my boss at the distributorship.

"Oh no, she has started her antics already?"

She was notorious for this type of outrageous behavior. *The Devil Wears Prada* had nothing on her. They told me to go up to my room, order room service, and take it easy that night. Come back down the next day refreshed and to just do my best. So, I did. In the elevator on the way up to their rooms to get refreshed for dinner at the hotel, Lillith had my direct report, Selena, call my room to ask if I was going to join them in the bar for dinner and drinks. "No, thank you. Not tonight." Every people-pleasing cell in my body reverberated in shock as if to say to the rest of me, *What are you thinking?*

Earlier, when I had told Selena that I was going up to my room to order room service, she said she would join me and I asked her what I could order for her dinner. By the time she called from the elevator, her dinner order was on its way up to my room. She had been enraged by the treatment she witnessed in the booth earlier and had said she would quit if I decided to walk out. But by this time, Lillith had bewitched her again, and she called to let me know she would not be joining me in my room for dinner after all, but joining Lillith in the hotel bar instead. When she set her sights on manipulating you, you don't stand a chance against her magic. She was a beguiling woman of power and influence, and when she turned her attention on you, you basked in it.

The next day I worked just as hard as I usually did, sold a ton of products, and avoided Lillith at all costs. When I heard her announce she was leaving for the airport, I crawled on hands and knees under the table skirt and pulled out more product to restock the display. I thought if I stayed there, I would not have to say goodbye. We began breaking down the booth that afternoon. I felt both afraid and proud that by refusing her invitation the night before, I had drawn what I believed to be a reasonable boundary. I believed in that moment that I was worthy of good treatment, worthy of protection.

I felt some measure of growth from the first professional experience I'd had working for the national clothing chain years before. I had only been twenty-two years old at the time and worked as an assistant buyer. When it was time to present the winter collection display to the sales team, I pinned the wrong pair of pants on the rotating display board. This was an easy mistake to make, considering the collections were extensive. Barbara, the senior buyer I assisted, grabbed me by the arm, yanked me hard, and sent me reeling backward on my heels. "What the hell is wrong with you? Are you stupid?"

She had scolded me harshly the month before about the top I chose to wear to a holiday function, saying through gritted teeth that I was more concerned with looking like a buyer than I was acting like one. I still don't know what that meant except I wonder if I was masking, trying to look the part in hopes of becoming the part—some manifestation of imposter's syndrome. If she meant to mentor me, she could've done a better job. By the time she'd grabbed me by the arm, we both knew she had gone too far. Human resources got involved before I'd said a word to anyone about it, gave me a few months' salary in a severance check, and continued to pay me while I looked for a new job. I never took it any further, but I should have. Did men experience this type of abuse in the workplace? Was there something innately wrong with me? I sure felt there was at the time. I called my dad. He told me what he'd do if anyone laid a hand on me again. That felt nice, but what I learned was not to tell him, or anyone else, when someone did treat me badly. All too often, I'd forgive it, justify it, because in my heart I always felt I was to blame when anything went wrong. Then I'd return to the situation or relationship, which was incomprehensible to those around me. What I now know to be an abandonment wound made it difficult to let go of the people in my life, for better or worse.

Here I was, nearly ten years later, this time advocating for myself, drawing a line at what treatment I would accept from my employer. I felt conflicting emotions, both invigorated, but also, *What the hell did I just do?* I had a family to support. We needed that health insurance. At the airport that evening I called my husband, and he said Lillith had called for me. "She's asking that you call her before you get on the plane." My fingers trembled as I dialed her number and they put me through to her office. She asked me if I was happy. I told her I wasn't sure what she meant.

"It has come to my attention after the last brand manager training that you are not happy, that you have made it clear you are not happy here." I got stuck on the word *happy*. I never had a single thought about what made me happy. No one had ever, not once, at any point in my life, asked me if I was happy. I was always in survival mode at work and at home, fight or flight, so my happiness had never really occurred to me.

She went on to say another brand manager had told her I was miserable. My face burned at the betrayal. This other brand manager was a friend of mine. But at the time, the friendship was not as strong as her desire to be Lillith's next beloved pet, something that would only be made possible in my absence.

"I love this product and I believe in this company, but you cannot talk to me like a child," I said. "You cannot yell at me and belittle me in front of clients and my direct reports." With my voice shaking, I said, "That is not okay."

Silence.

"How are you going to continue to represent my brand if you do not like me?"

"It's not a matter of liking you. It's a matter of how you treat me. I believe in this brand and I can do this job." I was full-on trembling now, and I was pissed that my voice was shaking. Something I had recently learned about myself was that I cried when I was angry or frustrated, which only served to make me more angry and more frustrated. I was grateful she couldn't see the hot, mascara-tinged tears running down my cheeks.

Then she screamed into the phone. "I am the product! The product is me!"

I was stunned. I had worked so hard. *Why does it always seem to end this way for me? What is wrong with me?* Were dysfunctional dynamics so normal to me that I didn't recognize them as such until they came to a flash point? Sick to my stomach, I hung up the phone, got on the plane, and headed home to my family.

The next morning at home, a certified letter arrived. It came while I was shopping for discount baby clothes at Marshalls. My husband called my cell phone to let me know it was from Lillith. It was a termination letter. As he read it to me, I began to remove tiny outfits from my shopping cart and put them back on the rack. They requested their laptop back, but I knew my employment contract and it said that after two years, the computer would be mine. I kept it.

Interviewing for a new job proved to be quite a process. Trying to make sure no one knew that I had been fired without cause from my previous position felt dishonest, but necessary. I did not want to throw my former boss under the bus, which I would have had to do in order to explain my termination. But Lillith's reputation preceded her. It would not have been a stretch for anyone in the industry to believe what had happened. I interviewed with a chain of spas that was purchasing the grandest, most innovative spa in our city and it went very well. I was certain that I had secured the position; however, the next day, I received a phone call from the man that interviewed me. He told me that the job had been mine as far as he was concerned, but that the chain of spas had been purchased by a Canadian company and the Charlotte location was to be staffed by the candidates selected by the new management. Panic was setting in. Failing my family financially was not an option. We had no safety net.

The next series of interviews was to be with a West Coast- and New York City-based skincare company. This was a skincare for the celebrities. I'd read about the owner in *US Weekly* and knew that she was as notorious for her narcissism and drama as my former boss, but I figured I could handle it if the salary was right. They would see that I had worked for Lillith and know that I had what it takes. My sales figures spoke for themselves. I had a series of interviews with the LA office and the New York office and they went well. The last interview was with the son of the notorious owner, and he asked what I liked to do in my spare time when not working. Naïve as all get-out, I told him I loved to take our children to the country where my in-laws lived and get out of the city for a few days. He was silent for a moment and asked, "How do you manage such a large territory with small children?" And in that moment, the truth was illuminated for me. I knew he had asked about my spare time intentionally. If they were to invest in me, they needed to know if I had children or was going to have them soon. I told him I did not know any different because I had always worked and mostly supported myself since I was seventeen.

What I had been feeling for the past few years had come to a head. I never felt like I was giving 100 percent at work or 100 percent at home. If I was killing it at work, I would feel like a terrible mother. If I was doing great at home, it was at the sacrifice of my work. In reality, I was doing the best I knew how to do. I'd later come to learn this balance was a delicate one and that it fluctuates for most women, but in the end, it would balance out.

There was a decision I needed to make. I prayed and prayed because I believed God would answer me, yet it still took me by surprise when I received an answer as clearly as I'd ever heard anything. God said, "It's time to stay home with your kids. It is time to dedicate yourself to raising your family. Do this now and your time will come later." I believed it with my whole heart. Over the next few days, "your time will come later" played over and over in my mind. I had never felt more certain of anything, and for a person who never felt sure of anything, this was monumental. On the next call I had with the owner's other son in the New York office, I told him I wished to withdraw my name from consideration for the position. He was stunned. He asked if I would tell him why. I told him based on his brother's reaction to my having children, I suspected I would be sacrificing too much when it came to my family.

In the weeks that followed, a beloved church member would give my husband her entire Charlotte territory of private music lessons and another would hire him in the mailroom of the mortgage company where she worked. And before long, he would become the manager of that mailroom. For the next five years he would be gone in the mornings before the kids awakened and then, after work, he'd teach music lessons well into the evening, getting home long after they went to bed. Most nights after lessons, he would have a rehearsal, a gig, or a studio session. It was exhausting for both of us, but I loved being a mom. I loved planning playdates and craft projects with the kids. Story time was my absolute favorite time of the day. I looked forward to reading to them every night after their bath, their bodies washed clean and smelling like heaven, cozy in their footed pajamas. I was so intentional about curating a child-centered home. We were young parents and liked to party on occasion, but never with or in front of our kids. Giving them a routine provided me with a routine. I thrived in the stability of it, even when I was desperately tired and burned out from doing the parenting and housework alone. Emotionally exhausted from the ups and downs of a young, and often-volatile, marriage. For the first time in my life, I understood what was expected of me and I was pretty good at it.

To have a happy marriage and family was the greatest desire of my heart. Second to that was the desire to finish my college degree and become a writer. We stayed in the pattern of Jason working two jobs seven days and nights a week for nearly a decade, when one day he finally told me that, financially, we would not make it through Christmas if I didn't get a job. It was November 2011, and I had already been accepted to Queens University to finish my creative writing degree. I was registered to begin classes the following January.

I decided if I was going back to work, it was going to be in my favorite retail store. I headed to the mall to apply. I interviewed and was hired on the spot. This began a six-year stint at Anthropologie while I worked toward my creative writing degree. A few months into my retail employment, I was offered a contract position in event management for a large local nonprofit that operated a gorgeous wedding and event space downtown. I accepted because I felt like I had to, and the next thing I knew, I was working two part-time jobs and going to school full time. With meals to cook and kids to tend to, I was overextended and my health deteriorated. The strain on my marriage from intense financial pressure and the absence of companionship made it feel like we lived two separate lives. All this stressed my immune system, and I was always getting sick with this or that virus or flu.

Most days, on my way to the beautiful oak-lined streets that bordered the Queens University campus, I was so tired that I cried at the thought of still having to make dinner alone and do homework when I got home, both my own and help with the kids' assignments. Learning to understand my limitations would be a lifelong journey. Something besides circumstantial exhaustion was brewing in my body. I had visited my doctor regularly for years by this point, begging him to find out why I was so tired. He always responded with, "You have two kids and a busy husband. It's normal to be a tired mom." Finally, one day he was away on vacation and I was seen by his PA. She took one look at my gray complexion and ordered a test to measure my iron but also one to test my ferritin levels. She explained that my blood iron could look normal based on what I had recently eaten, but testing my ferritin levels would show how much iron my body had in storage. Turns out, I had next to none. After returning to work the day after my first four-hour-long iron infusion, my manager at Anthropologie asked me if I had gone on vacation because I had color in my skin once again. The heart palpitations were gone and my energy was better for a while. The hematologist put it this way, "If you were going to bake a cake and realized you had no eggs, you would not bake the cake. Think of ferritin as the eggs you need to make a cake. The body cannot make new blood without ferritin and you had almost nothing in the pantry."

After many tests were run, including a colonoscopy, it was determined that my awful, heavy periods, a parting gift from a lifelong battle with endometriosis, were the culprit and I was eventually approved for a uterine ablation. This procedure changed my life. I barely had a period anymore and therefore began to keep my iron in my body where it belonged. My complexion turned from gray to pink and my energy levels improved significantly, for a while at least.

The day I finally walked across a stage to accept a diploma for the first time was one of the proudest days of my life. I had five colored cords of honor around my neck. Just like Wally World's Marty Moose in the closing scene of the movie *National Lampoon's Vacation*, you could not have punched the smile off my face. I looked straight into the eyes of the man that stood before me ready to hand me my diploma, his hand outstretched to me. He was on the college's board and I knew him as the CEO of the nonprofit where I worked as a special events manager. I thanked him and said, "I work for you!"

He smiled big. "I thought you looked familiar. Thank you for your excellent work and congratulations on your graduation!"

I floated off that stage and scanned the crowd. My whole family sat there out on the lawn with smiles as big as mine. I walked back to my seat, my eyes glistening with pride, shoulders back, and head held high. This high school dropout had just graduated college, magna cum laude. I wish I could say this great accomplishment was the antidote to my feelings of unworthiness and that my health began to improve from this moment. Unfortunately, that's not what happened, but I had earned this degree despite the most challenging of circumstances and no one could take that away from me.

A Ritual Prayer

If we have too many worries, fears and doubts, we have no room for living and loving. We need to practice letting go.
—Thich Nat Hahn

I have a confession. For far too many years I had the dangerous habit of adjusting my rearview mirror to where I could see my own reflection. I drove this way during the busy rush-hour drive to high school and at night on the way to and from parties when I was too stoned or drunk to have been driving at all. Many times, it felt as though the arm of God reached down and yanked my gaze forward where it belonged, just in time to ease my tires back onto the road.

I didn't study my reflection out of vanity. I carried so much shame, but it wasn't a part of me; shame *was* me. It informed how I felt about every aspect of myself and the way I moved through, and related to, the world. I asked the reflection, *who am I?* while I searched for my "self in the eyes of others." I am as I am seen. Each glance was a question: *What is it about me that is so inherently unlovable? Unworthy of the kind of love and attention others seem to gather unto themselves effortlessly? Why do I feel like I'm from another planet? From where does this deep, almost desperate sense of longing come? Why am I so lonely? Why do I not feel worthy of anything good?*

I fretted over the shape and tone of each freckle across my nose, whether concealed by makeup or revealed by a recent wash. *What do others see when they see me? Why do I feel like an alien among humans?* No matter my surroundings and circumstances, I seemed to be consistently the same ill fit. Can you truly know who you are if you're constantly searching for home? Can you ever be at ease in your own skin if your nervous system is stuck on high alert? Are rest and reflection possible when your family is in constant conflict? It was impossible to be reflective while in a chaotic and ever-changing environment.

While in the car, I was also busy with practice runs of conversations I had and would have. Sometimes I rehearsed what I should have said and sometimes what I might say if given the chance. I pondered the witty anecdotes I might share, if by chance I was blessed by a listening ear. This lack of personhood went pretty far back. When I was in middle school, I realized I didn't know how to smile. I practiced in the mirror, but those forced smiles never looked or felt natural. Only later in life would I pause to think that if one were truly happy, the smile would just appear. The smile I invented and practiced made me look like a tiny open-mouthed bird. As a result, Ken nicknamed me "Chirp." I remember pulling up to the skating rink and jumping out of my parents' sleek white sports car.

"Have fun! Let me see you chirp!" Ken called out from the car. Standing on that sidewalk next to the giant vehicle shaped like a roller skate, I died a million deaths while my parents drove off, most likely trying to figure out why my attitude was so crappy. That nickname found a quick retirement because the teen years brought about a sort of half smile (smirk?) that suited my brooding personality, but mostly because my original nickname, Death Breath, was still applicable. Damned sinuses.

What the mirror could tell me was limited solely to the facts visible to the eye. I stared at my dyed blonde hair, deep-set brown eyes ringed with black circles, and lips that seemed to disappear with an unflattering swipe of frosty pink lipstick. The mirror never gave me answers, only features to wish for (less cheeks!) and things to obsess over (ugh, freckles!). On the long journey to midlife, I grew to understand a few things about myself, both good and bad, that can't be captured within my reflection.

Since then, I have mostly come to realize my appearance isn't the entirety of me, so I have turned my search for self-understanding inward. I have come to understand that my brain is Grand Central Station for all manner of intrusive thoughts, but after a lifetime of anxiety, I have also come to realize they are not prophecies. These micro-nightmares are simply a marriage between my fears born of an insecure upbringing and my highly creative mind.

I won't describe the darkest of them because there's still a part of me too superstitious to go there, so I'll keep it light. Here's a glimpse inside my head. I step out of the tub, take my rings off, and set them on the bathroom counter. I apply my body cream very carefully because I have already started a risk assessment. Although it was only a temporary situation, it was a gamble to place my rings there and I knew it. I could easily lose my balance, as I often do, apropos of nothing, and knock them down the drain. I could grab my towel and send them tumbling down the sink's drain and into the p-trap. What if that heart-skipping, flippy-floppy thing in my chest happens again, as it often does, but this time I collapse? Jason will come running in when he hears my egg crack on the tile floor. He'll knock into the counter and off they'll go, deep into the plumbing of this old house.

When the EMTs arrive to get me, Jason will yell in Brady's direction, "Do NOT use the sink! Mom's wedding rings fell down the drain!" Our bright, yet likely distracted young son will only hear, "Mom's rings fell down the drain!" He'll be so sad for my loss and so worried about me while they're making me better at the hospital (A recovery! See? I'm not all death and darkness.) that when he goes to brush his teeth, he will inadvertently spit all over my most treasured jewels as they wash down to never-never land.

Here's another sample of the machinations of my mind. I'd been having heart palpitations, as I mentioned earlier, and more frequently than usual for a few days. I went on my regular run-walk and just as I was really getting sweaty and red-faced, I worried that I was pushing too hard. I imagined clutching my chest in a cinematic way and plopping over right there in the middle of the street. I would be able to manage a call to my husband (I always have my phone), but my speech would be almost incoherent. He'd panic and yell into the phone, "Baby! Where are you?" I decided in this imaginary moment that I would be able to eke out a breathless "On . . . Gainsborough Street!" Heroically, he'd find me, and hopefully, I would survive. I managed to laugh off this nightmare fantasy and stay with my workout.

These thought patterns are just a part of who I am, much like my deep-set eyes and the sun damage sprinkled across my nose. I was once ruled by these intrusive thoughts and would call on my friends and family to talk me down from the worry and panic. They'd patiently listen to my rambling thoughts and assure me all was well. I have learned to observe these thoughts, and I'm often quick to laugh at their absurdity. Except, of course, when they come late at night and my husband is out working and both our young-adult children are out and about, exposed to all manner of possible dangers and snares. Something about the quiet hours of darkness intensifies the fears that pass through me and I have to work a little harder to get through those.

There was a period of time when Jason was out on tour and I was home with our little kids. I would sleep, or more accurately, not sleep, with the light on, dozing. I'd wake every few hours to a fresh thought of what tragedy could befall him out on the road or us here at home in his absence. I'd think of what dangerous figures could be lurking just outside the walls of our home. Just as I had done as a small child, I recited the adult version of my prayer that covered every possible scenario and need. And sometimes I repeated it over and over again when my anxiety was high.

A turning point came when I had to travel as a part of my job responsibilities as a brand manager, and being just a year post the 9/11 tragedy, there were times the fear of leaving my family was so great I was paralyzed. We'd been staying at my in-laws' house, and I was supposed to fly out to Baltimore that morning, but I just couldn't do it. It felt so unsafe, so much like the wrong thing to do. I canceled my trip and promised to be there as soon as possible. I lay facedown on the carpet in my in-laws' guest room, and both kids came in to sit on me, one on my back and the other on my butt. I let the vibration of their giggles seep into my skin, knowing I would be leaving again soon.

That night I knew I'd come to a place where I had to make a choice between living a life of faith and living a life ruled by my fears. After all, I couldn't lose my job, my benefits, our health insurance. I knew that cultivating this type of faith was only as good as I allowed it to be a comfort in times of fear and uncertainty. My father-in-law dropped me at the airport the next day, and I stepped onto that plane with great confidence. If it was going down, I was gonna do it bravely, in faith, not fear, and I recited my prayer as the plane lifted into the sky. Right there in my window seat, I outstretched my hands, opened my palms, and imagined releasing my fears into the swirling atmosphere that surrounded me.

I practiced this ritual of prayer for many years until it became a habit that almost automatically redirected the fear into the prayer. Over time, the fears lost the power to paralyze me and I continued to observe them. Every once in a while, I entertain the idea that perhaps I should be worrying, that I'm too complacent, that letting my guard down made me all the more vulnerable. Instead, I quickly reframe this as "faith in action" and move on with my day. No more magical thinking. The intrusive thoughts don't stop, they're just as frequent as ever, but now I see them for the habit they are and they no longer rule my life. I say my prayers and then I reach to switch off the light, feeling safe in God's perfect care, at least for the moment, until the next dark thought arises.

Neurosis Diagnosis

"It's not appendicitis. My pain isn't, like, on the upper right side." My fourteen-year-old daughter gave me regular updates as she paced the kitchen floor with her iPhone in hand. For the ninth time today, she showed me, emphatically, with fluttery hands, exactly all the places her stomach hurt.

"Well, that's good news. Honey, I've told you before, googling your symptoms is a bad idea. There's so much information out there. It can really be scary to read about all the things that can go wrong."

My speech was careful and sweet and totally belied my annoyance at her persistent googling of symptoms and the play-by-play updates on her condition every thirty minutes. My precious child was sick, and I'm a terrible mother because her constant complaints made me want to skewer my own eyeballs. Two weeks prior, she had been diagnosed with a sinus infection and treated with antibiotics. These antibiotics were too much on her empty stomach and gave her an inflamed colon, otherwise known as colitis. She also has an intense fear of vomiting, which had her even more intent on googling her symptoms to ensure she was not, in fact, in danger of vomiting.

"I can't stop, Mama." She pushed her oversized glasses up onto the bridge of her tiny nose. "Look." She showed me the screen. "It could be stomach cancer. See, I have all the symptoms. Or it could be IBS, you know. I have all the symptoms of that too!" She twisted her long brown hair round and round her finger, creating a spiral, a nervous tic she's had since toddlerhood.

"Honey, you've seen two doctors. We've adjusted your diet and just started new meds. Your tummy just needs time to heal. The more you google, the more anxious you get and the more your tummy hurts. We've been over this. You've even had all that blood work done," I said. "If something terrible were wrong, we would know by now."

Against the advice of my recent read, *Yes, Your Teen is Crazy!*[5] I tried to reason with my teenager. Logic was of no value here. This was a frontal lobe issue. Logic is a language that teenagers do not yet speak. The book also wisely advises frustrated parents of unreasonable teens to hold fast to their sense of humor. This parental life raft is deemed crucial to survival.

What this obsessiveness and worry didn't remind me of at the time was myself and the carousel of horrible

---

5. Bradley, Michael J. *Yes, Your Teen is Crazy!* Gig Harbor, Washington: Harbor Press Inc., 2003.

outcomes that goes round and round in my own mind. It wasn't until a week after this exchange, after I'd been burning up with a fever for three days and experiencing what can only be described as the feeling of an elephant standing on my chest, I became manic. At night, marooned there in my bed in the dark, the room lit only by the light of my iPhone, I googled my symptoms.

Google Search 3:00 a.m.: *Prolonged fever in adults.*

Results: *Fever of 102 or more, or fever of 101 or more lasting for more than three days is a sign of something serious.*

Temp: *101.3*

With the flu and mono already ruled out by tests in the doctor's office, and true to my dramatic nature, I began to mourn my impending death, my youth cut short. *It's probably fatal.* I'd been on antibiotics for three days, and the fever persisted. The robin's-egg blue of my bedroom walls looked as black as doom, and these thoughts barreled through my mind like a freight train. During the day, I can think rationally; however, my neurosis and all her wicked sisters always arrive at night. I was now convinced that this fleshy, fatty cyst that lived above my collarbone for five years now was not fat at all, but a giant swollen lung-related lymph node as was first, erroneously, suspected by my doctor. I was certain my lungs were filled with liquid and cancer and by some tragic fluke, the doctor didn't hear any of it in the exam and declared it a simple case of bronchitis.

What about that kid that died of pneumonia a few years back? He even had a chest X-ray, but his lungs were completely full of fluid and therefore showed no line of demarcation. His pneumonia went undetected and he *died*!

This is when it occurred to me where my child may have learned such behavior. I am my daughter, or worse, she is me.

"Honey," my own words rang in my ears, "googling your symptoms is a bad idea. There's so much information out there. It can really be scary to read about all the things that can go wrong." I was the worst kind of hypocrite. I made a mental note not to *ever* say any of this to my kid again.

> **Google Search 3:30 a.m.:** *Symptoms of pneumonia in adults.*
>
> **Results:** *Persistent fever, chills and coughing up brown mucus may be signs of pneumonia.*
>
> **Temp: 101.7**

I was coughing up brown mucus. Convinced I would suffocate from it, I woke my man and asked him to bang the mucus from my lungs by whacking me on the back.

"You know, like we did to the babies when they were babies?" He is exceedingly patient when sleeping, and after five minutes of violently shaking him, he woke up and obliged. Well, at least he mimicked the use of force as I rammed my back into his outstretched palm. After a few weak attempts, he fell back asleep. While I cannot remember which color soccer uniform the youngest kid should wear for away games, I can instantly recall every single traumatic news story of preventable death I've ever heard. I wonder what kind of shape my dresser drawers are in. I'm not ready to die.

My neck was killing me, but I was sure it had nothing to do with tension or lying in bed for hours looking at the screen of my phone. It was definitely another symptom crucial to the discovery of the cause of my impending death. I began to experience a real—or possibly imagined—pain in my left arm, certain these symptoms were also related. My head hurt, but not like a headache. It was more like a weird, intermittent dull pain in the back of my head.

> **Google Search 4:00 a.m.:** *Symptoms of stroke*
>
> **Result:** *Numbness of face, arm or leg, trouble speaking and seeing; severe headache.*
>
> **Temp: 101.7**

A pop-up flashed in front of me. It was an ad for a game called Funny Farm and the irony was not lost on me. I wondered if they had one called Hypochondriac Hill and if I should download that one too.

Then I thought of Ken's brother-in-law, Uncle David, who is of course not an uncle by blood so no shared DNA, but an uncle nonetheless. He suffered with sinuses and allergies for years, just like me, and one day he ended up in the ICU fighting for his life. His sinus infection had crossed the blood-brain barrier. He had the most brilliant doctor and was miraculously saved. So naturally I went to see him a few years back when I had had so many sinus infections that we had exhausted options of antibiotics. Jason and I listened as the doctor told us I was a great candidate for sinus surgery, of the Roto-Rooter kind, as he explained it. Then he went through the disclaimer of, "Then there's a chance of a tear in the thin wall between the sinus cavity and the eye . . . blah blah, possible blindness . . . blah blah, requiring a quick surgical patch."

Our collective gasps of horror sucked that option right off the table. We decided antibiotics a few times a year was a much more appealing idea than what sounded like an unnecessarily risky surgery. In that moment, it was a comfort to remember the doctor telling me it was highly likely that due to my deviated septum, every time I had a cold it would likely turn into a sinus infection. *That's probably it*, I thought. The pain in my neck distracted me. I removed the pillow and lay flat on my back, hoping this would ease my neck tension. Bam! There's the sinus pressure. I was flooded with relief.

Of course! I'd just call the doctor the next day and ask for an antibiotic that treats sinus infections and pray that it works despite my overuse of them. My obsessive, anxious mind began its rambling again. I laughed at myself. Then I thought, *But what if . . . ?*

Google Search 4:30 a.m.: *Sinus infection crosses blood-brain barrier*

Results: *Visual defects, fever, confusion, lethargy*

Temp: 101.7

Revelations

These undies are going in the trash. That's all I could think as I pushed the grocery cart to my car in the Whole Foods parking lot. The pink patterned Jessica Simpson panties had betrayed me; the elastic gave up after only a few weeks of ownership. Normally whilst leaving this particular store, my thoughts would be consumed with anxiety over how much of my paycheck I spent on $9 pineapple salsa and tortilla chips that are free of gluten, dairy, soy, nuts, and grains, and a fresh bag of $22 cacao powder for my morning smoothie. Instead, I was uncomfortable and I recognized that something in my life was no longer serving me. This may seem like a small thing, trusting oneself to determine that something is no longer a good fit and recognizing a source of discomfort, but I've never been in the habit of either. It was a big deal. I am always the first to doubt myself and the last to trust my own feelings, opinions, and instincts.

I was parenting two young adults at the time, so the idea of nature versus nurture was on my mind. As I had the most feelings of anyone ever born, and was undoubtedly exhausting to be around, I imagine my own parents' instinct to tell me to just "get over" whatever it was that was upsetting to me was the least painful route when these emotional episodes would occur. Trying to convince me my feelings were wrong or misinterpreted or just inaccurate in general likely felt like the best approach.

Once when I was pretty young, say seven or eight, I went with my sister to stay with my dad for the weekend. It was the first time we'd stayed at his new post-divorce apartment and it was bedtime, an hour I always dreaded whenever away from home. I'd discovered that the space under the bed where I was to sleep was the storage space for my dad's rifle collection. Now, I was no stranger to guns. As young as I was, my dad had already made sure I knew how to safely handle a gun and that I had the proper reverence for them. When he took me hunting back then, I would lie on the ground on my belly, .22 caliber shells in my ears to muffle the sound of the rifle in my hands should a groundhog pop his head up. I always prayed I would never see one because I knew I could never pull the trigger, nor would I ever recover if I saw him shoot one.

With the guns under my bed, I threw an all-out shit fit, because not only did I not want to sleep there for fear the guns under the bed could go off, but more likely because I was far away from my mom and didn't understand, or couldn't articulate, that was the source of my anxiety. It didn't matter that I was with my dad and sister and that the guns (probably) weren't loaded.

It didn't matter that Dad had taught me how to look for the orange indicator that the safety was on and took the time to show them to me.

Dad was flustered and ill-equipped to handle my tantrum, so he told me to go to sleep or he'd give me something to cry about. I felt the odd sensation of feeling both mad at him and desperate for his comfort. I just wanted to be heard and comforted. It was about so much more than the guns. I was so young and there had already been so much change and uncertainty in my life. I was away from my mom and now with my dad that I hadn't spent much time with in my life. Now I can see that he was frustrated because he wanted to make me understand that I was safe, but I refused to believe him. As a parent now, it's clear to me how far removed adults can be from the perceptions and fears of a child.

I have a child that is so much like me in this way. I find myself shorting her on affirmations and not listening well because my first reaction is to be dismissive of the things she fears, things I am no longer afraid of. Like my parents, I, too, sometimes tried to assuage her many fears by dismissing them instead of comforting her. I tried to convince her that the fears she had—fears of vomit, of getting sick, of losing one of us, of rejection—were all things she needn't worry about because the worst of those fears were unlikely to happen and only caused her to miss out on the good parts of life. Sometimes, when I had the presence of mind to hold her hand and just listen, I noticed that she miraculously calmed herself. She spoke her fears aloud, felt a release, received comfort, and navigated her way through it. When I affirmed her feelings, she showed that she could draw upon the wisdom she'd retained from our many, many talks and a wisdom of her own that she inherently possessed. Oh, how life-changing this would have been for me and the generation before me.

When the kids were little, if I tried to work on a writing project in the morning hours, they would come up with exactly one million reasons to need me and call my name. I had read somewhere that a parent's attention was like a drug to young children and they would act like cracked-out fools until they got their fix. One morning I got up early, fixed my coffee and breakfast without checking my emails or getting on a marathon phone call with my mom or best girlfriend. Instead, I sat with them, played with them, and listened to their thoughts and ideas all morning. My presence was magical. They had been seen, heard, and engaged with all morning and for the rest of the day they gave me the space to tend to my freelance work without constant interruptions. I was the sun and the moon to them. I rose with them in the mornings and read them to sleep every night. Time with me served as an anchor for their day.

I wish I had taken this approach in the more frustrating and confusing era of parenting teenagers. Maybe

I did. The kids would probably vouch for me because they adore me and I've brainwashed them into always lifting me up instead of cutting me down. The tagline for parenting remains true: I could have done better. But, like a cheap, spent pair of undies and the ensuing chronic wedgie, these thoughts of regret don't serve anyone. They simply settle into your crack and make you miserable.

Every parent wants to do better by their kids than their parents did by them. My parents certainly did. I used to entertain my parents' friends when they would come over to visit. In my bulky gray sweatpants and pink knitted leg warmers, my bangs pulled back with a sweatband like Loverboy's Mike Reno, I held court in the living room with a hairbrush microphone, Journey blasting from the giant wooden stereo system. I sang along, complete with dramatic flourishes that made anyone watching believe I really knew what it was like to be a stone in love the way Steve Perry sang about it. I sock slid into a moonwalk and hogged the attention of anyone that might be passing through the living room to the bar to refresh his or her Chivas Regal. I knew and sang every word to Stairway while miming the lyrics, my cheeks flushed as I awaited their applause. I truly believed it was my destiny to entertain, but it was never nurtured. There were no drama camps, singing lessons, or music lessons. It's really not what baby boomer parents were up to back then. My poor parents were in survival mode too.

I found redemption in that warm, fuzzy feeling of full-circleness when I committed to seek what really lights my kids up and made sure those talents and interests were noticed and nurtured as best as our limited resources would allow. I thank God and all my lucky stars for this revelation every time I see our son in a passionate pursuit of the perfect photo of the rare car he just spotted. He is a brilliant photographer and his vast knowledge of cars is impressive. I am grateful when the melodies and lyrics our daughter has written and performed cause joyful tears to spring forth from my eyes. My children are known and seen by their imperfect parents and know they are loved and cherished by God. Their lives have purpose, and for that I put forth a constant refrain of thank you, but it's off-key because I never did learn how to sing.

The Most Fragile of Us All

The nursing home called in the middle of the night to alert me that Nana was experiencing chest pain.

"Mrs. Atkins, would you like us to send an ambulance to take her to the hospital? We see here in her chart that she is a DNR."

I always have my cell phone nearby. I'm always ready for things like this. I'm always *on*. The nurse confirmed that Nana, my dad's mother, was coherent and in pain, so, of course I agreed to have her sent to the hospital. The night nurse at the nursing home assured me that the emergency room would be aware of the family's DNR wishes and would simply make her comfortable immediately. They would evaluate her and let us know if it was a cardiac event. I informed them of my hospital of choice and that I would be waiting there when she arrived. I leaned in to kiss my husband goodbye. He stroked my cheek and said, "It's funny how you are the most fragile of us all, and yet, when these things happen, you are the first one to face it head-on."

With young kids and fledgling careers, it had been one thing after another for us. For the past few years, the shit didn't just hit the fan. It was as though someone just stood over the fan and kept shitting into the wind. We were like a well pump being primed. But he was right. When disaster, drama, or strife of any sort occurs, I'm right there on the front lines. I need to be needed, to have my existence valued. I gathered my things and headed to the hospital to care for a grandmother that never really cared for me.

I phoned my sister Angela, who is unlike me and sleeps like a rock; she needed a minute to process before she called back to say she'd meet me at the hospital. Nana had already doled out all her earthly treasures, mostly to my sister, but also to anyone that wasn't me. She gave my sister all three sets of her china. I've often wondered how she would feel if she knew my sister had given me two of the sets and kept only one for herself. Nana was a dying woman with nothing left to offer except embarrassment at the clumsy way she chewed her food and the rude way she spoke to her caregivers. She accused the staff of stealing from her. After my grandfather passed, she was living alone in their home for the first time when she began to accuse my dad and me of breaking in and stealing her things, mostly her linens. We knew it was dementia when she accused us of breaking in and putting them back.

Inside the hospital, Nana was already on a gurney, shrouded behind the Pepto-pink curtains that served to create a room in the emergency wing. The crisp white sheet was tucked up to her neck, and she appeared to rest peacefully. The fluorescent lights overhead gave her pale, papery skin a translucent effect. The young cardiologist confirmed that Nana had had a pretty substantial heart attack. Nana, always full of piss and vinegar, no matter her condition, waited until my sister, her favorite grandchild, went home before she woke from her deceptive slumber. We were sure she'd sleep for hours. I swear she did that on purpose, just to inconvenience me. I've never known the cause of why she didn't like me much. When I was little, she called my mom to ask if she could have my sister for a weeklong visit.

"Sure, Sylvia," Mom had said. "But you have to get Shelley for a week this summer too. You can't just take one of them."

Nana was furious. She'd always had a favorite. It seemed whoever came along first secured their place as her favorite. It was as though she felt it a betrayal to like both of her sons or both of her granddaughters or both of her daughters-in-law.

My dad has a bad back from years of boxing and couldn't handle sleeping in the hospital, so I stepped up. I spent three nights alone with a demented and dying woman, listening to her give voice to a mountain of regrets all night. Sundowner's syndrome is a freaky thing to witness in itself, but when the good doctor throws in a nice evening hallucinogenic, life begins to feel like something out of the Pink Floyd movie *The Wall*. The hallway outside her hospital room held the faint smell of cigarette smoke that drifted in from the stairwell. It was a small relief from the odorous mix of piss and antiseptic that had lingered in my nose for the past few days. The situation with my Nana was pretty dramatic, but I felt strangely calm. I am at my best when I am caring for people.

My nights with Nana were filled with cries for my grandfather, for her adoptive father with whom she was very close, and for her adoptive mother that resented that closeness. In her head she was a baby, and then she was my baby, and then she's a bird. She wailed and begged me to hold her hand when it had been tearing at her diaper and doing things down there that I won't mention here. She removed her hospital gown repeatedly, exposing what I never wanted to see.

She finally ripped out one of the IVs in her hand, the very one I'd hovered over for days and tried desperately to keep intact as she picked and picked at the frayed white tape with gnarled fingers—fingers that once graced the ends of long-sleeved Oscar de la Renta gowns. Fingers that used to spray Chanel No. 5 over her graceful neck and décolleté. She was elegant if anything, but never gentle, never nurturing. Not toward me anyway. Toward my sister she was attentive, though the attention couldn't always be considered kind. Once, when my sister was a teenager, Nana told her to never,

ever wear white tights. According to Nana, my sister just didn't have the legs for that. That scarred my sister enough to make me resent her.

The nurses, though it seemed they would rather be anywhere else, were surprisingly kind toward me. One older nurse in particular seemed to tend more to me than Nana. She ordered a real cot for me and insisted I accept extra pillows and blankets. One particularly trying night she gave Nana an extremely painful-looking shot in the shoulder. Nana let out a howl, and then her milky white eyes slipped away under heavy lids, her coarse, silvery bob spread out like a fan over the hospital pillow. I wandered out into the hallway to stare through the windows into the inky darkness of the courtyard. From the vantage point of the other windows, I imagined I looked like a ghost. I did some yoga stretches in the deserted corridor.

That peace was fleeting and I heard Nana's moans, "I don't want to die." Back in the room she tried repeatedly to get out of bed and begged me to help her "get out of this hellhole and get going." There was another dying man down the hall that kept yelling, "Water! Water! Water!" over and over again and switched it up with, "Help me! Help me! Help me!"

For forty-five minutes I lay across her body and entertained her with nonsense conversation in an attempt to keep her from ripping out her IV, her telemetry, and her catheter. I stood up long enough to duck into the hallway and flag down the first person I saw. Unfortunately, it wasn't the kind nurse that had cared so well for us, but some small, gray-haired man with a puckered face that gave the impression he'd just smelled something foul.

"Can you please help me? My grandmother is tearing at everything attached to her and trying to get out of the bed."

He pushed a button to silence the IV, one of the few things I could have done myself.

"It's up to you to make sure she doesn't."

About that time my mom strolled in and Nana was totally distracted.

"Hi, Mom, you ready to go dancing?" Mom asked her ex-mother-in-law. Nana was instantly captivated by her. For the moment, Nana was no longer hell-bent on escaping.

Despite a sixty-year nicotine habit and a pretty intense heart attack, Nana miraculously survived another night and was soon moved back to her room at the nursing home. I regularly drove the mile distance between my house and the nursing home to sit with her while family came in and out for visits. After a few weeks, her condition worsened and family began to say what they thought were most likely goodbyes. I was alone with her again, and at first I was terrified she would leave this earth on my watch. I had never witnessed anyone take their last breath. I had watched several chests rise and fall in anticipation of death, but had never seen the dying breath. As much as I was afraid, I also didn't want Nana to be alone when she died. And maybe, selfishly, I wanted to prove her wrong. When choosing her favorite grandchild, maybe she had made the wrong choice. I would be there with her in her last moments. I'd be there by her side, duty-bound, when she had nothing left to give and I had nothing more to gain. Around nine thirty that night, the nurse came in to take Nana's vitals and assured me nothing had changed since earlier that day.

"Go home and eat. Take a shower. We will call you if anything changes. You live so close you can be here in no time," she said. I felt that strange calmness again as I drove home. I walked through the door and into my husband's embrace. The phone rang the moment I took my shoes off. The nurse said Nana had passed.

"It happens that way a lot around here. Sometimes they just want to spare the ones they love any more grief, so they wait for the moment they are alone."

I couldn't help but hope this meant she did love me after all.

The Diner Prophet

My husband slouched down in the driver's seat as he hung up the phone. His broad shoulders hunched under the weight of what felt like the entire universe and all its troubles. He'd spent the previous ten minutes on the phone with his mother. His brothers were not in good health, and it was my husband's first Christmas without his father. A fatal asthma attack had sent him into cardiac arrest just two months earlier, a month shy of what would have been his sixty-ninth birthday. While he spoke to his mother, I searched my mind for a word more appropriate than *devastated*. His death had laid waste to us.

When it came to the business end of his death, there were frustrating delays. My mother-in-law's parents had changed her birth certificate so she could get her driver's license at the early age of thirteen. This made it difficult to prove her identity to the social security office now, but back then had enabled her to go to work and help her family. This revelation shed light on my mother-in-law as I've always known her. We are talking about a woman that digs her own footings when she wants to renovate the dilapidated porch on her "she-shed" and changes the door hardware on her own French doors when, as a project manager working in luxury home building, I paid skilled carpenters good money to do this because we simple folks fumble with them until the pieces go missing. But now she is alone and we can't fix anything.

For a while, the world seemed against us. Jason's mom had gone back to the social security office to see what was causing the delay in receiving his dad's check and discovered the woman she'd spent hours working with the month prior had gone on vacation for the holidays and left my mother-in-law's paperwork sitting on the desk unprocessed. Despite our grief, the world was still going to celebrate the holiday.

My father-in-law's absence from our lives made us feel unsafe in the world. He had always been there for us whenever we needed guidance or help in any way. When the hot water heater died, he made the ninety-mile drive to help Jason install a new one. When our cars needed repairs, he did them himself, saving us thousands of dollars. He and my mother-in-law loved us so well.

I had just completed a four-year degree in creative writing from an expensive private school. I had been searching for a full-time job to replace the two part-time jobs I'd been working while earning the degree. Finances were weighing heavily on us. We worried about hers and our own. We sat parked in front of the restaurant. Just getting out of the car felt like wading through whitewater.

Right there on the sidewalk, I boldly, desperately called out to God. "Holy Spirit, come," I begged aloud as I turned my face to a dull, cement-gray sky. We dragged our leaden hearts into the crowded diner and waited wordlessly for a table as a sea of voices gurgled around us. Surrounded by the happy chatter of families and friends visiting for the holidays, we felt like foreigners. When you're grieving, you resent the shit out of other people enjoying their lives. It seems nonsensical that life should go on.

I grabbed Jason's hands across the table. I said all the things that people say when they don't have the answers. I said, "God has a plan." I said, "He's going to take care of us and he's going to take care of Mom." This hushed conversation went on for a while, me encouraging him and him trying hard to let me lift his spirits. All the while surrounded by the loud clatter of dozens of other diners.

We eat at this diner at least once a week and sometimes more often than that, so we were surprised when a man we didn't know walked up to our table halfway through our meal. Jason is the organist for the local hockey team, so my first thought was that he might have recognized him from there. He was younger than our parents, but older than us, and we knew we'd never laid eyes on him before.

He turned to Jason. "The first thing I thought when I saw you walk in was that you look like John Lennon." I laughed, grateful for the distraction of this small talk.

"Wait," he said, holding up a gentle hand, cutting off my laughter. He didn't take his eyes off Jason the whole time. He was not there to speak to me.

"That's not why I came over. I have a word for you from God. You're going to write something very important. You're going to write very popular songs with an important message that God is going to give you. He is going to speak to you while you're in the shower. He's going to speak to you when you lie down to sleep. You'll need to keep a notepad by the bed or a recording device handy. You've been preparing for this for a while, but you weren't ready to handle the responsibility that's going to come with the success until now. It could be five or even ten years before it happens, I don't know when, but I do know it will happen."

I blinked furiously, trying to keep the tears from spilling over. His words of hope and purpose were like an ice cube on a parched tongue. Not an hour before, just outside the doors of that restaurant, I'd pleaded with the Holy Spirit to come, and he did. The man handed Jason his business card.

"I'd love to know how this works out."

We thanked him for being brave enough to come over and share with us the words God had spoken in his heart. He softened a little. "I've been doing this for twenty-five years. You could say, 'Hey, thanks,' or 'Kiss my ass.' Doesn't matter to me. I did what I was supposed to do."

As he turned to head back toward his table of friends, I told him that Jason was a professional musician, but he did not seem at all surprised or even remotely interested in discussing it further. That might have been the best part. He didn't need any worldly, human confirmation of the truth he'd clearly heard from God. That fact still leaves me speechless. That is faith, isn't it? There's no proof necessary, just an unwavering belief in the unseen, a faith that lives deep within the heart and defies the puzzles of the mind. When the coffers of hope run low, I reflect on moments like these, moments when God shows up magnificently. There is no need to seek proof by jabbing fingers into wounds when we reflect on what we know to be true of God.

Many Christmases have passed since that day in the diner. As of yet, there have been no new songs written, but a wealth of life has been lived—the kind of joy- and sorrow-filled life that inspires the kind of songs my husband once wrote years ago. It began with a simple request on the sidewalk that day. Holy Spirit, come. Once again, he comforted us in the form of hope brought by humankind, and that comfort carries us through the roughest days.

We Are All Stories

The nurse looked closely at the paper in her hand, counted out twenty-nine vials of blood, and placed them on the metal tray next to my head. I was desperate to determine the cause of the crushing fatigue and joint and muscle pain I'd been suffering with for months. I sent up a silent prayer that these labs would provide answers.

I can't recall a time in my life when I wasn't coping with some form of illness or pain. Whether it was repeated strep infections as a kid, debilitating endometriosis, or seasons of wicked migraines and stomachaches, my body has always been at war with itself.

Trying to determine the cause of the most recent onslaught of symptoms was like trying to cut hair while it's blowing in the wind. I'd landed in this functional medicine doctor's office because I thought my hormones had taken an age-appropriate nosedive. I was in my early forties and just the year prior, had undergone a uterine ablation, a process in which a surgeon cauterizes the lining of the uterus so no more periods—yay! It made sense that heavy periods were the cause of my anemia, so couldn't it now be possible that hormones were to blame for headaches, debilitating fatigue, and crushing joint pain?

Turns out, after I answered a lengthy questionnaire, the doctor suspected a biotoxin illness.

"Your symptoms are consistent with both Lyme disease and water-damaged building syndrome. Have you ever lived in a water-damaged building? Do you spend much time outdoors?" she asked.

"The crawlspace of our home floods every few years and we need to have it remediated for mold. There were many years this was the case, but we weren't aware of it, so it went untreated. And yeah, I love to hike and spend time outdoors."

"Is it possible you could have been bitten by a tick?"

I told her about the time my husband and I prepared to throw one of the kids a birthday party in the backyard. We spent the day clearing brush, picking up sticks, and raking up those pesky gumballs that fell from the half dozen sweet gum trees on the property. By the time the party started, I wasn't feeling well. I had a strange warm, pink lump on my chest just below my collarbone that could have been a bite and flu-like body aches. Once the party was over, Jason stayed home with the kids while I went to the emergency room to get checked out. This was around the time that MRSA was in the news and top of mind for anyone in the hospital. The staff was hesitant to take a sample from it, declared it a spider bite, and sent me home with no real answers and instructions to follow up with my doctor. By the time I was able to see him, the sore was deflated and hardly resembled what they'd seen at the hospital.

At first, my primary care doctor agreed it was some type of bite and then quickly excused himself from the room. When he returned, he had a new answer. "You have cellulitis. Just a skin infection." I didn't give it much thought after that, but I never forgot how bad I felt those few days. Over the next few years, it seemed like I was always sick with upper respiratory illnesses like bronchitis and walking pneumonia.

I hadn't thought much about the mold that hung from the dilapidated ceiling over our back porch until this doctor mentioned that mold might be an issue. I was embarrassed by it, so my sister came over before the party and helped me tack up some fabric in a pretty swag to hide it before the guests arrived. So yes, there was some exposure to a water-damaged building as well as a potential bite of some sort.

I flashed forward to the more recent past, when I took my friend Meg to the family cabin for some hiking and tubing on the river. We put on bikinis and rubber flip-flops, grabbed inner tubes from the basement, and started walking up the cabin road. We walked about two miles before a neighbor stopped to greet us, and when we told him where we were going, he told us to hop in the back of the truck and he'd take us to the river. As we rounded the hairpin turns of the mountain road, I felt a rush of adrenaline from the danger. As a risk-averse adult, this ride in the back of a truck wearing almost nothing was out of my comfort zone. He drove us to the drop-in point at the bridge. By the time we jumped out of the truck, I had a rash all over the left side of my neck, and as we floated down the river, it spread to my shoulder.

The next day I felt more rundown than usual and developed a hacking cough that continued over the next few weeks. Eventually, my bosses convinced me to go to urgent care where I was diagnosed with bronchitis and given an antibiotic. After a few weeks, the cough lingered and made me sound like I was near death, so I made an appointment to see my family doctor, Dr. H. I brought along the test results from the functional medicine doctor. I explained to him that upon receiving the lab results, the functional medicine doctor had called me to say that my inflammatory markers came back so high that she needed to refer me out to another practice; her office was not equipped to treat someone as sick as me. The tests she ran were not the same tests that a conventional doctor would run, so he questioned why they tested me for Lyme disease but didn't use the standard tests. He ran those tests and they came back positive for Lyme disease.

I began treatment right away with thirty days of oral antibiotics. When this did not result in significant improvement, I was prescribed two additional weeks of antibiotics. The cough persisted, so Dr. H gave me a shot of Rocephin. It would take years to get my stomach back to normal after all those antibiotics. I began seeing a chiropractor that performed muscle testing and provided support for illness and wellness by prescribing vitamins and herbal supplements. He suggested I adopt an anti-inflammatory diet, and since I'd already given up gluten and dairy in a general attempt to feel better, all I needed to further eliminate was grains. While I am sure it helped reduce my chronic pain levels, I also became hyper-fixated on my diet.

I began to realize, test after test, meeting with expert after expert, doing more investigations and readings myself, was how much grief I still carried with me in my body from my own childhood. On top of that, I was beginning to feel grief for my own children and the ways in which their lives were harder because mine had been. Jason and I had very little money and few healthy coping skills when the kids were growing up. He had trouble controlling his anger when he was anxious or frustrated, and I constantly heaped a world of doubt on him because my life had shown me that everyone leaves and everyone cheats. I was both anxious and so often sick that it made the kids anxious too. I saved piles of homemade get well soon cards made by my kids—proof my health impacted them tremendously.

We had not healed from the pains of our early lives before becoming parents ourselves. Hurt people hurt people. My father once said to me, "I came from a dysfunctional family, and now I've created one." Now I can say the same for my family of four. My husband and I had lived our adult lives in a steady stream of stress, and our kids were the collateral damage. With the help of gurus and therapists, they are now working to heal from their own chaotic childhoods. This is an ancestral gift that keeps on giving.

The decision to write about my life, following that night I read my essay aloud at Kelly's, had proven to be therapeutic and eventually led me to wonder how much grief and trauma affected my immune system. Studies indicate that the nervous system can become conditioned to fight or flight, which can then disrupt the normal function of the immune system. A 2020 article published in peer-reviewed journal, *BMC Psychiatry*, states, "Stress disorders (such as PTSD) may lead to impairment of the immune system and subsequent autoimmune disease." In a study conducted from 1995 to 1997, researchers coined the term "Adverse Childhood Experiences" to describe childhood adversities, such as experiencing physical and sexual abuse and living with an incarcerated or addicted parent. This list was eventually updated to include parental separation and divorce as well as socio-economic hardship, homelessness, community violence, emotional abuse, and neglect.

Research documents a link between ACEs and inflammation of the immune system and poor health outcomes. Additionally, chronic cortisol and adrenaline spikes can raise blood pressure, which can stress the cardiovascular system, deplete adrenal function, and negatively impact glucose levels. The higher the ACE score, the poorer the health outcome. The study indicated that people with ACEs are more likely to drop out of school and experience trouble maintaining employment and referred to them as having "low life potential." It is believed that, due to changes in brain chemistry caused by childhood trauma, issues with executive learning function and emotional regulation are often seen in those with high ACE scores. Lastly, these people are more likely to engage in risky behaviors such as hard drug use, alcohol abuse, sexual promiscuity, and cigarette smoking, which further threatens poor health outcomes. I was the poster child for all these risky behaviors. I had been a high school dropout and checked all those boxes during my youth. I lived most all of my life in a constant state of hypervigilance. It's been powerful and affirming to see my own experiences reflected in the study of ACEs.

When I first considered the possibility that healing could come from a deep dive into my past, I worried that it was possible the exploration would lead me to discover that chronic anxiety, and perhaps a depression I only was mildly aware of, were responsible for the pain and exhaustion I was facing every day. Somehow, that was scarier to me than the illnesses with which I had been diagnosed. I thought this connection would feel like another failure—a failure to cope, to overcome obstacles, and adversity. I could not just pull myself up by my bootstraps. But the truth is, I do believe my body holds within it the sorrows of my past and of my parents' pasts. Antidepressants called selective serotonin reuptake inhibitors, or SSRIs, do help minimize my pain and anxiety. While these medications are the go-to treatment for fibromyalgia and post-viral syndrome, when I was first prescribed that type of medication, I was pissed off. Not because I didn't believe in them and their value, but because it seemed like the conventional doctors just threw their hands up and pulled something off the shelf that shifted the blame back to me. Once I understood that fibromyalgia is a disorder of the nervous system, I began to see that a nervous system that had always existed on high alert could certainly benefit from the brain-calming nature of an antidepressant.

There is a dull, aching buzz that reverberates throughout my body, a tightly wound tension in the gristle of my insides. I was aware that I suffered chronic pain in my neck, back, and hips, but I could have never explained it as such before medication helped me experience its absence, giving me moments of soul-deep quiet stillness. SSRIs helped me in that way. I slept more soundly on them, which is to say I slept at all because my busy brain seems wired to switch on hyperdrive every night when I switch off the bedside lamp. But taking these pills is like a handshake with the devil. On the altar of sacrifice is my sex drive and enjoyment; my body confidence thanks to an extra five pounds in my thigh and ass area, known as the thass, that makes dressing my short, curvy body pure torture every day; and the increase in water retention that further worsens my chronic case of constipation. I am vain and I am a heathen because after periods of compliancy, I will quit taking them and choose sex and feeling good in my clothes every time. Eventually, the pain in my body will be too much and I will start the medication all over again.

The many side effects of SSRIs are something to constantly weigh against their benefits. So, I start them and stop them and switch medicines a few times a year. This is a terrible idea. I am not recommending or condoning this behavior. I'm just being honest about the rollercoaster ride it is for me.

When I first posed the question, "if healing past traumas and mistakes by naming them can heal my body, does this mean illness has been my fault and within my control this whole time?" I was so afraid that the answer was yes that I didn't consider what a gift it would be to know that if any of it *was* within my control, that meant I could influence my own healing.

Writing about my own personal history has been the one thing that has been the most impactful on my health. This self-awareness has paved the way for self-acceptance, and sharing it here within these pages has been a bold, brave declaration of acceptance and self-love. Self-acceptance is a revelation for the child within me who never fit in anywhere. *You mean I can just declare myself worthy of love, attention, and care?* This is where true healing begins. Author Toko-pa Turner wrote, "The difference between fitting in and belonging is that fitting in, by its very definition, is to parcel off our wholeness in exchange for acceptance." I will no longer parcel off my wholeness. Instead, I'll tell myself that wherever I am is where I belong.

Pamela Anderson wrote in her memoir that she felt it was almost like she'd lived her life just to write about it. I have enough inherent drama and vainglory to say the same about my own life. This is also true from a more altruistic perspective. I believe I was meant to be a student of God and self-discovery. I wouldn't exchange the person I am today for a different life experience, although I do fully intend to come skidding back Earthside, breathless and wild-haired, to take another stab at life. I plan to raise holy hell again, but this time as a dangerously self-possessed badass. Think Debra Winger's iconic Sissy riding that mechanical bull circa 1980. In my next life, heads are gonna roll.

I accept that I will probably always deal with intrusive thoughts. While I still repeat the prayer-mantra of supernatural healing and protection, it continues to evolve. It is the way of the spiritual sages to thank their deities for answering their prayers in advance of any actual answers in a show of great faith that it will be done. Instead of repetitive, pleading prayers for supernatural favor, protection, healing, and purpose, I began to offer great thanks in advance to God and all his angels for protecting my family, leading us to wisdom, healing, safety, joy, and lives of great purpose. Please note this applies to good parking spots as well as other highly sought-after life conveniences. This spiritual practice allows me to rest more soundly and hold less tension in my body, which helps reduce my body pain. In my mind, offering thanks in advance instead of continually asking and pleading is a show of deep and abiding faith. Nobody likes a whiny, pesky kid. Especially Spirit and his angel entourage.

I continue to work against the predicted poor health outcomes of my ACE score by practicing yoga, taking walks, and meditating daily. I try to get enough rest each night, hydrate, limit alcohol and caffeine, and eat an anti-inflammatory diet to help minimize my body pain. What I understand now is that physical, emotional, and spiritual healing is an ongoing journey of trial and error. What works for one season will need to be tweaked for the next, and recovery comes slow and steady when we are present and mindful in our lives. The path to healing never really ends and it isn't linear. I started this journey to better understand myself and heal my body, but I remain committed to it to help heal my children and the future generations to come. In her book *Moral Disorder*[6], Margaret Atwood writes, "In the end, we'll all become stories." I constantly ask myself, *what do I want my story to be?* Then I get to work, thanking the angels in advance for their help making it an epic one.

---

6. Atwood, Margaret. *Moral Disorder.* Nan A. Talese, 2006.

Needling

I sat in my work truck with an ice bag tucked under each butt cheek and reflected on what had just happened. I've feared needles for as long as I can remember, yet I'd just elected to be stuck multiple times with numerous needles in some of my most tender places. The management of chronic pain will make a person do things they would normally never do.

My fear of needles started when I was a kid. I came down with strep throat at least twice a year. My mom would have to drag me, crying and sometimes kicking, into Dr. Dixon's office, where he'd gag me with a long swab to the tonsils while whistling a snappy tune. I found this unnerving, foreboding. Without fail, he'd declare a shot of penicillin to be the best course of treatment. The smell of the alcohol wipe alone triggered pure panic in me. The measures taken to give me the actual shot are too embarrassing to recount here. My mom, sister, and I still laugh about the time I required surgery, my first ever, for the treatment of severe endometriosis when I was nineteen. The nurse wanted to get my IV started without my mom or sister in the room, and as they rolled me down the hall on the gurney I wailed, "Don't let them take me! Pray for me!" I caused them mortal embarrassment. One nurse calmly stated to the other, "She's gonna need some vitamin V." It took about two minutes for the IV Valium to calm me down. Years later, my sister confessed she had never prayed before that day, but did so because I asked her to. I scared her into praying. I *am* proud of that part.

In my early twenties, I got my belly button pierced. The fact that I went alone is the first indication that I hadn't fully thought it through. The moment the needle went through the skin I passed out cold. I awakened to a pair of blurry faces hovering over me. One guy waved a paper fan over me while the other guy mopped my forehead with a wet bandana while he scanned my waiver to recall my name. "Okay, uh, Rachelle? You still with me?" I thought, *Why is the bandana wet? Is there a hole in my belly yet? Why do you sound so far away?* When I'd recovered from my fainting spell, the guys declared me the first to faint at the precise moment the needle went in. *I would like some sort of formal recognition for that, sir.*

Two years prior to the belly piercing, I got more work done on the tattoo at the center of my lower back. After a few short minutes with the tattoo gun, I knew that something had gone very wrong in my body. Unable to determine which body system was going to fail me, I stumbled to the bathroom, leaving my tattoo artist friend and beloved local musician, James, exasperated by the interruption. He tried to insist on coming into the bathroom with me—for my safety, he said—but I refused. There I was in a cold sweat, pants down around my ankles with the trashcan between my knees *in a tattoo parlor.* From the other side of the bathroom door, he informed me that my low tolerance for pain spelled big trouble for me should I ever want to birth a baby. Ugh. James, a dude with a penis tattoo, ended up being right. When it came time to deliver my first baby, I could not handle the pain and demanded *all* the drugs.

During my first pregnancy, I had a large amount of blood work done, and subsequently, and almost predictably, I fainted. Much to the irritation of the nurses, I once again insisted on being alone in the bathroom because the truth was, I didn't know what my body's next trick would be—would I lose control of my bowels or lose my lunch? It wasn't as much the blood loss as it was the poke of the needle that caused this total nervous system failure in me.

I was expecting my first baby at the same time my friend Summer was expecting her third. She bestowed upon me the honor of driving her to the hospital and being present with her during the delivery. She settled in her hospital bed on that gray winter's day, and I leaned against a bank of windows in the room, ready to help however she needed me. When the nurse started her IV, I felt faint and had to lie down. I was then ushered out into the hall for some air. About that time, my OB-GYN rounded the corner. He looked panicked when he saw me. I still had four months to go.

"Rachelle, why are you here?" He had the kindest smile, but I easily registered the concern on his face.

"Oh, I'm here with my friend who's in labor. I wasn't feeling well so I came out here for some air."

"What's going on? Are you in pain?" he asked, concerned. I was embarrassed, but I knew I had to confess that her IV sent me on a downward spiral.

"Oh boy," he said in his gentle manner. "Well, it will be different when it's your turn. Your instincts will kick in and you'll do just fine."

Once I steadied myself with some deep breaths and a pep talk about how my friend needed me (she didn't), I got back to the room just as it was time for Summer to get her epidural. The nurse took me by the shoulders and positioned me in the doorway before she yanked closed the half-moon-shaped privacy curtain so I couldn't see the giant needle they were going to insert into my poor friend's back. It's probably best because had I known the size and location of the needle that was in store for me in a few short months, I would have been a flight risk. I'd have run away and ended up delivering my kid in the beach hut of some old surfer, named Indigo or Swami, who would have convinced me she could be my stand-in midwife. "Here, smoke this. You won't feel a thing!"

But back to the truck and the ice packs under my butt. I was recently referred to physical therapy for low-back pain due to a dislocated tailbone—which had been cracked all those years ago in birthing that first child. During my first appointment, the physical therapist determined the muscles in my lower back and butt were wound so tight it was certain to be a big contributing factor in my pain. Not surprising, since a lifetime of intrusive thoughts, stressful circumstances, and uncertainty had left me in a forty-year-long butt clench. She recommended I receive a therapy called dry needling. For me to agree to have needles poked into my back should be an indication of my desperation for relief.

During this process, eight laser-cut needles are placed deep into the tensed-up muscles of my back. While it was painful and the anticipation of needles made me anxious, I breathed through it and found some relief from my pain for a few days. The second time I got needling done it was in my hips and glutes. My therapist informed me he was going to place the worst, most painful needle first, and then the other three, before putting an electrical charge to them. There were four needles inserted into tightly wound pressure points that were painful enough to make me see a halo of unicorns when simply palpated by hand. By the time the fourth needle was in, I had the cold sweats and was in a full-on laughing-crying fit. Imagine little jumper cables attached to the needles. When he connected the wires to put the electrical charge to the needles, my butt and hip muscles started "jumping" at which time I experienced a debilitating toe cramp and developed a large black floater in my eye.

In an effort to distract me, the practitioner, John, told me a story about a refined, well-dressed female dentist that came in for needling. The moment the first needle went in, she yelled a hearty, manly, "Fuuuuuuuck" which could be heard by all the other patients throughout the office. Later, my physical therapist, Kim, added some color to that story by mentioning the fact that the petite dentist continued to say *all* the bad words throughout the procedure, and called John every name in the book. And then, once the electric charge made the muscles start to jump, she repeatedly shouted, "My butt is twerking!" Just before slipping into my own state of panic that disabled my ability to think, I thought, *I like this lady*. I admired her uninhibited expression of the intensity of what she was experiencing in that moment.

Most humans are morbidly curious about the painful experiences of others, yet when we are faced with others emoting, many of us get squirmy. When a child is crying, it's a reflex to say, "Shh, don't cry." We just don't like to see others upset. Crying makes us uncomfy. And sometimes, the timing is simply inconvenient for others. Maybe we should encourage our loved ones to cry and cuss when they need to. Doesn't everyone feel relieved after a good cry? I sincerely believe all the reasons we were taught to squash our messy emotions are rooted in patriarchal discomfort, but I won't launch into that now. I recently read a study that found cussing relieves pain, but society asks that we not yell those words in public spaces because doing so does not make for polite company. Selfishly, universal acceptance of crying and cussing in public would go a long way to normalize my compulsive over-emoting and nearly nonexistent pain tolerance. I feel *all* of my feelings, both emotional and physical. Even my feelings have feelings. I will even feel *your* feelings if you share them with me. This means you will never cry alone in my presence. For instance, if you tell me about the time you tripped on a crack in the sidewalk, fell, and bloodied your knee, I will experience an immediate weakness in my legs followed by a nervy sensation up and down the backs of my knees. If I hear of an injury more serious than a scrape, I may flop over and put my head between my knees to keep from passing out. My extreme empathy is like an opposite super power. I blame this on an over-reactive nervous system.

When my husband agreed to undergo a vasectomy, like the selfless king he is, I accompanied him for moral support. The surgeon was pretty proud of himself when he removed that little tube from the tender region just south of my husband's knackers. Holding it between a pair of forceps, he asked if I would like to see it, but he did not wait for an answer. Consequently, I got all swimmy-headed, so much so the nurse had to tend to me. My poor husband lay neglected on a gurney with a fresh incision and his ball region exposed while the nurse tended to me and the doctor watched in amusement. My presence is a liability in these situations.

I truly believe some people tolerate pain better than others, and I know beyond a shadow of a doubt that I'm *not* one of them. There are people that feel things so much more intensely than the majority of other folks, both physically and emotionally. Like the petite dentist, these, too, are my people. I used to spend a tremendous amount of energy pretending to be tougher than I was, unaffected by this or that thing, acting as though I wasn't in pain, be it physical or emotional. It's exhausting trying to be someone you're not. I don't recommend it. To be human is to suffer. What's the point of trying to deny you're hurting? Expressing and sharing our pain is how we process it and a good way to form healing connections with others. I'm grateful for having been told the tale of the well-dressed dentist and appreciate her for being the yelling, cussing, trailblazer of self-expression she is.

My Alter Ego

I dreamed I was at a Tom Petty concert, front row, center stage but a little more to the left, so I could check out keyboard player Benmont Tench. When they finished their set, I hung around for a bit as the crowd hesitantly began to empty out. I tend to miss certain social cues thanks to my severe hearing loss and it causes a lot of anxiety. I know the hearing loss has to be the culprit because I'm not terrible in social settings where I can actually hear and understand what's being said, but I'm terribly awkward when people yell across the yard or greet me in passing and I can't see their mouths. "The weather is beautiful!" they say. "Aw, gosh! Thank you so much!" I reply, realizing my mistake only when the weird look registers on their face. I am humbled when I realize this person thought the weather was beautiful, not me.

In this dream, I decided the show must really be over and that I should go to the bathroom, maybe locate my husband. I'm in the bathroom, mid-squat because, you know, God's hilarious like that, when I hear the first riffs of "Refugee." Of course, there's an encore! Hovering over the toilet, I throw my head back, sober, but nearly losing my balance and let out a deep, guttural, "Ohhhh noooo, Timmmm Petty!" Wait, what? Did I just scream that loud enough for the entire free world to hear me call Tom Petty "Tim Petty"? Yep. As a dedicated music fan and the wife and mother of musicians, I was horrified. I yanked up my pants and threw open the stall door to see a handful of super fans wide-eyed with confusion at my blasphemy. My dream-self felt the white-hot flush of embarrassment.

So even in my dreams, weird words—or more precisely, slightly altered versions of words—come out of my mouth. I just don't form them correctly. Maybe a vowel sound is off or I say the word too fast and it comes out wrong. Either way, it's horrendously embarrassing. My late friend, Mike, proud owner of some kick-ass hearing aids, once told me the root cause of this is a side effect of hearing impairment called loss of word recognition. Whatever it is, it has become an underlying fear of mine that I will do this in front of people that do not yet know I'm really an okay, relatively intelligent person. If you happen to talk to me and I speak slowly and deliberately, it's not because I'm stupid or I think you're stupid. I'm going slowly because I'm afraid my tongue will trip me up. Like recently, when I tried to say to my mom and sister, "My right boob is bigger." Instead, what came out was, "My right big is boober." But, seriously, Tim Petty? Would he have been the same had he been named Timothy instead of Thomas? Probably not. Different saints, different superpowers.

There really is something to a name. I was born Rachelle Leigh, but I don't ever remember having been called that name even once before I was eighteen and registering myself for community college. Unless you count the all the times my mother yelled it when I'd been in trouble. All of my official documents and forms of identification read "Rachelle." It is customary in Jewish families to name new members of the family after the deceased members of the family. This way the angel of death won't get mixed up when he comes for the elderly and snatch up the baby before her time. My folks dumbed down that rule further by simply honoring the first letter R, choosing to name me Rachelle instead of Rose, after my dad's late grandmother. My parents gave me the easier-to-pronounce nickname, Shellie, but as an adult, I decided not to volunteer this info at school registration, doctor appointments, or at the beginning of a new job. I always left the line blank when it asked for a nickname.

I tried "Rachelle" on and I liked it. No matter that now, all these years later, I have come to answer to the name "Rachael" because people rarely pronounce "Rachelle" correctly. Just recently, while in the waiting room before getting a mammogram, the tech called out "Rachael?" "Yes, right here." I didn't bother to correct her. Rachelle is sophisticated, and maybe a bit worldly, but Rachael is biblical and fearless. This perception of the name is based on one of my fiercest girlfriends, Rachael. If you need something handled, she's your girl. She might not even know the first thing about the problem she's tackling, but she will take charge and have you curled up in the corner sucking your thumb if you can't fall in line. This time, "Rachael" suited the situation, so she got up and walked her boobs right on back to the big boob-smashing machine.

One time at a job interview, the interviewer introduced himself as Andrew. I stuck my hand out and said, "I'm Shellie." Damn it all, Shellie showed up so this interview is as good as over. I'd really wanted to be Rachelle again. You see, Rachelle's put together. Her name hints at refinement, but not so much that she seems elitist or that you wouldn't like her. She mostly has all her shit in one sock, but when she doesn't, she lets go a charming, self-possessed laugh and moves on. Mostly, she doesn't have the shame-filled baggage Shellie has. Seven-year-old Shellie lied to her mom about raking the yard and when she was caught in that lie, she changed the spelling of her name. Shellie is still striving and she's kind of a mess. She's still trying to prove her worth and convince the world she's good enough to be in print on a birth certificate or driver's license. I'd wanted her to take the backseat in this new environment at a potential new job, but the second I opened my mouth to introduce myself, "Shellie" just came flying out. It's worth noting I didn't even get a call back.

It's my life's work to integrate these two personas into one. As a parent of two young adults, I consistently preach individuality. My words are full of constant reminders like, "God intentionally wove into you all these characteristics and life experiences to make you exactly the beautiful human you are today." "You'll never stand out in the crowd if you're always flying with the flock." Super annoying, I know.

One particularly trying day on the job site, I'd somewhat faked my way through a subcontractor meeting using my best interpretation of the plans we had onsite. As a rookie project manager, I had been honest with everyone about what I didn't know, but sometimes failed to hide my frustration with myself. This particular time I was annoyed because the interior trim salesman was openly enjoying my struggle and asking me questions designed to show how much he knew and how little I did. I said something along the lines of, "Well, that's what you're here for, so don't quiz me for your entertainment. Just walk me through it until it makes sense." He softened his tone before heading off to measure some other rooms, but I was pissed. "See ya, Shellie!" he called out behind me.

I walked down the two-by-ten plank we had propped up to cover for the front porch steps we hadn't yet built. The wood was wet and slick with rain, so of course my feet flew out from under me and I slid on my ass all the way down, landing with a thud. Stunned for a moment, I just sat there. Rachelle rolled her eyes, and Shellie thought, *Yep. That feels about right.*

Knowing I was going to have two red, mud-streaked butt cheeks when I stood up, I channeled Rachael and Rachelle and told myself, *You get up right now and own that shit*. I walked to my truck, laughing at myself the way I knew my schadenfreude-stricken family would when I tell them about it, grabbed a towel to sit on, and made my way home.

Crying at Work

"Is It Okay to Cry at Work?" This magazine headline caught my eye. I figured I knew the answer so I only skimmed the pages, both surprised and relieved to read the answer was yes. Revealing our true nature within the confines of the workplace can be daunting, but for us highly sensitive people, it's impossible to hide. While traits such as approachableness, loyalty, warmth, and kindness are universally welcomed in the workplace, the often accompanying traits of sensitivity, emotional expressiveness, and vulnerability are traditionally not as well received. I believed early on that this was an issue mostly faced by women, but later realized that many men carry this burden as well. In my formative years, men that showed any emotion other than anger were viewed as somehow weaker than their more stoic counterparts. It only takes a few rom-coms to see this idea of the emotionally intelligent man is now the more highly sought-after model.

One Sunday when my kids were younger, they left Sunday school visibly upset. My daughter told me that one of the coolest boys in Sunday school had opened up to the teacher about how angry his dad gets when he cries. "Boys don't cry. Suck it up and act like a man," the dad would say. I grieved for this child and simmered in anger at his ignorant father. Men that were never taught how to identify and deal with their emotions and the emotions of others had been a recurring cause of heartache for me and so many of my friends.

Growing up, I had the opportunity to be an extra in several TV shows and movies. Having been referred to as dramatic my whole life, this seemed fitting work for me. I was always more comfortable pretending to be someone I wasn't, and this made acting a perfect fit. Cry on demand? No problem. I'm a straight-up endless well of tears. Pretend to be someone I'm not? I'm here for it. Sadly, acting did not become my career, and I landed in the world of the steady, straight job, so I spend my non-working hours expressing myself freely on the page, figuring out life by writing essays. I'm always trying to contain that expression while in the workplace.

This has always been a challenge for me. This zebra just can't hide her stripes. In my thirty-some years of work experience, I have cried in absolutely every annual review and meeting that contained even the tiniest bit of criticism. This crying has ranged anywhere from "who knew she had so many tears in her head" to the slight head tilt so that gravity would cause the water to recede back into my eye holes.

"Keep going," I'd said, waving the general area of my face. "This is not about you," I'd assure my boss. I have no poker face. I have no thick skin. And dammit, I'm not sorry about it anymore.

The idea of women as emotional beings has long been viewed as a weakness to overcome. I have always found this an impossible feat. And now, in my second act of life as they call it, I find the idea of trying to squash that part of me repugnant. It goes against the nature in which God created me, and finally, as a grown-ass adult, I care more about being true to myself than I do the shortsighted judgments of others. I hope to encourage other highly sensitive people to do the same.

The same characteristics that make it possible for me and other tender beings to develop trust and genuine, meaningful relationships—both personally and professionally—are rooted in the same sensitivity that causes me to cry at work. For years, I have meditated on and ruminated over what might be the reason I cry when criticized. Old-school folks like to say it's a mark of maturity to be able to handle it with confidence and a touch of indifference, but I rail against that type of oversimplification and dismissal. Perhaps, for me, it is an underlying, overwhelming feeling of being undervalued and misunderstood, or possibly a deep-seated fear of rejection. I have long felt I am one mistake away from losing everything and everyone, and whatever the failure du jour may be, it could be the one to finally out me as an imposter, to make people realize I am not worth their time. I walk into work meetings feeling like a little girl in her mom's business suit, teetering in oversized heels and sporting a swipe of messy peach lip gloss.

I've mined the origins of this imposter syndrome for years and can't place blame on any one occurrence in my life. People everywhere are digging themselves out from under what the world has long told them they are or should be. I reject the call to assimilate. Men who were raised not to cry or show any emotion other than anger are often viewed, however archaically, as effeminate, and women who express themselves through anger or tears are labeled unstable, crazy, and angry.

And then there is the one that makes me want to kung fu donkey-kick the shit out of the person who refers to an emoting female as "off her meds." I was once shocked into silence by that comment, and therefore unintentionally complicit, but no more. From now on I will rage against this machine.

These gendered concepts land as outdated on the younger generation who seem to be experiencing much greater freedom of self-expression. I can scroll through social media and see a mind-blowing amount of what would once have been considered career-threatening oversharing had it happened around a conference table rather than on a digital platform. This content is peppered with f-bombs and teary rants and yet this dialogue contributes to their great commercial success. We connect with people when we see them in an emotional state. They become real to us in a way that is rarely welcomed in a corporate setting. Many of these influencers and product ambassadors are being paid six-figure incomes to share their personal lives and are not penalized for passionate outbursts, political rants, unprofessional language, and full-scale meltdowns. It took me a minute to come around to it, but now I'm shouting "hell yeah" to these young people. They do not question whether their authentic selves deserve a seat at the table. They've already pulled up a chair.

Former supermodel Paulina Porizkova posted on Instagram a one-minute-long video where all she did was ugly cry. At first, I wanted to hold my hand over the screen and protect her. I wanted to keep the world from seeing this vulnerable moment, but then I realized I had been conditioned to believe this part of our humanity should be hidden and private. For those to whom the idea of public emoting feels like stabbing straight pins into your eyeballs, I'm not trying to change you. I am just here in support of those who feel shunned when they accidentally open their suitcase of emotional baggage in the workspace.

It's been said that Generation X was the most under-parented generation. Our mothers were fighting for their place at the table professionally, while about half of them were also single-parenting their kids at home. Our fathers were exploring life outside the traditional confines of monogamy and the monotony of workaday life, rejecting what they saw as the unsatisfying lives of their fathers. We kids were at home alone watching *Happy Days* and *Good Times* while eating frosted chocolate Pop-Tarts for dinner. We have some shit to cry about, dammit.

Scores of latchkey kids were left to their own devices, navigating both the wider world and big emotions they didn't have the skills to process. Many Gen X adults, now parents themselves, bravely went on a journey of self-discovery while fellow Gen X teachers presented awards to their students just for participation, much to the disapproval of old-school baby boomer grandparents everywhere. We have raised an army of kids that know and believe in who they are and that anything is possible if they just show up and participate. This new generation isn't afraid to show their authentic selves to the world and they are cussing, ranting, and sometimes crying all the way to the bank.

Strangers on a Plane

It had been a long workday in Baltimore. A few flakes of snow had swirled under an owl-gray sky. I'd flown up that morning and just eight hours later, I was already headed back home to Charlotte. As we prepared for takeoff, I could hear the woman sitting behind me gently coaching her kids about what to expect on the plane ride. I strained to listen to her soothing explanations. She told them stories about previous trips she'd taken to Cancun and Las Vegas. I listened as she described how the lights of the city would dance and sparkle like stars once we got off the ground.

They asked a lot of questions and she was endlessly patient with them. What struck me was the way she clearly enjoyed the presence of her children. I was really taken by this and grateful that, although I'd lost so much of my hearing, by some miracle, I could hear her words so clearly coming from behind me when I often can't understand the words of the person right next to me.

Time and time again, life has taught me to never miss an opportunity to engage with a stranger when your gut nudges you to. "Are you traveling with your children?" She had gotten up to let one of them out of the seat and as that child hurried to the bathroom, she replied a friendly, "Yes, I am."

I told her that I had been listening to her talk to them for the past hour. "I just wanted to tell you that you are such a great mom."

Her voice caught in her throat when she spoke again. "Thank you so much. That's such a nice thing to say." A mix of gratitude and relief showed on her face, like maybe it was the first time in a while she'd stopped to breathe, or perhaps she'd been wondering if she was doing a good job. In the absence of hearing aids, I often resort to reading faces to guide my conversations.

"My husband just passed away last month." She nodded toward the front of the plane. "My parents are up there. We are all going to stay with my sister for the holidays. We've never traveled at Christmas, so this is new and different for all of us." I quickly told her how sorry I was for her loss, for their loss. I could barely swallow with the knot that had formed in my throat. My sister had just lost her husband; my nephews and my niece had lost their father. I'd lost my brother-in-law of more than two decades. We'd buried him just the day before.

Immediately, I was overwhelmed by the thought that this could easily be them and this conversation happening in some alternate universe, two weeks from now, when they board a plane to NYC for a momentary four-day truce with their grief. Someone could recognize the tenderness in which my sister speaks to her children, or the public affection they've taken to showing their mother, and might lean in to encourage her with their words, or perhaps, with a wordless, kind gesture.

My eyes welled with tears and my nose burned. Here I was in public and I couldn't stop the tears. In reality I am always ready to feel anyone's pain. My own is always just a fingernail's scratch away. As this stranger quickly learned, one will never cry alone in my presence.

Before I knew the real, irrevocable pain of my brother-in-law Paul's death, I carried a grief fueled by the fear that I could lose a loved one unexpectedly and by the inevitable pains of life experience. Perhaps the sorrow I toted along with me like so much baggage was the torch of generational pain. My parents both experienced abandonment in childhood. Regardless of their merit, hot, salty rivers of tears always simmer beneath the surface just waiting to be released, prepared to burst onto the scene screaming, "See! I knew this shit was gonna happen." Though for the dozens of terrible things I regularly imagined on any given day, only one had ever come to pass and it was fresh and raw.

I told her my sister had just lost her husband two weeks ago. She said she was so sorry. "What happened?"

"Gastric cancer," I said.

She nodded and patted my hand. "Brain cancer," she said.

I could tell by looking at her that, like my sister, she'd been so busy taking care of everyone else that it hadn't occurred to her to care for herself. Or perhaps, caring for these children, these souvenir gifts from a life taken too soon, was the very thing that kept them both putting one foot in front of the other when it could have been so easy to fold under the heft of their grief.

As the plane hurtled through the black sky, I vowed to always listen to that voice that urges me to connect with a perfect stranger. I bowed my head and envisioned this woman and my sister in a circle of protective angels dictating who can come close and forcefully flicking away those who are not allowed. Then I wrapped them both in a silent prayer of deep and abiding peace.

Love Thigh Self

After the global pandemic of 2020 knocked me on my ass with six weeks of illness and no exercise, I finally rolled out my mat and attempted a self-guided yoga practice. I made my way through a half-hour flow based solely on muscle memory and what felt right. The practice of yoga has come in fits and starts for me, spanning more than two decades now. It's not an advanced practice, and never has been, but it offers me a consistent home to return to. This is not about yoga.

In tree pose, I swayed while I gazed upon the place where my left foot met with my right inner thigh as I balanced on my right leg. Over the years my instructors have preached the value of fixing your eyes upon an unmoving spot, a *drishti*, in order to keep good balance. Most of us ladies agree the thigh area is not the most uplifting of places on which to focus one's attention. No matter your size or shape, thighs always seem to hold a lot of metaphorical weight. The weight I speak of is not always poundage, though that could be true as well, but more in terms of the attention they receive. The bulk of my weight in this petite body rests in this lower region. My tall and lovely friend Gigi once referred to her gloriously long legs as being "a whole lotta real estate." I adopted that expression for my thighs.

As I released tree pose and floated one leg into airplane pose, I lifted my eyes to the mirror. *There you are*, I thought, *in all your glory, larger than all my other body parts. Big and proud. Strong and sturdy.* It was then they spoke to me. Outnumbered two to one, my thighs had taken over my stream of consciousness, and in unison they spoke: "Let us be."

In that moment I felt a new tenderness toward my body and decided to call a truce with my thighs. I no longer wanted to change them. I wanted to love them. Beloved writer Anne Lamott, aka St. Anne, once wrote about lovingly rubbing lotion into her thighs before an upcoming beach trip with a lover and reported it did in fact help her enjoy her bare-thighed time on the beach. I have been the enemy of my lower body for so long, squatting it and lunging it until my hip joints were achy pits of hellfire and I could no longer lower myself to the toilet to pee without a groan. "Mom, you okay in there?"

"All good, kids. Killer workout yesterday." Vanity won't allow me to stop the workouts altogether, but maybe some days I should just do like Anne and rub some lotion on them.

Sure, I could blame the multitude of ads photoshopped to impossibility or the magazine articles in the grocery checkout line that always shout in yellow or pink bold print, "GET SHAPELY THIGHS BY SPRING" or "SUMMER THIGH SLIM DOWN," but that's too easy and not the whole truth. In my developing years, I watched in wide-eyed bewilderment as my legs morphed from the things I walked on every day to something that my shorts strained to contain. Their battle cry could be heard over the cacophony of the middle school hallways as they whistled in protest of their corduroy prison. I cursed their presence as their splay took up too much room on the barstool and when they fought for their freedom from my Daisy Dukes.

The admiration and image of the woman's body has changed over the years. A relic of primitive art known as the Venus of Willendorf represented a rather large woman and indicated the essence of her beauty was in her size. Renaissance-era painters chose the palest of subjects with soft, round bodies. Celebration of other body types such as these mattered little to me as I came of age during the reign of Kate Moss and a procession of waif models with boy-shaped bodies. It never occurred to me to celebrate my womanly shape. My only thought was to revolt against it.

When you sprout boobs in the fifth grade, you soon discover their power and also learn their fate; I would be neither a waif nor an athlete, but instead the picture of curvaceous fertile-looking femineity. In my twenties, I nurtured an obsession with trying to change my thigh shape and minimize their presence through creative outfitting, running, and, once, breaking a Suzanne Somers Thighmaster from overuse. To squelch their right to exist in their God-given shape was task one on my daily to-do list. You may work out for your health; I worked out to show my short, buttery legs who's really God.

Later, when my body morphed and underwent the changes necessary to grow and birth two babies, enduring the long years of putting their care first and caring for myself last, the softness of my body gained ground. When my kids were old enough to get through most of a day without me, I rejoined civilization, only to be bombarded with images displaying the highly coveted thigh gap and a million online and in-print articles on how to achieve it.

After dropping them off at school, I spent hours at the gym climbing the stairs to nowhere or clumsily dancing the rumba with a room full of gray-haired ladies when I could have been home learning to paint, play the piano, or become a master gardener. I could have been at the coffee shop working on the book I'd always wanted to write. Somehow, the person I wanted to present to the world possessed a thigh gap, knees that didn't look like mine, and arms like Angela Bassett's, but no real passions to speak of. Why didn't any other area of personal interest get as much time and TLC as the pursuit of changing my body? To think deeply about who I was on the inside would have meant inviting the pain of my past to the table, and I didn't yet have the space for that. The focus remained on the external, the superficial. I have stayed basically the same size all my life, which reduces the likelihood of many health dangers in a woman's golden years. But the arm definition? The highly coveted thigh gap? I learned they don't keep.

In all my unhealthy obsessing over my lower half, I overlooked the delicate bone of my wrist and the unexpected green in my brown eyes when the sunlight hits them just right. There were so many years of hiding my body in shame that had less to do with what it looked like and more to do with the careless ways people had treated it. There were so many years of suffering the summer heat in jeans because I couldn't bear to bare my legs. My dear friend, Christy, once declared dresses to be the most comfortable clothing on Earth and shorts to be a close second. "How can you wear jeans on a day like this?" she would often ask. Of course, her legs, along with her stormy gray-blue eyes and coy smile, are among her best features. I couldn't stand the thought of my thighs touching beneath a dress in the smothering heat of our Southern town.

Once, my son, who is an excellent photographer, took a picture of me while we were at a car show together. I remember him spontaneously turning the camera from a bright blue Lamborghini to me. Later that day, after he'd finished editing his photos, he brought me his camera. "Mom, I got this great shot of you today." I admired my strong little body in a floaty navy floral top with a cute half tuck into my favorite denim shorts.

I wore Converse low-top sneakers, with no socks of course, because that makes your legs look longer. The look on my face was all pride in this talented boy I had helped create, who cared about me enough to document my presence on this fun day. Then I saw it. He had edited the photo so that my knees were completely blurred out of existence. My legs just sort of melted into two flesh-colored stalks so well that others might have missed this alteration altogether.

"Honey, what happened to my legs?" I asked.

"Well, I know how you hate your knees, so I just edited them out."

Shit, I thought. I had focused on my thighs for so long I had forgotten how much I hated my knees. Worse than that, my youngest child had learned what I'd hoped to never teach him: how easy it was to fixate on something we don't like about ourselves to the point where it eclipses the fire in our eyes, the magic of our creative minds, the tenderness of our hearts. But did you catch the beauty of that story? I was out in the summer heat wearing shorts in public and my legs were the last thing I noticed when I looked at the photo. My eyes went there because sometimes, as my dad says, old habits die hard.

My foolishness and ingratitude for my body had other repercussions. For so many years I missed out on the sensation of a soft summer breeze as it tickles those leg hairs the razor always manages to miss. If an event required shorts, or God forbid, a bathing suit, I would decline and miss out on it altogether. I have since learned how much more fun a body can have while in shorts and in a bathing suit and that beautiful bodies come in many different silhouettes and sizes. I mourn the levity of the playfulness that was sorely missing from my uptight life in pants and jeans.

My husband knows the best angles from which to photograph me if my legs are out and proud, but he does so quietly, and only because he has seen firsthand how an awareness of their presence in a photo could ruin my day. That man kisses and caresses them at any given chance and does so as though they are the most precious thighs on Earth. For that reason alone, I continue to slide on my shorts, usually a size too big so they don't bind, or kick a bare leg out of the hem of my dress when I cross my legs in his presence. These thighs and knees deserve to be kissed and caressed by the trail of his finger. They deserve to feel the warmth of the sun on any given day. As my heart continued to heal from the traumas of my past, I began to understand I am more than just a body. A friend once told me that you can tell a lot about a woman by watching her move through a room. I think of this and realize when someone sees me walk through a room, they see more than just my body. I'm a collection of experiences, passions, and desires, embodying a carnal shape that is unique to me.

No matter what shape my body is in, my acceptance and gratitude for it continues to grow as I age. Don't get me wrong. Some days—okay, most days—it's still work not to care about the side profile, hip dip, thigh gap, or whatever body craze has taken over the world. After all, I am still the girl whose thighs just begged for mercy in the mirror during a yoga pose.

The Woman Who Ironed the Sheets

I pushed the iron back and forth across the gray-and-pink floral bedsheet. The set was a clearance score from twenty years ago. While on our honeymoon at a bed-and-breakfast in our favorite mountain town, we fell in love with our suite's floral Ralph Lauren bedding. When we returned home to our tiny urban apartment, we sought to replicate its beauty. I am ironing these bedsheets because my mother is coming to stay for a few weeks. Ironing the bedsheets had once been a dreaded childhood chore. Every Sunday I ironed five white oxford button-downs and three tartan plaid skirts for the week ahead at Catholic school. The ironing board was set up in the creepy basement of our historic home where the wood floors creaked eerily overhead, regardless of whether anyone was walking on them. I kept one eye on the door to the dark, musty wine cellar in the far-left corner, which would have made the cleverest hiding place for a braver child. But for me, it gave off Amityville vibes, like the walls could begin to ooze at any moment. Once the uniforms were starched stiff, it was time to iron the bedsheets. This seemed so pointless and tedious to me at the time, and honestly, for the next few decades of my life. It just felt like punishment.

One night, my sister and I left our kids and husbands at home and headed to Mom's for a sleepover. I pulled back the covers to find perfectly pressed sheets. It was clear no one else had slept on them. This effort was meant just for me. The crisp bedding was a warm welcome and, at first blush, such an obvious gesture of love and care. What I have come to understand now is that this simple act of caring for her home switches her mind from a state of anxiety to one of mindful purpose and provides a sense of control over her surroundings. I have come to view daily household chores as a form of meditation on gratitude, an active way to slow a busy mind.

Thich Nhat Hanh wrote in his book *The Miracle of Mindfulness*[7], "There are two ways to wash the dishes. The first is to wash the dishes in order to have clean dishes and the second is to wash the dishes in order to wash the dishes. . . . If while washing the dishes, we think only of the cup of tea that awaits us, thus hurrying to get the dishes out of the way, as if they were a nuisance, then we're not washing the dishes to wash the dishes."

Hanh proposes that washing the dishes, among other seemingly mundane chores, is a way to realize the

---

7. Hanh, Thich Nhat. *The Miracle of Mindfulness*, Beacon Press, 2016.

miracle of life, and if we are not completely alive at the sink, then we aren't going to be alive afterward while drinking our cup of tea. "While drinking our cup of tea, we will only be thinking about other things, barely aware of the cup in our hands." And so it is with the daily rituals required to have a clean and peaceful home.

I would be lying if I said I iron my sheets regularly. I don't. But if anyone, especially my mother, is coming to my house to stay, it is a ritual I pour myself into. I iron the sheets to iron the sheets. I press a steaming iron back and forth over the percale, infusing the fabric with gratitude and a lavender-scented prayer. Creating a sense of order in my home helps calm my busy mind. When I wash the dishes to wash the dishes, I find a contentment that grounds me.

What Does the Owl Say?

I had to face a painful truth. I was hard of hearing and needed to do something about it. I was a thirty-year-old with a four-year-old marriage, a four-year-old daughter, and a two-year-old son when I was finally prescribed hearing aids by an ENT doctor. Back then I still had lots of elasticity in my skin, but not much remained of my hearing. The doctor said things like, "You've lost more than 70 percent of your low tone hearing," and "Your hearing loss is substantial for someone your age," and "It's bilateral so no need for imaging, just some lab work to see if we can determine pathology."

At the time, spending thousands of dollars on hearing aids seemed selfish, impossible, and not a priority in my life the same way paying for preschool and life insurance was, so I did not get the hearing aids. For the next seventeen years, I missed out on conversations at parties and bars. I never knew entirely what was discussed in work meetings or the classroom when I went back to college in my late thirties, though I could discern the main points by asking strategic questions. I'd hold my breath and hope I'd gotten enough of it right. I was relieved when

I managed to make sense of what was being said and red-faced with embarrassment when I didn't.

Also troublesome was the one-liner muttered in low tones or under one's breath—you know the things that cause everyone to laugh or serve as a jumping off point for the next conversation which I could then sometimes kind of follow, but could never trace its germination. As the decades passed, I longed more and more to hear every word and sound. Oh, the sounds I missed! When our kids were babies, we would often ask them, "What does the owl say?" I taught them the answer was, "Hoot hoot," though I'd never heard it for myself.

"Do you hear that woodpecker?" my husband asked.

"Nope," I said.

"The train is coming," my friend said.

"I don't hear anything."

I'd been in a hearing deficit so long, it just felt like a personality defect more than a medical condition. I have come to realize that the conditions of the life we live become so familiar to us that it feels like our very own normal; we don't know any different. Much like when I was twelve and got my first pair of glasses. The world sprang to life like a vibrant Dr. Seuss movie! The details of the bushes and trees revealed shapes within shapes and the mortar between the yellow bricks of our house emerged. I hadn't realized all that I had been missing. Reality was intense and just shy of harsh in its detail. At night when I'd take those purple hexagon glasses off and rest them on the bedside table, I'd rub and rub my aching orbs till the darkness behind my eyelids filled with stars.

Right after I turned forty-seven, I shared an essay I'd written with an uncle with whom I'd recently gotten to know and had come to learn was a kindred soul. He shared stories of his childhood and early life with me and I shared with him essays I'd written about mine. In one particular essay I shared with him, I referred to my hearing loss not as the main topic, but as an aside. He loved the story, as he is a great encourager of my writing, but his focus was on the surprise of learning about my hearing loss.

Our communication had solely taken place through texts and a few emails. Talking on the phone has become especially difficult for me. Particularly when talking with someone new to me. If I had not yet learned their speech patterns, I'd repeatedly, awkwardly, talk over them. In addition to hearing loss, I have an auditory processing delay, which means I sometimes hear much like a drummer playing behind the beat, but it ain't groovy at all. This means I sometimes respond to people with "huh?" and then the sounds fall together in my brain just a bit delayed, causing me to respond before the person even has a chance to repeat themselves. I have been told more than once it's maddening.

This uncle-turned-dear-friend encouraged me to get the hearing aids and, to be sure I would, he graciously sent a check to fund them. He heard I had a problem, one that was written off as a fact of life I'd long lived with, and in a swift act of love, my life was changed. Sitting on the back porch one evening not too long after I received my hearing aids, I heard the strangest sound. At first it sounded like a woman having short fits of laughter and then screaming bloody murder. I couldn't really tell which.

"Honey, do you hear that?" I asked my husband, alarmed.

"The owl?" he replied.

"Oh my gosh! They cackle?" I replied.

The cackling of an owl was a revelation to me. The first time I heard the hammering of a woodpecker, my face burst into a smile. Somewhere down the road, a train would rumble down the tracks and I would stop dead in mine just to listen to its low whistle and hum.

There are some deficits my hearing will never regain, sounds made by the mouth and voice that are just lost to me because, as the doctor explained, I was without them for so long. Whenever the subject of my hearing aids comes up in conversation, inevitably someone will mention the difficulty their parents, some thirty years older than I, experienced with their hearing aids. This is not an experience I have with my peers, although, since many of them are lifelong musicians, I am sure that time will come for most of them. I'll be there to lead the way.

Much like hearing loss itself, I've learned hearing aids can be isolating too. The background noise in some situations causes the words of my companions to float right past me, undistinguished. Patient friends repeat themselves until I understand. Others simply give up and wave it away as unimportant. At times, the amplification of all the sounds becomes overstimulating, much like it was with the glasses of my youth. So, I take them out, carefully put them in their dehumidifier, and stuff spongy, purple ear plugs in their place.

For a while the silence is a gift, a break for my brain. I can still hear a frequency that is always with me. It's a hum more than a ringing, but that noise born from within me is all I hear. The rest of the world is drowned out. After a while, when my brain and nervous system have reached some level of homeostasis, I remove the earplugs and inevitably respond with "huh" to everything my husband says. I will forever celebrate the gift of being able to walk over to the tiny white box in the bedroom windowsill, pull out two tiny devices, and fully join the world around me.

Trip, Fall, and Die

I became a "trip-fall-and-die" kind of mom. It goes like this. When my child has to cross a road, I imagine said child (who never ties shoestrings) is going to trip in the road, fall, hit their head, and be struck by a motor vehicle. I imagine worst-case scenarios multiple times per day.

Perhaps we come into this world with our predisposition toward anxiety. It would be easy to blame my mother, with her certainty that terror and accidental death hovered just the other side of every decision, making the stakes of daily choices feel unnecessarily high, but the truth is more likely that I was born into this world with the same gene combination that made her that way. This DNA, combined with the burden of keeping us safe all by herself, and a strong case of PTSD from a tough upbringing by poor, often cruel parents in the hollers of West Virginia, kept her nervous system on high alert. Some nights she would have a bad feeling about something and ask my sister or me not to go out. "Just stay in this time," she'd plead. A few times her intuition was right. I would go on to repeat this pattern with my own kids.

It wasn't until I was in my forties that I recognized my anxiety as something like the angel and devil on my shoulder like I used to see in my beloved *The Flintstones* cartoons. On one shoulder, an angel of boundless faith, a caricature of a little figure in a floaty white smock always reminding me God is with me. She rolls her eyes at the demon of worry as he rages, jumping up and down on the opposite shoulder waving his flag of fear. He's more sinister and dressed in a dark cloak of foreboding, not the red devil of the horns-and-tail variety. This guy is easy to believe when he tries to convince me that it is my job to worry and obsess until I take my family down the rabbit hole with me. He's the real worrier I have to talk down off the ledge several times a day. This demon had long been with me, but I was learning to separate him from myself. Conversely, I was still getting used to hearing the angel's voice more clearly, a product of the Jesus-Zen-Buddha-tinged faith I'd cultivated.

My worrying became problematic when I saw my daughter begin to live her life in this kind of familiar dance and I know I contributed to this. When deciding whether to let her journey here or there on the highway at night with people I hardly knew, I remembered all the reckless nights I drove with one eye on the road and one eye on my headlight-lit reflection in the rearview mirror, more concerned with how I appeared to the world than focusing on where I was going. It is both figuratively and literally speaking that I tell you I ran off the road more than a few times, and yet God spared my life.

I have spent my whole life worrying and feeling unsafe. Whether by nature or nurture, and both could be argued, I have always considered the worst outcome when second guessing even the most mundane things. Should I take a walk? Go on a girls' weekend trip? Have dinner out or at home Saturday night? I was afraid of everything. The dark, the future, needles, the stranger lurking on the corner. Later on, there'd be a few times when I'd convinced myself that I was letting fear rule me, but then I'd struggle to discern fear from intuition. Like the time I took my kids for a walk through the neighborhood. I'd always been nervous to do this, and I soon found out the danger didn't exist solely in my imagination. Our neighborhood was sketchy. There was once an early-morning raid with sharpshooters crouched in the bushes at the house across the street and frequent late-night trespassers that would often greet my husband when he came home from a gig at two or three in the morning. "Hey, man. Can I charge my phone?" Absolutely not.

When Māya was about five years old and Brady was three, I took their little hands in mine and we set off down our street for a walk. We never saw any other kids playing in the neighborhood. What we did see was the occasional stumbling woman with crazy eyes, a mumbling drunk man with the thousand-yard stare, an antisocial dog walker with a giant stick, and an elderly man with his strict no-eye-contact policy in a full-tilt power walk.

Just when I was starting to relax into the blue-sky day, a large dog jumped the fence and came tearing after us. "Don't look back," I told the kids. "Don't run." I was trying to lift both kids on either hip when a large SUV came rolling up the street. With the dog growling and snapping at my heels, I thought the safest choice was to jump in the vehicle with this stranger. I flagged him down. It didn't occur to me that he would be anything other than a savior until we were in his car with the doors closed and he began to drive away.

"Thank you so much for picking us up. I thought that dog was gonna eat us alive." He looked at me awkwardly with no response and it sent a chill down my spine. The thought occurred to me that it's possible we jumped into the car with the second coming of Jeffrey Dahmer. He was not at all making me feel safe. "Uh, thanks. You can drop us down the street." We hopped out of the SUV and started toward home. A decade of gentrification passed before we dared to take another walk through the neighborhood. My body remembered this feeling of unsafety and added it to the many I already carried.

Sometimes I have to tell myself to just chill the eff out. I remind myself constantly that God is in control. I read once that when stressed or worried or even just exasperated by the struggle to yank on my skinny jeans, sometimes I just have to sit (or throw myself) down on the floor, close my eyes, and imagine myself in God's holy velvet-covered armchair. I remind myself that I am here for a purpose and I am not alone in my endeavor to fulfill it. I sought to unlearn my maternal grandmother's efforts to teach my mother and her siblings that God was a punishing God.

I honestly don't remember who it was that said, "Don't pray for patience or God will give you plenty of opportunities to learn it." In my memory, that person is just a floating body, with no face and no gender, but their words stuck in my brain for years. After believing for so long that life is a series of pass-or-flunk tests administered by God, I became exhausted by the notion that God tests me constantly. It was the exasperated cry of my seventeen-year-old daughter that called my attention to this learned thought pattern. She loves God, but wholly rejects the idea that God dangles carrots and hands out endless exams. The girl craves a deeply loving, protecting creator.

I know we have free will, and I won't claim to understand how God works. Just knowing this holy presence exists both inside me and around me, cultivating stillness in that knowledge, is enough for me. Not so much for my young adult daughter. She's a self-professed control freak (sorry about that, baby), and because she is wise well beyond her years, she already recognizes this about herself. She possesses a deep knowing that guides her spiritual journey, but it's accompanied by an almost ever-present sense of anxiety. Sometimes, if I look at her at just the right angle, I can still see her baby cheeks, and I'm reminded of how these fear-based control issues once masqueraded as the stubbornness of a strong-willed toddler hell-bent on getting her way. Try as I might, I can't download my experiences to my children's brains and help them skip past the faith-building, undergirding experiences life throws at us. I hear my childhood friend Christy's words in my head, "Apples, meet the tree you fell off of."

I've recently learned to disregard these thoughts of God testing me as soon as they come into my head, but they still come regularly. So, this morning when I went on my walk and my breath was short, my neck and knees hurt, my hips ached, and it felt less like a walk and more like pulling cinder blocks behind me, I thought, *You should be happy with your body when you're working out and you're eating right even when it doesn't look perfect, even when there are fleshy arms and chubby thighs and your body aches like all hell. You should be happy with your body when you can manage to move it, even when you feel like a ten-pound hen shoved into a five-pound sack.*

My habitual thoughts revert to the teacher-God. *Maybe I have chronic pain because I need to learn gratitude for this body whose shape I have fought against for decades?* Surely, that's toxic thinking, a product of a busy, anxious mind that convinces me that I am in control, that God would smite me with mysterious chronic illnesses just to undo a lifetime of hating my curviness. Mindfully, I try to counter that thought with this thought: *Hey, maybe your body needs rest today. Remember to express gratitude tomorrow whenever movement comes easier.*

Trip, Fall, and Die

When my kids were babies, and my husband was away or working late, I crafted a ritual prayer to combat the crippling anxiety and fearful thoughts that plagued all of my days and nights. It was sort of reminiscent of the prayers you'd say as a kid: "God, please protect my mom, dad, sister, grandparents, uncles, aunts, cousins, pets, friends, cousins' pets, friends' pets, the family of ants on the sidewalk . . ." This prayer said, "Please grant us supernatural favor, supernatural protection, supernatural healing, and supernatural wisdom. Send us help right when we need it. Please keep us on your path for our lives. Please grant us wholeness, health, and togetherness throughout the youth of our children, through graduations and marriages and grandbabies and their graduations too. When we need medical care, or miraculous rescue and healing, please deliver it to us in your perfect timing with a favor that transcends all human understanding. Let us always seek to be closer to you and love one another the way you call us to."

Every time those scary thoughts skittered across my mind, which was daily and sometimes even hourly, I met them with this prayer, taking captive each thought and holding it up to the light of what I knew about God and his promises. As far as I was concerned, we had a deal. I would pray and believe in him and in turn, he would protect me and honor my prayer. Because my anxiety was so profound, it was nearly debilitating, and I uttered this prayer multiple times a day. Like magic angel dust blown from my palm, it settled into all crevices of my mind and in every cell in my body. Eventually, I adapted a shortened version of it, looking heavenward and simply saying, "You know!" I was concerned that it could be insulting to God to continue to repeat this prayer ad nauseam. Eventually, instead of praying, I began to give thanks. "God, thank you for your supernatural favor, supernatural protection, supernatural healing, and supernatural wisdom." After a while, the shortened version became, "Thank you!" My editor and friend, Betsy, once shared this one with me, "I can't, you can. Please do, Amen." While I still have thoughts of all the worst-case scenarios, my prayers calm me enough that I can see these thoughts as simply a habit of my anxious mind, not an intuitive warning. Clinging to this abiding faith would sustain me time and time again in the years to come.

The Movie in My Head

When my nephew Grant was little, he always did this thing where he'd fight imaginary opponents in his head. He'd jump around as if dodging enemies and swinging a mighty sword. He called it "doing his movie in his head." Is the chandelier rattling in the dining room? Oh, that's just Grant doing his movie in his head. You could see the focus and joyous abandon of everything around him. It was clear he liked the way things were playing out. He'd created one with a good ending, and then later, I imagine, other variations of it, and he'd play them over and over again in his mind. In the movies in his head, he was always the victor.

When I was about seven years old, Mom was out late one night and instead of having the wild fantasies of youth, I imagined her car being crushed head-on by a semi. The adrenaline of those thoughts and the feeling of being unsafe, soon followed by the relief of the key in the door, created an underlying anxiety and chronic stomachache. It wasn't until well into middle age that I began to recognize these suck-holey thoughts as something I could try to manage by rewriting them in my mind. This would allow me to play out a new scenario, always with a humorous or happy ending, tinged with a warm cinematic light. I don't always catch myself before I spiral. Sometimes, it's mid-spiral, but I persist, reframing the myriad terrors in my mind.

One night while lying in bed, I closed my eyes to sleep and a dark, greenish-blue sea appeared in my mind. I'm in the murky water, a single leaf rippling beside me. I can see myself, as if from a distance. I'm laughing, head thrown back with abandon. My guard is down. First, I hear then feel the snap of my leg. The movie in my head shows my leg being crushed between the jaws of a shark. Sharks are the monsters of my dreams. I open my eyes to make it stop.

I realize that I will have to close my eyes again eventually, so I know I have to rewrite the story. Will I still get in the water? Yes. Will I be mindful of all the scary facts I've learned from years and years of Shark Week? Yes, one cannot unlearn those things. (You might be wondering why, if I'm terrified of sharks, would I watch Shark Week religiously? My dad once told me it's good to know your enemies, so I collect shark attack facts and statistics the same way I collect seashells from the shore.) No shiny metals on your swimsuit and don't wear any jewelry lest you appear as a fish to a shark passing by. Don't get in the ocean on your period. I broke all those rules as a stoned teenager, floating on my back in the ocean, adorned in silver jewelry from the local surf shop. Probably had my period at least a few times too. I shudder to think.

In my movie's rewrite, I'm still happy, still smiling, still enjoying the water. I imagine myself safe and guarded by God, by angels. Not just this once, but once and for all. Eternally held. Eternally shielded. Eternally safe and loved, warmed by that golden light of happy endings. It takes constant daily work to rewrite the movies in my head. In an act of solidarity, I wrote a letter to my children, who are similarly afflicted.

Dearest loves,

I know you fear endings, heartache, and unexpected change. When I think of you two out in there in the world without me by your side, I can feel that fear deep in my gut, gripping every inch of me. Some bad things are likely to come to pass, but in the present moment, instead of anticipating those events, try to let your shoulders drop and loosen your white-knuckle grip on what you think should happen next, because no matter what happens, you will always be okay again. You will smile again. God gave us the ability to feel so many emotions, so don't squander all that isn't happiness. Sadness, anger, fear, joy: feel it. Learn from it or don't—I know you hate the idea of pain as a teacher, but you're free to let that go too. Few of these things are permanent. They all pass eventually. Knowing this is the key to surviving anything. You are so strong.

I know you worry about making mistakes and being vulnerable. I learned the secret to surviving both from American-Tibetan Buddhist nun Pema Chödrön, who said, "Everything that occurs is not only usable and workable, but is actually the path itself. We can use everything that happens as the means for waking up."

I know you fear losing loved ones. The younger version of myself was often stricken with worry about this terrifying possibility. But every morning when the day broke (the terror is always worse in the absence of light) I was less afraid. During the day I moved through the world on high alert and at night I often slept with the light on, but the key is I continued to move through the world. Over the years, worry, fear, and self-doubt have begun to ease up, and most of the time, I'm quick to reframe the intrusive ideations with a more positive bent. From time to time, I have to talk myself down from the paralyzing fear of my runaway thoughts. It takes practice.

You see, those feelings of fear and worry become habits, creating deep neural pathways in our minds. That pathway becomes your mind's default until you start to tell yourself a new story. A story that says, "I am safe. I am protected. I am enough." Then your thoughts have a new path to take and that path is the way to freedom. I think this is what it means to have a childlike faith. Say this out loud when you need to, "I am safe."

Before we know it, we've lived enough anxious, self-conscious days to decide we want to live the rest of them so completely, with such abandon, that we long to make up for those we've squandered on fear. That's the wrong word because nothing is truly squandered here. Everything we experience, both good and bad, fortifies us and we become more enlightened humans.

I know that scares you because you're tender and nostalgic and you want to take the past into the future with you. And you will, but just know this: you will never long for that former version of yourself. Every day you become the truest, wisest, best version of yourself. So, keep doing your movie in your head and make it a magical ending.

*All my love,
Mama*

The Dinner Party Guest

Not too long ago, I went to a dinner party at my sister's house where I hit it off with a friend of my sister I'd never met before. She was a decade or so older and possessed a striking natural beauty and poise. I filed away her image in my mind as something to aspire to one day. We started talking about wellness and natural approaches to disease. This conversation usually starts when a thoughtful host, in this case my sister, points out to me what all I can and can't eat based on food intolerances and in consideration of the anti-inflammatory diet necessary to manage my chronic pain.

Of course, whenever natural approaches come up in conversation, talk of pharmaceuticals usually follows, and this conversation was no exception. When this happens, I always have to tell the Chris Rock joke about the drug ads on late-night TV that list symptoms that we all experience from time to time. In a commercial-like voice he says something like, "If you go to bed at night and wake up in the morning, this medication could help you." "Oh shit! I go to bed at night and I wake up in the morning! I need that drug!" My paraphrasing and comedic timing was polished by having told it many times, but I don't think she got it. She's polite and fun so she laughed.

Before long, somebody else mentioned all the side effects they always list off in the advertisements, and this is when my new friend piped up, very matter-of-factly, and wrecked me. She said, "You have to understand, the drug does both what it says it's going to do *and* all the things that the warnings say it might do. It's not, perhaps, you may or may not have the side effects. You will have these side effects because it's doing both the good and the bad, not one or the other."

"Both!" she said loudly, like an exclamation point. She went on, "It is a trade-off because all pharmaceuticals are *poison*." I suddenly couldn't focus on anything else anyone was contributing to the conversation. Poison was all I could think about. Was I really poisoning my body? Poison? My OCD engaged with that word.

Poison. Poison. Poison.

I couldn't focus. After doing the work of managing an entire lifetime of severe anxiety and daily, nay hourly, intrusive thoughts, I'd finally allowed my doctor to put me back on medication. This medicine had worked for me when I had postpartum depression after our second child was born, and even before that when I went through a tough time just after high school.

This time she'd prescribed it to me to help with the exhaustion and brain fog of having long COVID, but I quickly found some relief from my anxiety along with help in overcoming post-COVID symptoms. Sometimes we grow so accustomed to a prolonged state of being, like say, anxious, that it's only in the absence of it that we recognize we had been suffering all along. That's what happened in my case.

At only a half of a dose, this medication seemed like a good trade, a safe trade from the spiraling bad thoughts for which I was particularly adept. I have a track record with medications: after being on the medication for a while, I sense it could be even better, that my relief from anxiety could be even greater, so I move up to the full dose, the therapeutic dose. I usually do well on the baby dose, considering my small frame, so when being medicated for anything, I rarely take the adult recommended dose. Unfortunately, not too long into the treatment, the medicine seems to stop working. Maybe it builds up in my system because my metabolism is as slow as an ancient sloth, and I begin to have bad side effects. Regardless, I usually freak out and quit. Then, at some point, I will inevitably start all over again with the low dose.

For a while my symptoms improved even more and my chronic pain, which was said to be from a condition called fibromyalgia and believed to be a result of having had undiagnosed Lyme disease for a decade or more, eased up. Once, it was mysteriously gone for two whole days, which was a record amount of time. I tried to sort this out in my head. *I did take NyQuil one night around that time because I had one drink earlier in the evening.* I can't even have one drink because my constitution is that of a delicate flower and if I have even one alcoholic drink, then I won't sleep at all. Instead, I'll lie in bed and launch into Olympic-level overthinking matches.

That run-on sentence is an example of how my mind operates when it's time for sleep.

My body: Oh hey, girl. It's time for sleep. Yay!

My mind: Naw, you got ninety-nine problems to solve before dawn and sleep ain't one.

So maybe the acetaminophen that's in the NyQuil is the reason I didn't have any pain for two days? For most everyone else it only lasts for a few hours, maybe twelve, but like I said, I'm a slow metabolizer. Either way, I was headed in the right direction because my mind wasn't screwing with me all day every day. I wasn't having scary, anxious thoughts or creating terrible scenarios in my head. And then this elegant, easy-going stranger just took a wrecking ball to all that because, hear me on this, *anxious people are anxious about taking medicine.*

In a recent interview with Russell Brand, Michael Singer, author of *The Untethered Soul*[8], talks about the

---

8. Singer, Michael. *The Untethered Soul*. Oakland, California: New Harbinger Publications, 2007.

"personal mind" that tells us, "I believe this, I don't believe that. I really like this, but I don't like that. I hope this or that happens. I really hope this or that doesn't happen." He tells us to challenge the voice in our head that says if something is uncomfortable then it was not meant to be. He calls these thoughts "personal noise" and says they cause us to judge life and tell us how to make life be our way instead of honoring and respecting life and letting it unfold as it may.

My takeaway from that is this: our thoughts/emotions/fears can't always be trusted. Neither can our long-held fears and beliefs. They need to be reexamined. When we let those restrictions be the guiding force in our lives, perhaps we miss out on a lot. To paraphrase Singer, "Your great-great-great-grandmother had to meet your great-great-great-grandfather, all those years ago, for you to be here today. Every single event that has occurred, both good and bad, had to happen in order for the thing in front of us to happen that we are now judging." So, what if we listen to life instead? Why not do what my friend Bob Graham always says when things get tough, and just "stay in the river"? Flow with it.

So if I need medicine and it works, why should I conversely be led by my fears about the medication's side effects? Why not gratefully accept that I benefit from Western medicine? If I think like Singer and listen to life as it unfolds, I would see that it is helping me in this stage of my life and I would allow that truth to guide me and not some fear or preconceived belief in my head. I would not subscribe to the voice that says this medication should be feared because it is poison. Perhaps it's blanket statements like hers, "All medications are poison" that have the potential to do us the most harm.

Singer's whole idea of judging or not judging the events of life reminds me of this parable.

A farmer and his son had a beloved horse who helped the family earn a living. One day, the horse ran away and their neighbors exclaimed, "Your horse ran away. What terrible luck!" The farmer replied, "Maybe so, maybe not."

A few days later, the horse returned home, leading a few wild horses back to the farm as well. The neighbors shouted out, "Your horse has returned and brought several horses home with him. What great luck!" The farmer replied, "Maybe so, maybe not."

Later that week, the farmer's son was trying to break one of the horses and she threw him to the ground, breaking his leg. The neighbors cried, "Your son broke his leg. What terrible luck!" The farmer replied, "Maybe so, maybe not."

A few weeks later, soldiers from the national army marched through town, recruiting all boys for the army. They did not take the farmer's son, because he had a broken leg. The neighbors shouted, "Your boy is spared. What tremendous luck!" To which the farmer replied, "Maybe so, maybe not. We'll see."

When I first read this parable, I was giddy at the idea of perceiving negative circumstances as potential impetus for something good and perhaps even celebrated in the long run. Interestingly enough, when I shared this parable with my stepmom, she saw just the opposite. "So that means what I perceive as good might actually be bad?" Perspective is everything.

Ultimately, I decided to stay the course and let my time with this medication offer me some relief which thankfully it did. I had been worried that it would numb me. I worried I wouldn't be able to tap into my deeper, more contemplative (i.e.: darker) side as easily, and the well of humor I use to cope with my anxieties would dry up. I feared the writing wouldn't flow. (Rest assured, friends, I'm as tortured and deeply disturbed as ever. What writer worth their salt isn't?) I had no trouble weening off the medicine and will be quick to take it again in the future should I need it.

As for the woman at the dinner party, I'm grateful for having met her. I'm okay with people challenging my beliefs and sharing theirs. I am learning to trust myself to know what's good for me. I'm learning to examine long-held beliefs that might be challenged when held up to the light. Are all medications poisons? Maybe so. Maybe not.

You're Exhausted

I sat across from the intuitive healer, eager and open, awaiting a revelation.

"You're exhausted," she replied. Holly, the healer, was beautiful, and something in her eyes told me she knew things.

It was true, if not anticlimactic. I'd expected her to point her all-knowing finger at which among my cadre of ailments was the worst offender, thus illuminating the path forward toward healing. Instead, she declared me bone-tired and said my home was extremely dusty, both of which are true.

Rest is not something that has ever come easily to me. Turning out the lights at night seems to send my mind into hyperdrive. Everything that I should be worried about dances to life, doing the do-si-do with giant exclamation marks behind my closed eyes. DANGER! WRONG WAY! WHAT IF? I am overcome with the need to know the exact whereabouts of my young adult children. What are they even doing with their lives? Do they know? Do they have a plan? Are they safe?

Most of my life I had felt afraid of being alone at night, which made me cling to people and rituals of comfort that didn't always serve me. Let's recall that I married a musician who is almost never home at night. My body ached from being in a constant state of tension. Darkness was more foreboding. I have spent too many hours of my precious time on Earth shadowboxing because I'd be ready when life landed its punch, dammit. I wonder now why I didn't think myself qualified to keep myself safe. Why, when the kids were little, did it never fail to surprise me that I was the only adult in the house?

After a childhood and young adulthood of flailing nonachievement in academics, I built a life around being productive and centered my value on my accomplishments. I had children that people enjoyed being around, in part because they are lovely humans, but also because I raised them to be palatable to others. I taught them, unknowingly and by example, to morph themselves into accommodating, polite people that can assimilate into any environment, and also, regrettably, to tamp down their self-expression whenever it didn't suit the occasion, whenever it was messy, whenever they didn't fit. I'd handed down the message I had received as a child: abandon yourself in order to be accepted by others. Squash your big feelings in order to be easy and likeable. I'd been a chameleon, morphing into the type of person the social situation called for, whether it was true to me or a total abandonment of self. When your early life is shaped around an abandonment wound, you tend to be loyal to a fault, regardless of whether it is deserved, lest you be abandoned or rejected.

For the longest time, I identified with the label of the black sheep, the high school dropout, the free spirit at my best, the wayward daughter at my worst. At some point, I realized that if I could identify with my failures, then it only made sense that I could also define myself by my accomplishments. I went back to school at age thirty-eight while working two part-time jobs with kids still at home. After graduation, I launched myself into a project management position building luxury custom houses, an occupation my creative writing degree had left me woefully unqualified for. That turned out to be yet another exhausting three-year uphill climb. Whatever mojo I had left would soon give out.

Over the years, nagging ailments and recurring illnesses continued to worsen until I was faced with a choice: continue working and forsake all other activities that threatened my ability to get through the next workday or wave the white flag and hang up my hard hat. We are not independently wealthy, so quitting wasn't an option. Betraying my true God-given nature and talents in order to better assimilate into what was expected of me, I continually put myself in workplaces I didn't belong, only to realize it in retrospect. Like the time I interviewed for a job and my potential new boss said the entire executive leadership team expressed doubts about my being right for the position since my resume indicated I was a "creative." *Creative* was almost whispered, like a dirty word, the way my elders often whispered *cancer* or *heart attack*. I was awarded that job and as it turns out, it was a terrible fit due in part to my being "a creative." Trying to make that job work was exhausting. Square peg, round hole, square peg, round hole, ad nauseum.

In two and a half years, I'd lost my brother-in-law to cancer, two uncles to COVID-19, a childhood best friend in a mysterious sudden death, and my dog to a fatal cluster of seizures. I got sick with COVID-19 twice, resulting in long COVID, and had over ten thousand dollars in car repairs and ten grand in vet bills in less than a six-month period. During this time, my daughter experienced two health crises that landed her in the hospital twice and made it difficult to get back on her feet each time. My mind was foggy, my body a house of pain. I felt brittle, like I might shatter into a million tiny shards. I couldn't focus on work much less follow new and complicated processes put into place during the pandemic. I was flailing at work. Since I was accustomed to being hit by the battering ram, I didn't recognize these were extenuating circumstances. I should have shouted "mercy" and asked for help. Instead, I just kept going. Punched in the face? I seemed to respond with, "Thank you, sir. May I have another?"

What I learned about trying to earn a valuable spot in people's lives by giving all of yourself away is that eventually there's nothing left to give. You're left with just your "being" and not your "doing." If your self-worth is based on your doing, then what is your value now? Was this lovely clairvoyant woman spot-on when she said sheer exhaustion was responsible for this life of chronic pain, fatigue, and recurring illness? Had I worn myself out by always being on guard and ready for the shoe to drop because as a child it always had? Was I beat down from imagining worst-case scenarios over and over in my head? Was it because my dad had been right all those years ago when we were young, broke, and uneducated and we told him we were pregnant and he said, with a heavy heart, that we had taken the hardest path?

What if I wasn't the one that answered every call from a distressed friend or family member? Would my loved ones spontaneously combust without my constant attention and care? What if I said to myself, "you're okay, you're okay," until I actually believed it?

What if I simply prayed about where I should put my energy and asked God to show me who to help and what to do each day instead of exhausting myself trying to do it all? What if I accepted myself for my tender heart and creativity, not solely for what I can provide to others? Finally, what if I sat on my porch for hours with the ceiling fan tousling my hair and my hammock swing cradling me like a big baby? I could learn the art of resting. I could abandon the idea that I should always be striving, earning, working on some project, worrying over something, or dusting the baseboards? What if I began to imagine the best-case scenarios and told myself that I was talented and kind and worthy just as I am with nothing to offer but my heart? Is this akin to putting on your own oxygen mask first? What if I had been more self-accepting and self-aware to have said to that interviewer, "Yes, I am a creative. If that is not a valued attribute at this company, then perhaps this isn't the right place for me." Would that self-acceptance have saved me from trying so hard to be something I'm not and therefore less tired?

After that ill-fitting job, I had a few weeks off, and eventually I began to sleep at night for the first time in more than two decades. The kids were in college and while they still needed me, it wasn't constant. Our epileptic dog had passed away the year before, so the need to administer meds every twelve hours and the ever-present possibility of seizures no longer loomed constant. Upon hearing about my job loss, an attentive and caring family member quietly anticipated a need and made sure our bank account was such that we could rest easy, and for a while, we did.

Toward the end of my session with the healer, she had me lie down on a massage table while she moved energy around my body with her hands. It's okay if you think this is all hoodoo voodoo, but I am here to tell you that I felt it. I'd told her nothing of my symptoms, so when she declared, "We gotta do something about this low-back pain!" it further solidified my belief in her abilities. Low-back pain had been my worst and most consistent symptom for decades.

"It's been there as long as I can remember yet nothing ever shows up on an MRI or X-ray," I told her.

"That's because it's emotional pain. Imagine a worm-like creature wrapped around your lower back and beginning to push into your gut. I'm going to get it out of there."

She proceeded to move energy around and tell this spirit of pain it was no longer welcome in my body and it needed to go. I felt its exodus and my eyes flooded with tears. *Fuck it*, I thought. I have always tried to hold back my tears, ashamed and embarrassed of how easily they flow. I let them go. I whispered to myself, "I accept your tenderness," as I let them flow down my face, drip into my ears and onto my neck. Whenever there is an emotional scene on television or in a movie we are watching, my husband and kids have always turned to me to see if I'm crying. I used to hate how it made me feel weak and predictable. Now I think maybe it's my superpower.

Going to California

If only she hadn't decided to take that trip, she'd still be here with us today. This was the intrusive thought that I'd been ruminating on for weeks, and the impetus was a wedding invitation. The midnight-blue, gold-speckled invitation arrived in the mail and was accompanied by a gossamer slip of velum that announced further details such as the attire, which was called "celestial romance." I wasn't sure exactly what that looked like, but I was up for it. My friend and former coworker Erika had moved out to Los Angeles a few years prior and was now getting married in February. Her guest list was intimate, only about fifty people or so. I was honored to be included. From my home in North Carolina to her wedding destination, Malibu, California, was a distance of 2,500 miles. I had enough frequent flier miles for the trip, thanks to the extensive travel required of me by my employer at the time.

I booked the flight and then almost immediately began doubting the wisdom of my choice. I imagined reckless Uber drivers, faulty plane equipment, random sidewalk attacks, numerous trip-fall-and-die scenarios. In the few weeks leading up to the trip, that Alanis Morissette song looped annoyingly in my brain. It wasn't ironic.

Was it? There was an ongoing battle, an occupation in my brain, where the valiant idea of spontaneity was always chopped down by the sword of fear. Would I be safe? Was this a good choice? Could I travel safely alone?

I had a lifelong history of making choices very few people in my life understood or agreed with and this fact left me second-guessing my own judgment. Another roadblock of spontaneity and fun was managing a chronic pain illness that required carefully measuring out my activities and the energy they required so I didn't end up bedridden simply because I wanted to have a little adventure. If I was lucky, I might have an experience that awakens my atrophied soul and reminds me there's life to be lived outside the cycle of earn, sleep, spend, repeat. These adventures I say yes to often end up being a transformative experience, and ultimately something worth writing about. Still, I almost always need a week to physically recover.

The flight to LAX was blessedly uneventful. The weather was surprisingly comfortable for February and the sun was bright. My friend of more than two decades, Yushing, gathered me from the airport and took me out for poke bowls and a long overdue evening of catching up.

The next day I awoke with the familiar gnawing of chronic pain throbbing in my head and aching in my back. Going from East-coast time to West-coast time had made for an uncharacteristically long day, and my body wasn't having it.

I relished the fact that I did not have to respond to the work emails that regularly piled up two or three dozen an hour. I grabbed an orange and a sparkling lemon magnesium and CBD-infused water from the mini fridge in my room and slid open the balcony door that overlooked Marina Del Rey. The warm air surprised me. The forecast showed it was going to be a chilly week. I pulled an ottoman over to a patch of sunlight and watched as a paddle boarder made his way around the bay below.

Once the magnesium water and Motrin eased my pain, I got dressed in my comfy wide-leg jeans, high-top sneakers, an ivory button-up sweater, and green army coat. Traveling alone for pleasure for the first time seemed like an occasion to document, so I took a selfie in the full-length mirror. Did I look hip enough for a day in Venice? I decided probably not, but I was comfortable and feeling decent so I called an Uber.

I ate a glorious vegan cheese pizza with a cauliflower crust at The Butcher's Daughter. I'd stalked this pizza via IG posts for many months now. I poked around the shops, falling in love with a hand-knit alpaca and wool sweater from a boutique called Flannel—a purchase I could never justify. I took a few photos of myself wearing it and sent them to my indulgent yet sensible husband with a note saying, "Lord help you. I have fallen in love with a sweater that costs more than a car payment." To which he generously replied, "Valentine's Day?" When I protested, he countered with, "Well, if you find you can't be without it and want an unforgettable memento from Venice, then get it." I didn't, but I can't stop thinking about it.

I ended up purchasing a beautiful hand-dyed, hand-sewn, 100 percent cotton, locally made peasant top from an eclectic boutique full of Moroccan imports. It wasn't cheap, but it was a fraction of the cost of the sweater. Though I absolutely adore this beautiful and unique piece, I have yet to wear it. However, I have visited the sweater online and in my camera roll an embarrassing number of times since returning home.

I made my way back to the hotel to dress for the wedding. The invitation said the ceremony was to take place at Malibu Dream Resort, but in the weeks prior, while planning my trip, I could not find such a place on the map. Why were all the hotels an hour away from the venue? I slid on a long-sleeved, rose-pink satin dress with a pattern of dark-green serpents that was a memento from a work trip to San Jose two years earlier. I paired it with wool socks, sleek dark-brown Frye cowboy boots, and topped it with a navy wrap and my army jacket. The bride and groom were of the younger, hipper set, so I thought this was an appropriate deviation from the usual stuffy, formal attire of the weddings I often worked as a side gig. Celestial romance? Not sure if I nailed it, but it would have to do.

The drive down the Pacific Coast Highway was straightforward and the views were stunning. My driver was an older gentleman whose accent indicated an ethnicity I couldn't confirm, so communication wasn't easy, but he possessed a fatherly warmth that was universal. He seemed to make a last-minute decision to exit the PCH with a hard right turn onto California State Road 23 (23 is my lucky number!) and took us up through Decker Canyon. We wound our way up and through the Santa Monica Mountains and the vistas were breathtaking. As we climbed farther and farther from the Pacific Ocean, the road became a harrowing succession of hairpin turns and narrow switchbacks. Some of the curves were so sharp that my driver had to nearly come to a stop to complete the turns. In anticipation of oncoming cars, I held my breath as we rounded each one, but never passed a single car with the exception of a McLaren that was parked on what could barely be considered the road's shoulder about a mile into the ride. My driver had pointed him out to me. I couldn't understand what he said behind his mask, but it was clear he was entertained by the sight. His chuckle I could hear and understand. The man sat in a folding camping chair with his empty hands in his lap, taking in the view. It was not lost on me that the driver of this lightning-fast car appeared to be practicing the art of slowing down.

I laughed too but my laughter immediately gave in to the familiar feeling of fear. My Spidey senses were up. Were there so few cars because this route is so dangerous?

As we climbed higher, I noticed the absence of guardrails. I know I have an anxious disposition, but I am pretty sure that the steep, jagged drops just off the side of the road would have alerted even the most adventurous and carefree passengers. I popped a Zofran under my tongue to counteract the motion-induced nausea that was brewing in my stomach. I zoomed out and took in the long view of the scenery around me. The mountains have a different color here. Different texture, maybe? They looked like yellow petrified sand castles versus the red-clay and evergreen-covered mountains of the Southeast. I'd never traveled through a coastal mountain range, but it made sense they would stand in great contrast to the piney ridges of the mountains back East.

In approximately twenty minutes of being on this stretch of road we'd still passed no cars, save for the McLaren. When a phone call from my stepdad, Ken, ended abruptly, I discovered I'd lost service. Would I be able to get an Uber to pick me up after the wedding? My driver ended up passing the road to the resort, because he misinterpreted the "Private Road" sign as "Do Not Enter."

Once the driver found the space to make the gut-wrenching twelve-point turn that was needed to turn us around without tumbling down the cliffside, we headed back to the road he'd passed and climbed nearly straight up for about a mile. At which point I saw nothing and no one.

"Just take me back to the hotel," I blurted out. "I'll pay you for both trips. I'm afraid I'm not going to be able to get an Uber back here to get me." I was sick with panic at the thought of not being able to get back to LA.

"Are you sure? You want me to take you back?" He was in disbelief.

"Yes, I'm sure. I don't want to be stranded here."

He asked again, "Are you sure?"

I told him I was sure, so he turned around to head back down the steep road. When we finally passed a sleek silver Mercedes driven by an older woman with a matching sleek silver bob, he waved her down and pulled up next to her. "Is there a club up here?" my driver asker her.

"No, not around here," she smiled and waved her hand around.

I called out from the back seat. "I'm supposed to attend a wedding up here. It's somewhere on this road."

She thought for a moment. "There is a private residence at the top of the canyon road that hosts events sometimes. Could be there."

"I'm nervous I won't be able to get an Uber back to town tonight and honestly, the drive up Decker Canyon

Road was terrifying." I started firing off my concerns: no streetlights, no guardrails, tight turns, low visibility, and the narrowest lanes I'd ever seen.

"My friends Uber up here all the time. I've been living here thirty years and never had a problem. As long as you get an experienced driver you should be fine! Don't be scared." My thoughts raced but my mouth failed me. Ubering up here clearly wasn't the issue since I was already in an Uber, lady, and when you call an Uber, you don't get to vet your driver. They can send anybody!

We continued up to the top of the canyon and found a little nondescript marker sitting low to the street that matched the street number on the invitation. The resort ended up not being a resort in the traditional staffed, amenity-filled sense, but a gorgeous oasis in the form of a privately owned mansion that operates as an events space.

My driver had already confirmed Decker Canyon Road was an extremely dangerous road, a road I would later read on dangerousroads.org is described as "long known to locals as the deadliest stretch of road in California." This is the same stretch of road that had claimed the life of Iron Butterfly bassist Phillip Taylor Kramer back in 1995. His wrecked van and his remains were found deep in the roadside ravine by a group of hikers years after his mysterious disappearance.

I arrived just as the ceremony was starting. I slipped into my seat in the back row. I would later learn I was not in Malibu, but in Oxnard, and Oxnard was experiencing what my weather app referred to as a "wind event." The Santa Ana winds were blowing at twenty to thirty miles per hour and punctuated by forty-mile-per-hour gusts. The men maneuvered their bodies to drape themselves over their dates in an attempt to provide warmth and protection from the wind. A few empty chairs were blowing over and we all did our part to hold them in place. My friend and her fiancé, both scientists, stood in front of the officiant with smiles that could light up the darkest black hole. It was the sweetest wedding I'd ever attended. Although I didn't know a soul other than the bride, the love among these people was palpable. When the officiant announced them as the bride and groom, they made their way down the aisle and that's when she saw me. "Shelley!" she mouthed in surprise. I smiled at her with my hands clasped in prayer position, and in that moment, I was so very happy I had made the journey. I loved this girl and if she didn't know before, she knew it now. I would later see a photo of this exact moment of exchange between us. A gift I will treasure forever.

At the top of this rugged mountain overlooking the Pacific Ocean, my dress flapping in the wind, I tried to stay steady. I was among complete strangers so far away from the safety of home. The road back to town was devoid of street lights, gas stations, and guard-rails. Erika and Luke were taking photos and would be occupied for a while, so I decided I would attempt to call an Uber now. If I was successful, I would stay for dinner and dancing. If not, I would figure out a plan B. I tried to call an Uber but I couldn't get a signal.

As the sun began to slip behind the mountain and into the Pacific horizon, that skinless, vulnerable feeling returned. Memories of the time I was a teenager lost on Marijuana Mountain at night in Sleepy Hollow, Kentucky, resurfaced from the vault of my memory. It had been daylight when a friend and I had found our way to the hangout site of a few older boys earlier in the evening, but had turned pitch black when it was time to head home. Away from the light of the campfire, I went from comically stoned to scared sober in a matter of minutes. I walked through those woods in a shiver, certain this would be how I died. We had to find our own way that night, guided by a Holy Spirit whisper nudging us to follow the creek babbling in the darkness down to the road below.

A similar memory of the looming darkness of the mountains surfaced in my mind: years after the incident in Sleepy Hollow, when I followed my mother through the mountains on the way to that new, friendless university to start a life apart from my already splintered family. I strained hard not to lose sight of her for fear I'd find myself stranded. Then again the following evening when I'd decided to go for a short drive only to have the car slog to a dead stop, the mountains looming large and ominous as the sun sank behind them. These fearful, mountain-themed memories, newly resurrected from their long-buried home within my muscle and bone.

I stepped through the courtyard at the center of the mansion and out to the curb, where the valet guys were huddled around a tall kerosene heater. I told them I wasn't able to get an Uber and asked if they had any suggestions.

"We could call you a cab," one of them volunteered.

"That would be great! A cab, a limo, whatever it takes," I replied.

"Hmm. How do we do that?" He turned to his coworkers for advice.

I explained that I didn't know anyone at the wedding besides the bride, and I wasn't about to bother her with my problem and I definitely didn't want to ride down the perilous mountain road with any guests after they'd been drinking all evening. We stood around, spit-balling ideas.

"Once our boss gets here, he'll know what to do. Maybe even give you a ride," one valet offered.

"I could give you a ride to Marina Del Rey if you pay me what you paid for an Uber to get here," offered the only valet that I definitely wouldn't get in the car with.

The other two seemed genuinely concerned about my well-being.

"Well, thanks, but if you didn't kill me my husband certainly would just for getting in the car with you."

After what felt like an eternity, a lady that appeared to be in her late fifties strolled past us toward the parking lot.

"Excuse me! Did you drive here?" Once the words were out of my mouth, I realized what an odd question I'd asked.

"Yes, I drove here." She had such a warm smile and calm demeanor I immediately trusted her.

"I know this is odd, but I am thousands of miles from home and I don't know a soul other than the bride. I took an Uber here, but my app says the service is unavailable in my area. I have tried for over an hour. Is there any chance you would be willing to drive me down to civilization where I might be able to call an Uber? A gas station, restaurant, or a hotel?"

"Hi. My name is Bonnie," was her reply.

"Oh, right. Sorry! Hi. I'm Rachelle. Er, Shelley." I forgot for a moment who I was at this event.

"Let me go get my harp and I will give you a ride. Be right back."

I smiled with relief. Leave it to me to find the musician. She had been clinging to her instrument on the side of the mountain during the windblown ceremony. I turned around to catch two of the valets smiling and giving me a thumbs-up. I was flooded with relief, but it was short-lived. Twenty or so minutes had passed and she hadn't returned to get me. I thought maybe I'd made her uncomfortable and she'd ditched me. After all, to put a stranger in her car was too much to ask of a woman traveling by herself.

"Y'all, I think she ditched me. Would she have to drive back by this way to leave or is there another way out?"

"I don't think there is another way out. She probably didn't ditch you."

"Okay. I'm going to go back inside and see if I can find a house phone so I can try to call a car service."

The guys agreed to come get me if she came back while I was gone. I found the wedding planner pretty easily and she handed me a cordless phone. Between the noise of the guests and the incompatibility of the phone and my hearing aids, I couldn't even hear a dial tone. I handed it back to the planner, who was busy with another task, and caught sight of the valet guy in the courtyard knocking on the French door.

"She came back for you! Come on!" His face was lit with excitement.

Bonnie was waiting for me in a Toyota Highlander, the exact car I drive every day back home. I got in and apologized for putting her in the position of having a stranger in her car. The ride down the mountain was slow and gentle in an almost exaggerated way. It was as though God himself had picked up the car, gingerly carried it down the mountain, and set us down carefully on the PCH. We chatted comfortably and discovered we had writing in common. She was writing a book too.

Bonnie pulled into the Miramar on Wilshire where the concierge, an older gentleman with gray hair and a wide smile, stepped out to greet me with a warm handshake. He called a car to take me back to my hotel in Marina Del Ray while Bonnie and I said our goodbyes. I waited inside the golden-lit hotel lobby and swallowed the lump in my throat. I had been cared for and protected every step of the way.

God had showed up for me in the form of a Holy Spirit whisper that dark night on Marijuana Mountain and again years later when I was following Mom through the mountains on the way to college. I never lost sight of her as I feared I might. The next day, when my car broke down in the small mountain town, an angel dressed as a police officer guided me safely back to campus. I thought back to the saviors of my past: Sandy the Hippie, MaryAnn the Psychic, the Diner Prophet, and now Bonnie the Harpist.

A particularly enchanting song, "Infinity and Beyond" by Ennio Morricone, came on during my Uber ride home from that trip. The coincidence of the song title was not lost on me. This trip had proven there was no great distance I could travel that could separate me from God's perfect care, care that stretches from East to West, and to borrow from the song, to infinity and beyond. I'd spent my whole life searching for one thing I could hold onto only to discover I had been holding it loosely all these years: faith in one hand, fear in the other. Now I knew it was time, once again, to open my palm and release the fear.

The day after I returned home, I was tired and sore, beached like a sick whale in our king-size bed, my husband beside me, our limbs overlapping. There was the usual pain, yes, but something new and different was within. I felt a burning ember, a powerful knowing in my core that God was with me. I mean really with me. Not just with me if I stay geographically local with carefully made plans, where loved ones can look out for me, guide me to safety, and care for me when I am sick. Within me was a knowing that I'm allowed to embark on adventure without fear of certain doom the way it so often plays out in my head. God and the angels had provided me perfect care in the faraway Santa Monica Mountains. As my friend Jen Pastiloff, author of *On Being Human*, always says, "I get to have this."

True to form, a few days after my return from LA, I felt awful. My chest tightened and buzzed as though it were filled with a swarm of bees, making it hard to breathe. My hands and feet went numb. I'd been having stomach issues as I am prone to do, likely from taking so many Zofran and Motrin on the trip. I debated going to the hospital and instead asked my husband to get me a baby aspirin and tried to convince myself it was my usual ailments combined with a panic attack. It had been nearly two decades since I'd had one. This one had started in my body and not as a result of anything ruminating in my mind, for once.

Just a few months ago, I'd gone to the ER after having chest pains and shortness of breath and it was a miserable all-night experience. Jason had arrived straight from a gig and was visibly annoyed at being there since he believes that if you're well enough to drive yourself to the ER, you're probably safe to wait till the next day for the less expensive and less miserable experience of the urgent care variety. I wasn't having a heart attack, though it had felt like it. I'd had a reaction to an IV solution I'd received the day before as part of my ongoing treatment for Lyme disease.

As I lay there weighing my options, I remembered my prayer. I'd always prayed for supernatural healing just when we needed it, supernatural protection, and supernatural favor. Didn't God just show me that in the Santa Monica Mountains? Is my memory that short? Will I always be a Doubting Thomas, searching for the holes pierced through flesh? Would God go to all that trouble just to wipe me from this Earth right here in my bed? No, I prayed for supernatural healing and I believed I would receive it. I released the fear and held onto my faith with both hands. I calmed myself with a few deep breaths. Despite the tightness in my chest and my pounding heart, I told myself this was a panic attack, not a heart attack. I anchored myself in this truth and in this moment. I was safe and I belonged here. The tightness in my chest started to ease.

All my life I had longed for people that would stand by me and I'd found them. I searched high and low for a place I could call my own, and I'd found it here in my perfectly imperfect family and in our community of friends. I wished for love and acceptance and I worked to cultivate it within myself and to give it to others. I sought after God and ended up finding the God of my understanding outside the walls of the church, deep within my heart where God had been all along. I found a spirituality that aligned with my beliefs, a faith whose fight song claims one love for all who seek it.

I reflected on this as my body continued to shift from tense to calm. Muscle, tendon, and bone easing, releasing. In this moment, I was not skinless. I was covered, protected, seen, heard, and loved. My fiercest guard, our hound dog Pearl, settled into her spot near my feet. I took off my glasses, reached across the king-size bed, and gave my husband a kiss goodnight. I bowed my head in thanks for my life, for all the pain and joy of the past and all the goodness the future surely holds. While I knew I was safe in this moment, I knew full well that my mind and body would likely turn on me again tomorrow. I settled in for rest, legs and arms spread wide. Like a starfish.

A Streak of Tigers

There's a feeling I've chased for as long as I can remember. It's a peaceful flutter, not in the belly but closer to the solar plexus. It's similar to the butterflies, but instead of a sense of anticipation or excitement, it's a feeling that all's right with the world. I described it to my friend Allison once and she recognized it right away. I needed to know that other people had felt this too and hoped they'd know the secret to calling it forth. Best I can tell, it seems to happen during special moments, like when my kids are home from college for a holiday and my husband is not out gigging but at home with us. We're all getting along and laughing together, the dogs curled up like half-moons around us. I think it's a sensation that only comes in the absence of fear and the presence of gratitude. Fear and gratitude sound like such simple words, yet they're not simple concepts for those whose bodies remember trauma.

I recently started chasing another similar feeling that occurs about ten to fifteen minutes into an acupuncture session. Shortly after the needles are in place, the light is dimmed, and the door is closed, the sensation arrives. It feels like I have a power adapter and someone has yanked the cord free from the wall. It's a welcome and rare feeling of complete relaxation that I look forward to. Only recently did I come to understand that it signals a powerful process is taking place in my body. My spirit, along with a chaotic energy that often runs a few feet out ahead of me, lands in my body and melts into the table beneath me. It's a reunion of mind, body, and spirit, yes, but something critical to my health is happening on a biological level.

A deeper understanding of what was happening in these moments came when I met a new acupuncturist, Ben. My friend Meg had been working with him and she felt he could get me to a deeper place of healing, both spiritually and physically. When I arrived at his office, my neck was killing me because my right shoulder was on an uphill climb toward my ear. An aching tightness had begun to restrict my mobility. I've always had neck and back pain, but since I'd undergone treatment for breast cancer the month prior, it had become unbearable. Scar tissue and tension from multiple surgeries, a month of radiation with my right arm awkwardly stretched over my head, and holding that right side in a protective posture could easily explain the pain. But I knew I'd been walking around in a sort of what-the-shit-just-happened-to-me-and-what's-gonna-happen-next posture and couldn't relax my mind or my upper body.

I'd been diagnosed with breast cancer just three weeks after my mom's breast cancer diagnosis. Mother and daughter marooned on the same island, but unable to do much for one another while we recovered from surgeries and tried our best to manage our fear and exhaustion. Somehow, two weeks post-mastectomy, she rallied enough to sit in the waiting room, with four drains protruding from her chest, while our surgeon removed the cancer from *my* breast this time. Her presence that day is proof there's no other earthly force as powerful as a mother's love.

During our initial appointment, Ben reviewed my medical history, his salt-and-pepper eyebrows knitted together, head nodding with the kind of deep knowing acquired by his five decades of experience. He scanned the page: Lyme disease, fibromyalgia, chronic inflammatory response syndrome, Epstein-Barr virus, breast cancer . . .

"I think I know what might be going on with you, but I'd like to do some muscle testing to confirm."

He instructed me to hold my right arm out straight and strong while he tried to push it down. This was to gauge my strength, and in this position I was strong.

"Great. Now put your left hand on your head, palm down, and try again."

I had zero strength, which indicated to him what he'd suspected. I was what he called switched.

"Your nervous system is switched on. You're in a state of fight or flight. It happens like this. If you encountered a tiger, you'd panic and your instinct to either fight the tiger or flee from the tiger would be activated. Your heart would race, adrenaline pumping through your body. When the tiger is gone, your body should switch back to rest and repair. You've just not switched back. You're stuck. There's no point in treating anything else until we can get your body back to rest and repair so you can begin to heal. Cancer is often the last stop on this journey."

He placed some needles in my ears and instructed me to zone out. There I was on the table, in the dark, consciously trying to relax, when, through no effort of my own, my whole body shifted on what felt like a cellular level, a place so deep I couldn't reach it in my own power. It can best be described this way: my power switch was flipped to the off position. This was the feeling of being in a state of rest and repair, a place where the body can truly heal itself. If bliss really exists, this is it. Though I have experienced it several dozen times now, I recall so clearly how foreign it was to me.

Through writing this book, I have come to understand I have been switched on, ready for battle for as long as I can recall. Growing up, I'd been knocked down by one big, scary wave of change and trauma after another. No sooner had I pulled my feet from the quickening sand, another would come fast in its wake and flatten me. A streak of tigers had been chasing me as far back as I could remember and they'd followed me into every relationship and every job I'd ever had, making me a time bomb of emotion and my body a host for illness and pain. It was in this state of dysregulation that I started a family, causing further instability for myself, my husband, and, most regrettably, for our children.

Jason had also come to this marriage young and emotionally ill-prepared for the challenge of raising a family, one that always teetered on the brink of existence. For decades there would be more tigers in the form of outrageous bills, dying cars, dying parents, dangerously low bank accounts, ongoing and sometimes frightening dysfunction in our families of origin, and a glaring lack of tools to keep misunderstandings from becoming more traumas. I don't think we are special in this experience by any stretch of the imagination. The more I talk about trauma and its effect on the body and post about it on social media, the more my contemporaries share how close they are to losing their marriages, how their health is suffering, and often how their children are showing signs of having inherited ancestral trauma.

The concept of something as simple and accessible as regulating a dysregulated nervous system is potentially life-changing. Trauma therapy, talk therapy, meditation, mindfulness, and other methods such as EMDR (eye movement desensitization and reprocessing) can help heal our minds and bodies, improve our relationships, and change the legacies of the generations to come. Could this be the way to end generational trauma? When we can identify and examine our triggers, we can lower the tension we carry in our bodies and we can affect our immunity by working to stay in a state of rest and repair. I believe that recognizing this dysregulation in ourselves and others could help us heal our physical bodies and our spirits by awakening a deep sense of compassion for one another, recognizing that sometimes long-buried past hurts can cause us to react harshly to one another.

If we can stop the vicious cycle of impulsive responses and refuse to believe our lizard brains when they try to convince us the world is ending, our bodies can settle and remain in a state of ease. In the beat it takes to examine our impulsive reactions, our relationships can be saved and our bodies don't have to pay the high price of dysregulation, thus we can begin to live our lives with a true authenticity of spirit. When we embrace our authentic selves, a feeling of true belonging radiates from within. This allows us to honor the feelings and reactions of others without perceiving their actions as personal attacks. From what I can tell, this is a process that gets easier with practice but never really ends, and I'm okay with that.

This quote by Eckhart Tolle is one I return to time and time again when I'm triggered by feelings of impending abandonment.

"To offer no resistance to life is to be in a state of grace, ease, and lightness. This state is then no longer dependent upon things being a certain way, good or bad. It seems almost paradoxical, yet when your inner dependency on form is gone, the general conditions of your life, the outer forms, tend to improve greatly. Things, people, or conditions that you thought you needed for your happiness now come to you with no struggle or effort on your part, and you are free to enjoy and appreciate them—while they last. All those things, of course, will pass away, cycles will come and go, but with dependency gone there is no fear of loss anymore. Life flows with ease."

Through an understanding of what my body has been through on a cellular level, and working to regulate my nervous system, I am beginning to feel healthier, experience less pain, and rest better. When I am centered physically and emotionally, I can approach life from a neutral place, not one of reactiveness, shadowboxing, and fear. There's a new softness to my formerly jagged edges and more room for compassion for myself and others. This, I believe, is how we heal.

Acknowledgments

Thank you to my content editor and project manager, Betsy Thorpe, for guiding this ship into harbor with your expertise and your big heart. This book would not be here without you. Thanks to copy editor and proofreader Katherine Bartis and interior book designer Robert Kern for making the inside of this book as beautiful as the outside. I'm so proud of it.

Thank you to Gigi Dover for creating the cover art that made this book come to life and to Lib Ramos, who laid it out like a dream. Thank you to my tenacious writing coach turned dear friend Jaime Handley for getting me to the finish line with my first draft. Many heartfelt thanks to Judy Goldman, Allison Hong Merrill, and Tommy Tomlinson for the lovely blurbs. Thanks to Charles Israel for reading the early version of this book and telling me to go for it.

Thank you to my husband, Jason, my one great love, for believing in me and working so hard to make my dreams come true. Avis and Brady, it is the joy of my life to be your mama. When the world around me is chaotic and burning, you three are the home I return to, time and time again. Thank you for encouraging me and letting me share a bit of our story.

Mom and Dad, thank you for the selfless act of giving this book your blessing and encouraging me to publish it. In doing so, you have set high the bar of parental love. Our legacy is the undoing of the ancestral trauma first unjustly enacted upon you both. I love you, Mom and Dad, oceans deep.

Thank you to my sister, Angela, for being a steadfast champion of my writing and my soft place to land. I love that we speak our own language and how much we laugh when we're together. Sissy, you are my ride or die. To your children, Cole, Grant, and Hayden, I adore you. It is a privilege to be your Aunt Shel. Thanks to Paul, who will be forever missed.

What happens when a young man finds himself with a feisty seven-year-old to raise? He never gives up on her. He teaches her to ride a bike, drive a car, and makes her believe she can build a house. Thank you for always loving me like your own, Ken.

Dear Bebop, thank you for your love and dedication to gathering us as a family. The traditions you worked so hard to create wove a rich tapestry of memories I wrap myself in. I'll cherish them forever.

My dear mother-in-law, Kaye, you have given me the best gift. I carry with me your example of love and faith as a guidepost for my life. Thank you to my father-in-law, Vance. Your example of fatherly love lives on in the way my husband loves his kids. You are greatly missed.

Aunt Brenda, your prayers save my life and your humor and love save my sanity. Thank you.

Uncle Benny, your friendship (and uncle-ship?) has been an extraordinary and unexpected blessing in my life. Thank you for reading everything I send, within hours, even the long, early version of this book, and always answering my texts with thoughtfulness.

Thanks to Aunt Carmen, Aunt Martha, Uncle Neil, Uncle Dave, Uncle Jimmy, Aunt Mary, and my cousin squad, Kelly, Ronnie, Paul, Tracy, David, Jay, Aaron, Chad, Morgan, Jolynn, Kelly E, Bill, and Trey for coloring in the background of my life and loving me so hard.

To Dana, Jeff, Chase, Jackson, Emily, Trevor, Chelsea, Winnie, Kacey, Tony, Brian, Tammy, Darrell, and Aunt Regina, thank you for calling me your own.

Huge thanks to the best girls—Rachael, Paige, Summer, Megan, Yushing, Michele P, Christy, Shonda, Shana, Gigi, Kellie, Mechelle, Angel, Brittany M, Candy, Liz, Sumanah, Reeve, Julie, Anna, Cat, Michele H,

Therese, Dana, Makayla, Jen W, and Whitney—for making me laugh and holding my paw when I need it.

Thanks to my brothers, Eric L, Tate, Daniel C, Steven O, Greg, David, Johnny, Bob, Joe, Pat, Flavio, and Ethan, for the encouragement and support.

To Leebo, there are not sufficient words to describe your beautiful heart, brother. Thank you for your friendship and all the ways you helped bring this book to life. I love you.

Special thanks to Dr. Dimitrios Hondros, Dr. Neal Speight, and Dr. Stuart White for the excellent medical care you provided during the years I was so sick. To oncology surgeon Dr. Peter Turk, oncologist Dr. Dipika Misra, radiation oncology doctors Wilson Brooks, PA-C, and Dr. William Warlick, and plastic surgeon Dr. Blair Wormer, thank you for the excellent care and kind bedside manner.

Milton Keynes UK
Ingram Content Group UK Ltd.
UKHW032325221024
449917UK00004B/383